Henry Wace

Christianity and Morality

Or the Correspondence of the Gospel with the Moral Nature of Man. Fifth Edition

Henry Wace

Christianity and Morality
Or the Correspondence of the Gospel with the Moral Nature of Man. Fifth Edition

ISBN/EAN: 9783337260187

Printed in Europe, USA, Canada, Australia, Japan

Cover: Foto ©Lupo / pixelio.de

More available books at **www.hansebooks.com**

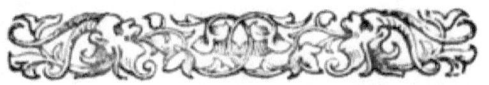

CHRISTIANITY AND MORALITY

THE BOYLE LECTURES

FOR 1874-5

CHRISTIANITY AND MORALITY

OR THE CORRESPONDENCE OF THE GOSPEL WITH THE MORAL NATURE OF MAN

THE BOYLE LECTURES

FOR 1874 AND 1875

BY HENRY WACE M.A.

PREBENDARY OF ST. PAUL'S PREACHER OF LINCOLN'S INN
PROFESSOR OF ECCLESIASTICAL HISTORY IN KING'S
COLLEGE LONDON

ALDI DISCIP ANGL

FIFTH EDITION

LONDON

PICKERING AND CO.

1882

Hazell, Watson, and Viney, Printers, London and Aylesbury

TO MY WIFE

IN GRATEFUL REMEMBRANCE

OF LABOUR SHARED AND FAITH SUPPORTED

PREFACE.

THE general subject of the two courses of Boyle Lectures contained in this volume is the Evidence in behalf of the Christian Faith afforded by the Moral Nature of Man. The author proposed to deal more particularly with those objections which, admitting the supreme obligation of Morality, deny that it requires any such religious support or superstructure as Christianity affords. Starting from the sense of Right and Wrong, he has endeavoured to show that it can only be explained upon the supposition of our standing in intimate relation to a spiritual world and to a Divine Person, and that it involves spiritual cravings for which Christianity alone offers an adequate satisfaction. He has at the same time attempted to vindicate Christian Truths from some of the misapprehensions which are displayed respecting them in current objections, and to exhibit their correspondence with the conscience and the experience of Man.

In the second course of Lectures this general subject is treated with especial reference to the objections prominently urged of late, especially by Mr. Matthew Arnold and Mr. W. R. Greg, against the possibility of our recognizing a Personal God, and of receiving a supernatural Revelation from Him. Speaking generally, the author has endeavoured in the first course of Lectures to exhibit the moral and spiritual reality of Christian truths; while in the second course he has dealt with the vital question of the validity of the primary assumptions which those truths involve.

January, 1876.

ADVERTISEMENT TO THE SECOND EDITION.

IN this edition the text has been carefully revised, and in some instances, as in the Lecture on *The Province of Faith*, the argument has been more fully or more clearly developed. In this part of his task the author has been greatly assisted by the criticisms bestowed upon his work, and he takes this opportunity of expressing his gratitude for the generous appreciation with which his efforts have been received.

November, 1876.

ADVERTISEMENT TO THE FIFTH EDITION.

THIS Edition, like the two former, is a reprint of the Second.

June, 1881.

EXTRACT FROM A CODICIL TO THE LAST

WILL AND TESTAMENT OF THE

HON. ROBERT BOYLE.

DATED JULY 28, 1691.

"WHEREAS I have an intention to settle in my lifetime the sum of Fifty Pounds per annum for ever, or at least for a considerable number of years, to be for an annual salary for some learned Divine or Preaching Minister, from time to time to be elected and resident within the City of London or circuit of the Bills of Mortality, who shall be enjoined to perform the offices following, viz.—To preach Eight Sermons in the year, for Proving the Christian Religion against notorious Infidels, viz., Atheists, Theists, Pagans, Jews, and Mahometans, not descending lower to any controversies that are among Christians themselves; these Lectures to be on the first Monday of the respective months of January, February, March, April, May, September, October, November, in such church as my trustees herein named shall from time to time appoint;[1] to be assisting to all Com-

---

[1] The Boyle Lectures are now preached in the Chapel Royal, Whitehall, on some of the Sundays following Easter Day, in the afternoon.

panies, and encouraging of them in any undertaking for Propagating the Christian Religion in foreign parts ; to be ready to satisfy such real scruples as any may have concerning these matters, and to answer such new objections and difficulties as may be started, to which good answers have not yet been made. . . . . I will that after my death Sir John Rotherham, Serjeant-at-Law, Sir Henry Ashurst, of London, Knight and Baronet, Thomas Tennison, Doctor in Divinity, and John Evelyn, sen., Esq., and the survivors or survivor of them, and such person or persons as the survivor of them shall appoint to succeed in the following trust, shall have the election and nomination of such Lecturer, and also shall and may constitute and appoint him for any term not exceeding three years, and at the end of such term shall make a new election and appointment of the same or any other learned Minister of the Gospel, residing within the City of London or extent of the Bills of Mortality, at their discretions."

CONTENTS.

FIRST COURSE.

SECOND COURSE.

"'All this means only morality.' Ah! how far nearer to the truth would these men have been had they said that morality means all this."—
COLERIDGE. *Aids to Reflection. Conclusion.*

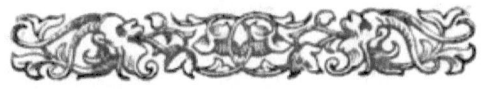

BOYLE LECTURES

FIRST COURSE

1874.

LECTURE I.

CHARACTER OF THE PREVALENT DOUBT.

ROMANS i. 16.

" For I am not ashamed of the Gospel of Christ ; for it is the power of God unto salvation to every one that believeth."

THE Lecturer on this Foundation is enjoined to preach eight sermons in the year "for proving the Christian Religion against notorious Infidels—viz., Atheists, Theists, Pagans, Jews, and Mahometans—not descending lower, to any controversies that are among Christians themselves." It would seem to be the first duty of any one entrusted with this commission to endeavour to ascertain what are the peculiar forms of unbelief against which it is most urgent at the time to prove the Christian Religion. Each generation has its difficulties and dangers ; and it would be a waste of opportunities if successive Lecturers did not endeavour to adapt their arguments to the successive needs of their times. From this point of view some of the subjects suggested in Boyle's

B

will may at once be put aside as unsuitable to the
moment. In proportion, indeed, to the development
of commerce and the spread of Christian races over
all parts of the earth, the relation of Christianity to
the other Religions of the world becomes of increasing
interest. A very short time ago it attracted, on a
special occasion,[1] a remarkable share of public attention; and it may be that the discernment of the
great man who founded these Lectures led him to look
forward to a period when the controversies of Christians with Pagans and Mahometans would be of
greater importance to the welfare of mankind than
controversies which, in his day and in ours, are nearer
home. Indeed, one of the most distinguished of my
predecessors vindicated **not** long ago the foresight of
the Founder in a memorable series of Lectures on this
subject.[2] But apart from the presumption which
would be involved in an attempt to follow him, this is
not the topic which now forces itself most strongly on
the attention of the Christian apologist, as he surveys
the state of religious thought in England and in
Europe.

It is scarcely possible to mistake the result of such
a survey. That which is chiefly to be discerned, alike
among friends and foes, is a deep conviction that the
Religion of the Christian nations is gravely menaced

---

[1] On the Day of Intercession for Missions, Dec. 20, 1872.

[2] The late Rev. F. D. Maurice, in his Boyle Lectures on "The
Religions of the World, and their Relations to Christianity."

from within. It is not from Pagans or Mahometans, it is not from Jews, considered only as the professors of an antagonistic religion, that the danger arises; it is from the dominant philosophies, from some of the most distinguished men of science, from some of the most acute critics of Europe. Few competent observers will doubt that these writers have been successful, to a degree which cannot be viewed without apprehension, in shaking the confidence both of cultivated and of uncultivated society in the truths of our Religion. The doubts thus generated are diffused far more widely than is generally avowed. That they are as firmly rooted as is sometimes alleged may, indeed, well be questioned. But that the very air is heavy with them, that they pervade alike literature and society, that they are not confined to the learned, that they perplex parents and confuse the young—these are the facts with which the apologist has in the present day to deal. It is no time for him to be contented, as in happier days, with addressing himself to the pleasant task of adorning or elaborating some of the outer defences of Christianity, bringing out its undesigned coincidences, or its more delicate harmonies with human nature or with history. He has to deal with influences, open or disguised, which are sapping the very foundations not merely of orthodox Christianity but of Christian civilization. He has to confront men whose writings he reads, whose faces he sees, whose friendship he shares, but who have abandoned for themselves, and for as many as they can legitimately influence, the characteristic elements of his Faith.

But the gravity of this state of opinion is at once alleviated and aggravated by one important peculiarity. Bishop Butler, in the Advertisement to his great work, says—" It has come, I know not how, to be taken for granted by many persons, that Christianity is not so much as a subject of inquiry ; but that it is, now at length, discovered to be fictitious." Subject to the exception which I proceed to notice, such a statement would be at least as true in the present day. But something is implied in the tone of this observation which is more fully explained in what follows. Butler adds—" And accordingly they treat it as if, in the present age, this were an agreed point among all persons of discernment, and nothing remained but to set it up as a principal subject of mirth and ridicule, as it were by way of reprisals for its having so long interrupted the pleasures of the world." No such statement as the latter could now be written with justice. The foes we have to meet are more worthy of our steel. The complaint has sometimes been made against the chief Christian writers and preachers of the last century, that they were too exclusively moralists. It may be suggested by such passages in Butler as I have just quoted, whether this tendency was not forced upon them by the circumstances of their time   He frequently speaks as if he were deeply

concerned to argue, not merely against impugners of
Revealed, or even of Natural Religion, but against
men who doubted the very obligations of Morality—
men against whom it was necessary, by considering
the constitution of human nature, to defend such
truths as that Duty and Interest coincide, and that we
are naturally adapted to a virtuous course of action.
Contrasting with this the state of feeling at the present
day, we may see reason to think that, if the writers of
this school directed their energies in a special degree
to this part of the struggle, they there, at all events,
won the day.   Controversies, indeed, of the gravest
importance are now prevalent respecting the foundation and the nature of Morality; and these controversies are perhaps pregnant with deeper consequences
to the practical observance and determination of
moral conduct than is generally recognized.   If the
theory of Utilitarianism were victorious, it has already
been made evident by the speculations of some of its
advocates that it would not leave Christian practice
untouched.   But, at all events, the supreme necessity,
and, in some sense, the supreme obligation of the
more conspicuous principles of Christian Morality is
fully admitted by all the writers with whom we have
practically to deal.   It is, indeed, more than admitted;
it is erected into the one sole pillar of the new edifice
they would establish.   Their chief position is that it
is really the sum and substance of Christianity itself;
they pay homage to what they designate the " sublime

morality " of the Sermon on the Mount and of our Lord's character, and they complain that this beautiful and simple revelation has been overlaid and obscured by the theological speculations of St. Paul and of the chief Christian theologians.

Two examples will afford a sufficient illustration. One writer[1] is eager to dissipate, by the shafts of wit and ridicule, the metaphysical abstractions with which, as he says, Greeks and Latins clouded the simple religious conceptions of the Hebrew mind ; but his aim is to bring into greater prominence the existence of "an Eternal Power which makes for righteousness,"[2] and he recalls the Christian Church, with an insight from which, in some respects, it may derive no little instruction, to the truth that its essential principle is departure from iniquity.   Another writer,[3] not less influential, protests that his only object is to vindicate " the grand and simple creed " which he discerns in the teaching and example of Christ.   That sacred Character, respecting which the Christian feels it presumptuous to speak in terms of praise, has in this age asserted in an extraordinary degree its claim as a

[1] Mr. Matthew Arnold ; especially in his book, " Literature and Dogma."

[2] Mr. Arnold generally speaks of " the Eternal not ourselves " which makes for righteousness ; but as he sometimes calls it a Power, I trust I may be excused for preferring, as a rule, to quote the latter, and the more English expression.

[3] Mr. W. R. Greg, especially in " The Creed of Christendom ;" see Preface to third edition, p. xciii.

moral standard for homage and imitation; and scarcely any one who has a right to the public ear would venture to speak in depreciation of the moral example of Christ.   All this, moreover, is obviously no passing homage paid to virtue.   It is the expression of a deep and sincere desire to know what is good and to do it. If such is the attitude of the chief writers with whom the Christian apologist has now to contend, it is certainly not less the attitude of those perplexed souls to whom he has to offer guidance.   The dominant feeling among them is that they would believe if they could.   They feel the want of a religious faith, but there are some things in what they have been taught to regard as the Christian Revelation by which their intellectual and moral nature is repelled ; and mean- while they cling to the faithful discharge of their duty as to a sure foothold.   The danger, in short, of which I spoke at the outset does not arise from men who have any private interest in disbelieving, but from men who have a sincere desire to know the truth and to follow it.

This characteristic, I observed, is at once an aggra- vation and an alleviation of the dangers in question. It aggravates them, because objections urged in this sincerity, and with this earnestness of purpose, carry a weight which, in all ages and all circumstances, has been wanting to frivolous or immoral objections.   If righteousness could be produced and sustained without Christianity, it might indeed be a question for grave discussion how far there would remain any practical necessity for Christian doctrine. I speak, of course, of Christianity and of Christian doctrine in the general sense affixed to them by our Church. Some of the writers I have referred to claim, indeed, to be the true exponents of Christ's teaching. But it is of no avail in this controversy to dispute about words, still less to distinguish minutely between various Confessions of Faith. The substance of that which has been hitherto called Christianity is sufficiently embodied in our Creeds and Formularies, and it is this which is menaced. When this Faith is widely pronounced to be an unnecessary subtilty of human philosophy, not by reckless sceptics, but by men of high aims and noble efforts, it is obvious that the forces arrayed against us become more formidable than ever.

On the other hand, there is this immense alleviation of our difficulty. The substantial acceptance by our opponents of the moral teaching of Christianity affords us at once a common ground. We are pursuing, at least in respect of the present life, the same object in principle ; and the sole question is by what means we may attain it. They tell me that I am complicating and obscuring a grand and simple truth with obsolete theological subtilties ; I contend that they are obstructing the realization of the very truth they admire, by abandoning the only sure way to it. But if we both can fix our minds on that truth itself and ask ourselves what it involves, we have at once common pre-

mises from which to start and a common purpose to
guide us in our inquiry. Probably, indeed, this has
always been the case in a greater degree than has
been generally recognized ; but it is so conspicuous in
the present day as to afford us a vantage ground of
which we are bound to avail ourselves.

Such appears to me the peculiar aspect of infidelity
which now chiefly demands attention. Its ultimate
causes are various, and for its full confutation it needs
a proportionate variety of argument. Certain scientific
assumptions or deductions are held to be incompatible
with those allegations of miraculous facts on which the
Christian creed is based. On philosophical grounds
objections are raised to the very possibility of a true
Theology. Undoubtedly, unless objections of this kind
could be answered, the only effect of presumptive argument would be to reveal a distressing abyss between
our desires and our knowledge, our wants and our
capacities. The Christian creed reposes on a historic
basis ; and if that could be shaken, no pleas derived
from the cravings of our nature would sustain the superstructure. On the other hand, the character of the
evidence necessary to command our belief in an alleged
occurrence necessarily varies in some degree with its
intrinsic probability. There might be evidence sufficient to compel our belief of anything not intrinsically
asburd, however improbable and inconceivable ; there
may, on the other hand, be allegations which no amount
of evidence, however apparently trustworthy, would

induce us to believe. But between these two extremes, the value of the evidence and the probability of the event are concurrent elements in determining our assent. If, accordingly, it could be shown that the most vital necessities of man's moral nature could be met without the miraculous facts alleged in the Creeds and the doctrines based upon them, it would be far more diffi- cult than at present to gain a hearing for the evidence on which they rest. But if, on the other hand, it should appear that those doctrines, and those alone, satisfy the imperious cravings of our moral and spiritual nature— if the conviction can be aroused that they supply a fatal deficiency in the highest moral teaching, and in the noblest efforts of moral practice—in this case, I do not say that we raise a presumption in favour of the facts having occurred, but we certainly diminish the difficulty of procuring assent to them. They are brought within the sphere of experiences which it is not unreasonable to expect; they acquire a character of verisimilitude, and find a place in the general consti- tution of human nature. In another course of Lectures I hope to meet some of those philosophic or scientific objections, just referred to, which are directed against the primary assumptions of Christianity; but it ap- peared to me that it would clear the way and would help to put the mind in a right attitude for considering them, if, in the first instance, we inquired into the practical signification of Christian truths in reference to that Morality which is, on all hands, admitted to be essential.

Such is the course of thought to which I invite attention in the present series of Lectures. The state of
mind with which I propose to deal may be briefly
described. I hear men who admit the paramount
claim of right over wrong setting up as the sole
standard for right the utilities and necessities of the
present world. I see others throwing scorn, if not
ridicule, on the notion of the idea of righteousness being
in any way dependent on the belief in a Personal God.
As a necessary consequence, all notions of personal
satisfaction rendered to such a Being are rejected as
superstitious figments. The great truths of Christian
Theology cease to have a practical meaning. The
doctrine of the Trinity becomes an idle speculation ;
Atonement and Justification are forensic fictions.
Such are the explicit allegations of the chief represen-
tatives of this moral school. If you listen to its
simpler and less advanced disciples, they will speak
in something of the following strain :—" I am sure that
God is good, and that there must be many ways of
coming to Him, and not one only—or that one would
have been diffused over the whole earth ages ago.
To be honest and conscientious, and in spite of many
falls to struggle all our lives after our highest ideal of
good—I cannot now believe that this will not satisfy
Him. We cannot justly be held responsible for many
sins to which the tendency is inherited ; and though we
may have free-will, it is not so free as is sometimes
represented. And if we feel it would be unjust for
God to punish us in the way the Bible says, I do not

see that the injustice would be remedied by the sacrifice of a perfectly innocent person." This, I apprehend, is, to say the least, a very prevalent form of disbelief, and has a great influence in inducing men and women to lend a favourable ear to the more scientific difficulties to which I have adverted.

It is an unwelcome task to give expression in a Christian church to negations of our faith ; but the first duty of a disputant is to understand his opponent's case, and to indicate the points to which his argument will be directed. It will be my pleasanter duty in the succeeding Lectures to consider one by one the truths which modern moralists would thus evacuate of any practical import, and to show that they are, at all events, far profounder interpretations of the facts of human nature than the bare moralities which are left to us without them. There is, indeed, something amazing in the fact that such a vindication of the reality of Christian doctrines should be necessary. The strange thing is not that they are denied and attacked, but that they are treated as mere obsolete subtilties. It would be pardonable to indulge in some indignation at the easy confidence with which they are thus contemptuously dismissed, did we not remember that Christians themselves may be in great measure responsible for such an eclipse of faith. I venture to assert that, even from those who have discarded them, Christian truths, or the dogmas of the Christian Church, demand a more patient and a more respectful consideration than they often receive. Be they true or false, one thing cannot be denied of them—that they have been associated with the mightiest revolutions in human thought, and with the noblest of human aspirations. Christianity is different from all religions in this— that, from the time it was promulgated, it has been inseparably blended with the progress of the human race, and that it has moulded the civilization of the nations upon whom all hopes for the future depend. It is easy to say that the doctrine of the Trinity at one time, or the doctrine of Justification at another, were mere philosophical or scholastic conceits. The fact is undeniable that they were believed by the best men of the day to be inseparably bound up with their intensest struggles. They were real to them, whatever they may now be to others ; and we owe at least so much respect to such men, as well as so much consideration for ourselves, as to make sure that we understand what that reality was before we reject it.

In fact, by some means or other, it has come to pass that even thoughtful and intelligent minds are possessed by utter perversions of Christian doctrine, and betray what can only be called a total ignorance of its real meaning. Here, for instance, is a short passage from a work republished recently by a man of mature and cultivated mind. " In Christ's grand and simple creed," he says, " expressed in His plainest words, ' eternal life ' was the assured inheritance of those who loved God with all their hearts, who loved their neighbours as themselves, and who lived purely, humbly, and beneficently while on earth :—in the Christian sects and churches of to-day, in their re-cognised formularies and their elaborate creeds, all this is repudiated as infantine and obsolete; the official means and purchase-money of salvation are altogether changed ; eternal life is reserved for those, and those only, who accept, or profess, a string of metaphysical propositions conceived in a scholastic brain and put into scholastic phraseology "¹—and so on.   Now, if statements like these were made by ob-scure or reckless writers, they would not be worth notice ; thoughtful and well-instructed Christians know what a miserable travestie they are of the real Revela-tion of the Gospel, and one would have thought no writer who deemed himself competent for such a vast task as the purification of religion could have put them forward.   But we have to deal with facts ; and the evident fact is that Christian Theology seems, for numbers of inquiring minds, to have lost its meaning. It is, unhappily, true that Christian theologians and Christian sects have contributed thus to narrow and obscure the great truths of the New Testament.   They have too often petrified them in hard " schemes of salvation," and have lowered them to the level of their own conceptions.   But the Creeds and the chief Christian Formularies themselves, and the Scriptural language which they interpret, stand on independent

¹ Mr. Greg's " Creed of Christendom," 3rd ed., Introd., p. xciii.

grounds, and claim a more thoughtful and impartial judgment.

There is nothing, in short, which the Christian apologist may more justly demand of his modern opponents, than that before they finally reject these dogmas they should once more endeavour to understand them. You tell me they are obsolete, and if not dead, are doomed. Be it so; but let them, at all events, "die in the light." I do not say that such dogmas are capable of demonstration; but this may certainly be demonstrated—that they mean an infinite deal more than the critics in question suppose; that they go deeper and touch human nature more nearly than such objectors at all apprehend; and that to dismiss them thus summarily is to leave out of account one of the vastest and noblest spheres of human experience. I am here to argue, and not merely to proclaim a belief, or to indulge in exhortation; but this at least I may be allowed to say—that I am jealous for some of the grandest characters who have illustrated human nature, when I find the doctrines to which they clung as their very life cast aside as having no essential human meaning. As a mere matter of fact, the souls of men have been stirred by these truths into deeper, grander, and more lovely harmonies than by any other influence that can be named. Augustine may sometimes be a rhetorician; but those profound and ennobling emotions which are betrayed in his Confessions are part of the heritage of the world, and no theory

can be accepted which does not worthily explain
them.   Luther may have been rough and impetuous ;
but the exquisite childlikeness and faith of his character demand to be explained and justified, and there
can be no doubt that, as a matter of fact, they were
mainly created by his religious belief.   When I contemplate such characters I can exclaim, in the words
of the text, "I am not ashamed of the Gospel of
Christ."   Admit, for the sake of argument, at the
outset of these discourses, that its truth is open to
question.   Yet, at all events, even the dogmas which
are most obnoxious to modern thought have had a
noble and inspiring influence ; and even amid the
perplexities of argument one is continually tempted
to exclaim, " Malo cum Platone errare quam cum istis
recte sentire."   I had rather experience those profound
emotions which history shows to have been evoked by
these dogmas, and by none others, than share the
apparent superiority of the most serene philosophy.
It seems necessary to vindicate the significance of such
dogmas once more to the ears of the present generation.   I propose in the following course of Lectures to
make this attempt ; and, at the same time, to argue
with our opponents from assumptions which they fully
admit.   May the Spirit of God aid this imperfect
endeavour to elucidate the truth, through Jesus Christ
our Lord !

LECTURE II.

THE PRIMARY MOTIVE OR ULTIMATE DESIRE.

MATTHEW v. 3.

" Blessed are the poor in spirit, for theirs is the kingdom of heaven."

I HAVE already indicated the point from which I propose to start in the present course of Lectures. What we find admitted on all hands, among those whose doubt or denial of Christianity is now of any serious import, is the supreme obligation of Morality. In other words, we may take it as an admission that, apart from any question of Religion, there *is* Right and there *is* Wrong ; that right is the highest and wrong the lowest, and that those whom I address prefer the highest at any sacrifice to the lowest without any apparent sacrifice at all. The question is, What does this admission involve ? and does it not, if pushed to itsconsequences, point to the Christian religion as the only satisfactory answer to its de. mands ?

2

Now, on entering upon that subject this afternoon, it may be as well to refer, once for all, to a class of speculations which at the present day possess peculiar interest, and which cannot, therefore, be passed over ; but which, nevertheless, for the purposes of this inquiry, it would seem not merely possible but necessary to put on one side. I mean the various speculations of modern science into the origin and development of the Moral Sense in general, and of our perceptions of Morality in particular. Whatever may be the final result of such inquiries, it is unquestionable that the moral faculties and perceptions of mankind have, in some important points, been gradually developed ; and science must be trusted to investigate the ultimate germs from which this development has proceeded. Probably we are very far yet from understanding in how extensive a sense it is true of our nature that "from the dust we are taken." But the question of what elements a thing is composed, or the question of the manner in which it is developed, is so entirely distinct from the question of its capacities and relations when in a developed and compounded state, as, for many purposes, to throw little light on the latter. Water, for instance, is a compound of two gases in a certain proportion ; but no idea whatever of the qualities of water could be gained from merely considering the qualities of those two gases in their uncompounded state. The mysterious action of Nature's laboratory unites and

converts them in one moment into a liquid, with uses,
relations, characteristics wholly different in kind from
those of its two elements.　Doubtless, our knowledge
of its elements is of value to us in the employment of
it ; but still the properties and uses which it possesses
in this compound state may, for general purposes, be
considered independently of its origin.　Similarly, in
considering the general significance of man's moral
nature, we have no need to embarrass ourselves with
the discussion of theories which are solely concerned
with its development.　Some philosophers may explain that development by the principle of association, others by the preponderance of permanent over
transitory instincts, others by the unconscious operation of perceptions of utility.　Others may think that
all such influences have co-operated.　But our moral
nature presents certain facts and relations as actually
existing, which are, for all purposes of action, independent of such considerations.　We have desires and
duties which must equally be satisfied, no matter how
they arose ; and, for the purposes of our life, we have
to accept them as realities without inquiring into their
origin.　In times when philosophical analysis is peculiarly successful, there is, perhaps, no more common
fallacy than to suppose that when we have resolved a
feeling or a substance into its elements we know
all about it.　On the contrary, its importance and
significance as a whole are, as a rule, absolutely
distinct from those of its component parts.

We may therefore, without the least disrespect to these philosophical theories, discard them from our consideration so far as our present purpose is concerned. If it were necessary, indeed, to enter upon them, it would be impossible to find in this field of inquiry any sufficiently solid basis on which to found an appeal in behalf of so intensely practical a matter as religious belief. Science on such subjects is in a state of flux, and it would be hard if we had to wait for its final conclusions. But the main facts of human life, the dominant needs of human nature, are subject to no such uncertainty. The Christian preacher or apologist is on perfectly clear and independent ground in appealing to the experience of his audience to say what Right and Wrong mean to them at the present moment, and what are the moral obligations and spiritual cravings of which they are conscious. The main facts of the Planetary System were known before the Law of Gravitation was discovered ; and, nearly two centuries since the discovery, we are still groping after a knowledge of the elementary constitution and development of that System. Similarly, the great relations in which the soul stands may be firmly interpreted and thoroughly grasped, while inquiry into the philosophical laws of its action and growth is left in abeyance. Having rendered this homage, therefore, to philosophy at the outset, we may, in the sequel of our inquiry, deal with the ordinary facts of life, use its ordinary language, and consider ourselves to be talking less of human Nature than of human Beings. I wish to ask the kind of questions which are proposed rather by poets than by philosophers; not by the mere intellectual faculty, but by the soul itself, with its various faculties of heart and mind—by each human being in his complete individuality. It is on this broad basis that any solid faith must be founded; and if it can be thus established, philosophical inquirers may the more securely pursue their laborious task of analysis and explanation.

To turn, then, in this spirit to the question of the significance of Right and Wrong, it will be observed that the inquiry divides itself into two distinct branches. There is first the question of the idea of Right and Wrong in itself, and secondly the question of what is right and what is wrong. In other words, there is a distinction between the general principle that I am bound to do right, and the subordinate principle that this or that thing is right. The obligation of Morality and the standard of Morality require separate consideration. It may be, indeed, that from the Christian point of view the answer to the one question is the answer to the other. But in the facts of life they are distinguished, and it is from those facts we are starting. It is right for a man to act according to his conscience; but it does not follow that because he is so acting the action is right in itself. On the contrary, persons acting conscientiously have committed acts which violate any recognized

standard of Morality.   If the actors believed that they
were under an obligation to act as they did, we may
abstain from condemning them personally, though we
may have to condemn their acts.   They obeyed the
highest principle of their nature, though, from prejudice or want of instruction, they were grievously
mistaken in applying the subordinate principles.   A
man can only act up to his knowledge ; and if he
does this, it may consistently be said of him, in a kind
of paradox, that he is doing right although he is doing
wrong.   This, it may be observed in passing, affords
an adequate explanation of some passages in the
Scriptures, in which persons are applauded for acts
which are in themselves indefensible.   At all events,
these instances are sufficient to remind us that the
sense of obligation to do right is one thing, and the
recognition of a true standard of right and wrong is
another.

It is in relation to the former of these questions
that Morality possesses its highest significance ; and
its bearing in this respect may be discussed in a
second course of these Lectures.   But it will be con-
venient to consider the latter question first ; and it
will be best for our purpose to consider it in the
manner in which it has been approached by independent moralists—namely, by considering the ultimate
desire of the human heart.   I do not say the ultimate
object of life, for that would be to look far beyond
the horizon open to our natural faculties.   But we

are competent to observe what is really the dominant desire of the soul, and we cannot avoid the conclusion that the course of action which satisfies this must be that which we were intended to pursue. From this point the great Greek moralists started; and from this point, also, the most distinguished of recent English philosophers commenced his defence of his utilitarian scheme of Ethics.

I do not know that there is really much doubt about the answer to the question. The most observant of Greek philosophers commenced his great treatise on Ethics, more than two thousand years ago, by defining the chief good of life as Happiness; and that, too, is the definition which, with some modification, to be presently noticed, the modern English philosopher accepts. It is an estimate of human impulses which the Christian, it would seem, is least of all in a position to contest It has indeed been made a reproach against Christian morals that they set before us selfish aims, and call on us to do right, not for the sake of Right in itself, but for the sake of the reward which it brings. The answer to such a reproach may be found in a passage[1] of the Greek philosopher already referred to; who shows that the ideas of virtue and happiness are inseparable, though that of happiness is the larger and the more comprehensive. But it would, at the least, seem evident that the Scriptures recognize fully that happiness is not merely the desire of

[1] Arist., Eth. Nic. i. 5.

mankind, but the legitimate desire. All their commandments are "commandments with promise," expressed or implied. One of their most characteristic
words, perhaps, is that which opens the text—the
word "Blessed." Blessedness, indeed, may be distinguished from happiness, but only as expressing a
higher degree or kind of it; and for the purposes
of the present argument the distinction is unimportant. The key-note of the Psalms is struck in their
first verse: "Blessed is the man that hath not walked
in the counsel of the ungodly." But the teaching
of our Lord offers the most conspicuous of all examples of this characteristic. The Sermon on the
Mount, which is recognized as the embodiment of
His moral teaching, is based, from beginning to end,
on this principle. It commences with a series of beati-
tudes; it ends with the assurance that the observance
of His word will be followed by permanent security.
"Whosoever heareth these sayings of mine, and doeth
them, I will liken him unto a wise man which built his
house upon a rock." The key-note of His morality is
blessing. He is the greatest of all preachers of self-
sacrifice. But how does He recommend it? "He that
saveth his life shall lose it; but he that loseth his life
for my sake and the Gospel's, the same shall save it."
Thus, in the very words which command self-sacrifice,
He sanctions the instinct of self-preservation. It
would be difficult to name a single passage from the
Gospels in which self-sacrifice is recommended without

reference to an ultimate blessing as the result ; and such, at all events, must have been the impression left on the mind of the Apostle who commences his epistle with the words, " These things write we unto you that your joy may be full." There appears no sense, in any of the writers of the New Testament, that they are making any real sacrifice in the cause they have adopted. It was not in days of real martyrdom that men spoke as if their sufferings demanded the admiration or even sympathy of others. " What things were gain to me," says another Apostle, " those I counted loss for Christ. Yea, doubtless, and I count all things but loss, for the excellency of the knowledge of Christ Jesus my Lord, for whom I have suffered the loss of all things, and do count them but dung, that I may win Christ and be found in Him." A deep joy pervades the souls of all the Apostles ; and they supply, perhaps, the most vivid illustration of the Aristotelian definition that happiness is the energy of the soul in its highest excellence.

But does not the experience of our own hearts compel us to admit the truth of this estimate of human impulses? It need not be said that every sin which men commit is due to the pursuit of happiness in some mistaken form ; but do we, in point of fact, ever separate that pursuit from our highest ideal of virtue ? Bitter as any present denial may be which we either impose on ourselves or recommend to others, do we ever fail to say, either to them or to our own hearts,

that the truest happiness lies in the path of duty?
Far be it from me to deny, what the Greek philosopher
already quoted admits, or rather asserts—that virtue
and righteousness are desirable for their own sakes!
But they are also desirable for something beyond them
—for that complete satisfaction of the energies of our
nature, of which they are the necessary condition.
It is not difficult, indeed, to understand that noble
indignation of the soul, exemplified in many great
heathens, who, despairing of themselves and of their
kind, clung to righteousness as the one good thing
they could secure, protesting that this, at all events,
was a certain blessing, though every other happiness
should be denied. If the Psalmist exclaims, " A day
in Thy courts is better than a thousand," the Roman [1]
could also exclaim, that a single day spent well, and
in accordance with the precepts of philosophy, is to be
preferred to an immortality spent in error and sin.
But magnificent as are these expressions of heathen
virtue, they lacked that animating and satisfying element which rendered Christian virtue contagious, and
which sent martyrs to the torture and to death, not
merely with resignation, but with joy. Doubtless
martyrdom has been similarly borne in other religions ;
but, putting aside those expressions of noble despera-
tion to which I have referred, it has been everywhere
under the same belief that martyrdom was the path

[1] Cicero, Tusc. v. 2.—" Est autem unus dies bene et ex præ-
ceptis tuis actus peccanti immortalitati anteponendus."

to bliss. In thus indissolubly combining duty with happiness, and the pursuit of the one with the pursuit of the other, the Scriptures do but reflect the universal verdict of human experience.

No fault, therefore, can be found, from the Christian point of view, with a philosophy which accepts happiness as the dominant aim of human life, and tests the rectitude of actions by their tendency to produce it. The fault to be found with it is that it fails so lamentably to satisfy the conceptions it arouses. In many cases it has to abandon, as practically unattainable, the greatest happiness of the agent who most faithfully pursues its dictates; and, above all, it has to relegate to an uncertain future the possibility of extending its benefits to the majority of those with whom it deals. Great numbers of mankind, it observes,[1] have been satisfied with but a moderate share of happiness; and, in the course of a long succession of generations, who will perish in the breach—I am quoting the language of the modern advocate of this doctrine—the grand sources of human suffering may be "in a great degree, many of them almost entirely," conquered. Meanwhile every one who has a moderate amount of moral and intellectual requisites is "capable of an existence which may be called enviable." It has to be recognised that, in a certain very imperfect state of the world's arrangements, a man may best serve the happiness of others by the absolute sacrifice of his own;

[1] Mr. J.S. Mill on "Utilitarianism," 5th Ed., pp. 19—24.

and the standard of right, we are told, is not the
agent's own happiness but that of all concerned. Now
far be it from me to deny the nobleness of such conceptions, considered in themselves ! But what I would
ask is whether they offer any adequate satisfaction to
the wants of human nature, and whether they take
any sufficient account of that dark side of human life,
which they admit it must require a long succession of
generations to remove ? It is hard enough to believe
that the noblest souls are doomed to disappointment ;
and it would mar even that moderately enviable existence, which is described as the lot of the human race,
to know that it had been bought by the sacrifice
of their own greatest happiness by some of the greatest
of men. But that which all such philosophies leave
out of account is the question, What is to be done
meanwhile, and even at the best, with the vast mass of
sorrow, suffering, and disappointment in the world ?
Taking things as they are, and as they must be for at
least generations to come, it is absolutely impossible
that the mass of mankind can find lasting happiness
in this world. There is much more of it, perhaps, than
we often realise ; and divines are too often liable to
the charge of conventionally depreciating the enjoyment of the present life. But if we wish to know
which aspect of life in the long run prevails, we have
only to consider what is the tone of the books, and the
temper of the writers, who have most touched the
world. There is, as I have been saying, a deep source

of joy revealed in the Bible ; but it is not the joy of
this world's enjoyment.   Is it by tragedies or by
comedies that the heart is most touched ?   The sadness of a great poet like Dante is an essential element
in his power, and the greatest poem in the world ends
with a lamentation over a tomb.

Such speculations, in fact, are comparatively easy so
long as they remain in their philosophical generality ;
but when we come down to individual human beings,
when we think of those with whom we personally have
to deal, when we realize distinctly the millions of disappointed or bereaved or injured hearts of which the
world is full, we feel that a doctrine which points to a
remedy in the course of successive generations is clearly
inadequate to our need.   Consider the life of one of
those suffering souls which, from no fault of its own, is
doomed through life to bear, perhaps unseen, the burden
of the sins or the vices of another : and is it possible to
rest satisfied with a view of life which, if it does not
deny, at least puts out of sight as a matter of entire
uncertainty, the prospect either of present relief or of
future reward ?   Granted that there is the deepest
pleasure in serving, at any sacrifice, one you love.   But
what is to be the remedy for that deepest of all anguish,
so often endured—to know that the sacrifice is made in
vain ?   Is nothing needed to sustain the soul under a
long strain of fruitless endurance ?   A manifestation
may now be noticed in European thought which may
not unreasonably be considered the natural result of

such philosophy.   I mean the popularity of writers like Schopenhauer or Von Hartmann, who reproduce the pessimism and the hopelessness of Buddhism. The sadness of life is far too real to be long left out of sight ; and if you erect a philosophy which disregards it, you will find it creating a philosophy or a religion of despair.

It may, however, be replied that, after all, such a view of life does but accept facts as it finds them. Over the greater part of the world, and for the greater part of history, men and women have had to face, and have succeeded in facing, this terrible burden of woe ; and nothing more has been possible than to produce in the long run, for the greatest number, the greatest amount of happiness practicable.   The mysterious fact, indeed, must be acknowledged, that the great majority of mankind have been left without the alleviation for which they crave.   This is not, however, a difficulty peculiar to Christianity ; while it is equally observable that the great mass of men have sought a refuge in imagining some happier future, and embodying their imaginations in a religion.   But it is Christianity alone which has at length met these cravings and miseries directly ; and it may now be perceived what a presumption is raised in favour of its truth by the very philosophy which would supplant it.   The text I have taken is the opening proclamation of the Sermon on the Mount ; it is the key of our Lord's teaching.   He came announcing the kingdom of heaven—a spiritual realm, different from that we see, but not less real, not less present, not less open to our enjoyment ; and He proclaimed that within this realm there was to be found satisfaction for all the wants which the world fails to satisfy, and a remedy for the miseries it inflicts. The poor in spirit, the meek, and the persecuted—the possessors of those gentler virtues which in an age and an empire of successful force were apt to be trampled out of sight—might here find their shelter, their exercise, and their reward. It was a proclamation which swept with a master-hand that vast mass of sad and suffering life of which I have spoken : and is it any wonder that, if sustained by revelations of miraculous power, illustrated by a perfect Example of suffering, and vindicated by a glorious resurrection, it enabled the weak things of the world to confound the strong, that it bestowed on the suffering a greater tenacity of purpose than on the happy, and that the very symbol of sorrow became the most victorious standard in the world ?

Let it be observed, moreover, that what our Lord revealed is no mere future compensation for present sorrows, but a spiritual realm in which the noblest energies of the soul may be continually developed, in spite of the adverse circumstances which surround it here. The poorness of spirit, the patience and meekness He describes, are not like the oriental characteristic of blank resignation ; they are the hopeful endurances of a soul clinging to spiritual realities, and developing new energies of faith and insight. " Not

only so," says the Apostle, "but we glory in tribula-
tions also, knowing that tribulation worketh patience,
and patience experience, and experience hope, and
hope maketh not ashamed ; because the love of God
is shed abroad in our hearts by the Holy Ghost which
is given unto us." Thus the great work of the martyrs,
in their lives and deaths, was not merely that they
bore testimony to the creeds they professed, but, still
more perhaps, that they revealed to the world new
spiritual realities, tempers more heavenly, and virtues
more divine than it had yet dreamt of, and that they
thus gradually brought its spirit under the spell of the
kingdom of God. From the moment this Sermon on
the Mount was preached, there was not a suffering
heart which had not, so to speak, a new spiritual
career opened to it. Christ had revealed a kingdom
"in which every one could work and no one could be
defrauded of his labour,"[1] and in which absolute satisfaction was to be obtained for all the permanent needs
of the soul. Christ in the Gospels asks of no one the
sacrifice of his highest happiness for the good of others.
On the contrary, He assures all that they will find their
own highest and absolute happiness in seeking that of
others at any apparent cost. " There is no man that
hath left wife, or children, or friends, for my sake and
the Gospel's, but shall receive a hundred-fold in this
present life, and in the world to come life everlasting."

[1] Preface to Bacon's " Novum Organum," edited by the Rev.
J. S. Brewer, King's College, London.

There is not one, however burdened, to whom He does
not promise peace and rest.

In short, taking this world by itself, you have to
admit that happiness is the desire of men's souls ; and
you are not less compelled to allow that, in a vast
number of instances, if not in the majority, it can
never be attained.   But admit into your consideration
that spiritual region which Christ unveiled, and you
have then an assurance that, even in this present life,
no soul need be maimed of its aspirations, that the
hardest duty may be alleviated by spiritual sympathy,
and the darkest path illumined by a heavenly light.
Ask your own experience whether it be not so.   Have
you not seen many a face, marked perhaps by years
of mental or bodily pain, but nevertheless brightened
by internal gleams of spiritual radiance ?   These
characters are not merely enduring—they are living,
acting, developing their deepest energies, and feeling
all the increasing joy of a heavenly existence.   Here,
too, is that "complete life" which the philosopher
deemed requisite to fulfil his conception of happiness.[1]
The spiritual energy is at work now, and it will last to
the perfect day.

Must it not, then, be admitted that Christ, at all
events, spoke to men's deepest thoughts and feelings
when, instead of proclaiming to them mere sublime
moralities, He commenced His work by unveiling to
their vision this new world?   It is upon this revelation,

---

[1] ἔτι δ' ἐν βίῳ τελείῳ.—Arist., Eth. Nic. i. 5.

as reflection will convince you, that the whole teaching
of the Sermon on the Mount is based. Christ does
not rely merely upon men's apprehension of the necessity of purity of heart for pureness of life. He warns
them that they are brought under the searching laws of
a spiritual kingdom; He speaks of spiritual condemna-
tions more terrible and inexorable than legal or moral
judgments; He exhorts men to lay up for themselves treasures in heaven. He bids them do their
alms and say their prayers in secret, that their Father
which seeth in secret may reward them openly.
Accordingly, it may be true that some of the injunc-
tions in the Sermon on the Mount are not reconcilable
with the dictates of utility or even of morality as
calculated solely for the horizon of this world. Christ
did not say that they were. But He came to reveal a
new kingdom with new laws, and He calls on us to
guide our conduct by reference to it.

We may, then, fairly bring our inquiries to-day to
this conclusion :—We have seen that nothing could be
more in harmony with the souls of men and the needs
of their position than the revelation of a realm of
existence beyond that which is afforded to their moral
nature in the present world—a realm both future and
present, in which the most important parts of their
lives must be passed, and which would have the power
to transmute morality, as much as morality has the
power, even in this world, to transmute their physical
nature. Did a message which proclaimed such a

Revelation deserve to find that presumption in its favour which, as a matter of fact, it obtained? If so, then we are led from the most elementary truth of ethics to conclude that the standard of our actions must be furnished by something beyond the facts and persons we have to deal with in the visible world; that we must take account of realities beyond our natural ken, and revealed by Christ alone. I do not say that this affords more than a presumption; that is all I am at present offering to show. But it is a presumption which, at the outset, should bespeak the most favourable consideration of the further claims of Christianity.

LECTURE III.

RIGHTEOUSNESS A PERSONAL RELATION.

ROMANS i. 28.

"They did not like to retain God in their knowledge."

THE considerations adduced in my last Lecture led us to look beyond the world of our visible relations for a sphere capable of satisfying that longing for happiness which is one of the most elementary instincts of the human soul. Admitting the legitimacy of that craving, we saw that it was only by leaving out of account at least one-half of life that we could find in the visible world any response to it; and so far as the standard of right may be determined, as it certainly may in some sense, by reference to this ultimate instinct, it followed that it was necessary to take into account, even for our present guidance, the relations of our spirits to an invisible and spiritual realm—in short, to a Kingdom of Heaven such as Christ proclaimed.

There are, in fact, several types of character which moralists who have abandoned the Christian basis

have condemned, but which the Gospels especially
applaud, and which have at all events this testimony
in their favour—that they never fail to enlist sympathy
and homage.   How much reason, for instance, have
we not continually to be grateful for that meekness
and patience under injuries, that endurance, at once
sorrowful and hopeful, which has been a characteristic
virtue of Christian saints, and which has won so many
desperate souls back to their true allegiance !   I am far
from saying that no such virtues have been practised
apart from a knowledge of Christianity.   It is the
very thesis of these Lectures that the Moral Nature
of man anticipates the answer which Christianity offers
to its aspirations.[1]   But does not history bear witness
to the fact that these suffering virtues have been immeasurably strengthened and diffused by that new
element of hope and sympathy which was opened to
them by the Sermon on the Mount ?   They all existed
in human nature, like plants half developed in some
gloomy shade ; but since the moment when Christ
poured upon them the light of the Kingdom of Heaven, they have flourished with a new luxuriance.
This argument, however, though it may have weight
with many minds, appeals, perhaps, somewhat too
much to distinctly Christian sympathies ; and the
question of the standard of Right and Wrong leads on
other grounds to the presumptions now contemplated.

[1] "O Testimonium animæ naturaliter Christianæ."—TER
TULLIAN, *Apolog.* 17.

It has been observed, by the distinguished writer to
whom I referred last Sunday,[1] that, though no question might seem to lie more closely at the root of our
practice, there is nothing which has been the subject
of more doubt and discussion.   To judge of Right and
Wrong is what we have to do every day of our lives ;
and yet philosophers are even now disputing with
respect to the ultimate tests by which they are to be
determined.   It is the dominant question in those
Socratic dialogues which first awoke in the West a
deep interest in ethical inquiries ; and it has been often
observed in what tentative conclusions the Athenian
philosopher and his disciples seem to end.   Whatever
definition or description is propounded fades into
indistinctness under his analysis ; and that profound
solution, which seems ultimately to be suggested in the
Platonic theory of Ideas, has been at once the admiration and the perplexity of the world.   Now, without
entering on these or later disquisitions, it may be
asked whether there be not one important fact in the
case which is independent of them.   If we examine
the ordinary matters in which righteousness is concerned, we shall find that they mainly consist in a
certain relationship between persons.   It is as impossible now as in the time of Plato to define them adequately by any abstract or external measure.   The
acts, indeed, are comparatively few which may not,
under some circumstances or other, be justifiable ; that

---

[1] Mr. Mill on "Utilitarianism," pp. 1 and 2.

which constitutes, as a general principle, the rightness or wrongness of an act consists in the relationship of the actor to the persons whom it affects. What have been called the self-regarding virtues, such as Purity and Manliness, and, in particular, the duty of Truthfulness, as applying to the soul under all circumstances, may at first seem to offer an exception; but it will appear in the sequel that these instances also fall under the same general rule when duly enlarged.

It would seem, indeed, we may go further, and say not merely that the rightness of actions depends on the relation of the actor to others, but that the righteousness of each individual consists in his personal relation to other persons, and must be estimated by that relation, and not by the bare acts which he does. The soul of man in this respect is very different from his body; and the neglect to distinguish between the characteristics of the two is, perhaps, especially in days when science has concentrated our attention so much upon the body, a frequent cause of misconception. The excellences and defects of man's bodily nature may in great measure be determined by the separate consideration of each individual; excepting, indeed, the intimate interdependence of the sexes, in which we observe an especial reflection of moral laws of health. With this exception it is generally possible to pronounce whether the organism is in a healthy state or to describe its maladies by reference to itself alone; and if it be diseased it can be cured independently.

It is, in this respect, like a plant, or any other external
thing of which the life is solitary, and of which the
main characteristics may be described without reference to any other plant or thing of the same kind.
But in the familiar saying, that man is a social animal,
we are pointed to the distinction I am now observing
—a distinction which separates him, as that saying
implies, from even the highest part of the lower creation.   The fact that he cannot live alone renders his
moral condition at any moment dependent on his relations to the other persons who surround him.   If a
moral observer wished fully to describe the condition
of any one of us, he would be baffled unless he could
not merely see into our own hearts, but were also
informed of our various family and social connections
past and present ;   nay, unless he also had an insight
into the hearts of those with whom we are connected.
We are not merely individuals with a certain organization ;   we are parents or children, husbands or wives,
masters or servants, friends and citizens.   The question
of whether we are right or wrong is a question of how
we feel and act towards the many persons with whom
we thus have to deal.   The characteristic virtues of a
child depend both upon his feeling a certain relationship towards his parents and upon his acting accordingly.   The virtue of a husband or a father does not
consist merely in his exercising, to the best of his
power, and for the general good of his family, the
faculties called out by his work as an individual man,

but in a certain constant state of feeling towards his wife or his children ; and this state of feeling will itself necessarily be modified by their feelings towards him.

It is this consideration which renders the definition of Right and Wrong so impracticable in detail. Law accumulates rule upon rule, but can never overtake the multitudinous variations which spring from our personal relationships. Equity itself is obliged continually to confess that it fails to grasp them exactly ; and the utmost justice it can render is often but rough. It cannot take fully into account honour and affection, and all the delicate shades of feeling, which, in their accumulated effects, go so far to determine characters and to characterize actions. Not the least remarkable witness to this truth is borne by the acute observation of Aristotle. If any man could have defined virtue by a rule, it is he. His definiteness, his logical exactness, are points in which he is most conspicuously contrasted with his great rival. Yet what is his memorable definition of virtue?[1] I need not trouble you with the whole of it ; but he says it consists in a relative mean, to be determined by reason. He cannot, however, stop here ; and he is obliged to add, "Such a mean as a wise man would determine." In other words, he is obliged to introduce, for the determination of what is right in each case, that personal estimate which only a living person can exercise. It

---

[1] Eth. Nic. ii. 5.—Ἐστιν ἄρα ἡ ἀρετὴ ἕξις προαιρετική, ἐν μεσότητι οὖσα τῇ πρὸς ἡμᾶς, ὡρισμένη λόγῳ καὶ ὡς ἂν ὁ φρόνιμος ὁρίσειεν.

will be observed, moreover, that these personal relations do not merely form a part of life ; they determine, for moral purposes, the whole of it.   There is no
work we do which is not done either in obedience to
or for the benefit of others ; and our moral excellence
in doing it cannot be judged without reference to the
spirit in which we act towards those persons.

If these observations be just, it follows that, so far as
ordinary morality extends, the righteous state of our
souls depends essentially on the personal relations
which we bear to others, and upon those they bear to
us.   Both elements have to be taken into account.   A
man's nature cannot be fully developed unless those
with whom he has to do are rightly disposed towards
him.   Without that, he may, of course, act rightly towards them ; but if you wish to bring out the full play
of his moral nature, it is necessary that his parents,
his wife, his children, his friends, should feel towards
him as they ought, and should thus evoke the true instincts of his nature.   If you wish to develop all the
righteousness of which a man is capable, you must
have a wise man and a philosopher constantly by his
side ; you must put righteous people around him ; and
in proportion as his heart answers to their hearts will
he himself become righteous.   It is seen from this
point of view that righteousness is distinguished from
love as being only a partial aspect of that higher excellence.   Righteousness, we might almost say, is the
metaphor ; love is the reality : because the reality of

life consists in the relation of persons to persons, and
not in the relation of persons to a rule.

Now, it would seem obvious to what these considerations point. If the essence of righteousness consists
in personal relations, is it probable that this characteristic of our nature stops short at the point where our
highest development and deepest interests commence ?
Are we not strongly impelled by the argument from
analogy to conclude that a characteristic which clings
to us up to the last verge of direct observation continues to attach to us beyond it ? Let it be remembered that it is in the highest characters we know
that this personal relation is most strongly developed.
Men have tried continually to separate themselves from
such relations ; and the effort has not been made only
in Christian times and countries. On the contrary, it
has probably been more often witnessed under the
influence of heathen philosophies and in pagan society.
The conception of the highest excellence as consisting
in self-sufficiency was not suggested by Christian divines. But it is not in Stoics or hermits that our
hearts recognize the highest types of human character.
It is in those who have followed that supreme Example
whose whole life consisted in the constant discharge
of the offices of love. Now, without asking you to
contemplate that moment when the earthly relationships which have thus, to the last hour, been identified
with the best energies of our souls cease to live save
in the memory of those who are left, it is sufficient to

take into account the circumstances of our present life, in order to recognize that the soul has necessities and energies into which human relations cannot enter. Are not some of the deepest struggles of the soul those which force it actually to disregard human affections? Has not the demand to hate father and mother, wife and children, been often exemplified in great lives? Even in humble careers are we not, sometimes by bereavement, sometimes by still worse wounds, thrown back upon something within ourselves? What is that something? Is it credible that the soul should exist in a region of personality in all else, that this personal relationship should grow more and more intense as the deepest feelings of nature are successively experienced, and that when the sympathy and love of wife or husband fail, we should be driven into an uninhabited region of mere law, order, and necessity?

It may, indeed, be admitted, even by many who reject the Christian conclusion, that the transference of the idea of a personal relationship from that which is temporal to that which is eternal, from that which is human to that which is divine, was due to an irresistible impulse in the mind. They will only say that the conclusion is not justifiable, and that with more careful reasoning we must cease to assert it. Such objections will need a more full examination.[1] But, meanwhile, can it be fairly denied that an analogy which harmonizes with the whole verifiable experience

[1] See the second course of these Lectures.

of human nature carries the strongest presumptive
weight? The Scriptures do but assert that our highest
spiritual relations are similar in kind to those into
which they merge, and from which they can often be
scarcely separated. The whole of morality is summed
up by them in the saying, "Thou shalt love thy
neighbour as thyself." What more probable, what
more natural, than to presume that all the spiritual
life which reaches beyond our relation to our neighbour is summed up in the expression, "Thou shalt
love the Lord thy God with all thy heart"? Again, I
must reserve the explanation and justification of that
great conception of the Divine Being. But that there
must be some being, in our relationship to whom consists the higher life of our souls, is a conclusion which
at least harmonizes with the whole of our other experience. The righteousness of the soul then becomes
of the same character, in whatever sphere it is exerted.
As moral righteousness consists in love, so spiritual
righteousness consists in it ; and there, as here—in
heaven, as on earth—it is in the influence of Person
upon Person that the health of our nature consists.

I will venture here to point out that this consideration meets that apparent exception to the relative
character of virtue, which, as I observed before, might
perhaps be noticed in the obligation to such duties as
purity and truthfulness. Under one aspect, indeed,
all such virtues are essentially social ; and it appears
some confirmation of the view now urged, that self-

respect itself is most effectually developed, not in a
solitary, but in a social life. It is only in association
with his fellows that a man fully learns what he owes
to himself. But I think that those who value truthfulness, for instance, most highly will acknowledge an
instinct that its deepest hold upon their allegiance
does not lie merely in its importance to their fellows.
Truth in the inward parts, even if they had nothing to
do with externals, they feel to be the foundation of all
virtue in their nature. I would observe, then, that
this demand for truth does seem to be laid at the
foundation of righteousness in that summary of
human duty which is based upon the Faith now in
question. The Ten Commandments are, perhaps,
primarily to be regarded as the constituent laws of a
nation; but they have been not less justly regarded
at all times as embodying the substance of private
morality. Accordingly, after the command to have
only one God, comes the command not to take God's
name in vain—a command which, in a time when all
solemn promises were oaths, would naturally be
understood as demanding, in God's name, truth in
word and deed. To men who believed that in their
inner and permanent consciousness they were always
in immediate relation to a supreme spiritual Being,
the observance of truth became the first necessity of
their lives. Similarly, it will hardly be denied that
Christianity has quickened intensely the sense of
obligation to purity in thought as well as in deed;

and it has done this, in accordance with the exhortation of St. Paul,[1] by teaching men to regard themselves as members of Christ, and thus bringing them in their most secret consciousness into relation with a perfectly holy person. The moral motive of self-respect has thus been incalculably enhanced, if not superseded, by the spiritual motive of reverence for Christ.

It may still be replied, perhaps, that to give these presumptions the validity demanded for them, we ought to be able to point to some definite indications in human nature that we are in connection with such a Being as we have been surmising. Granted that the supposition harmonizes with our experience and our wants, still, how can it be more than a supposition, unless we have actual experience of such a Person? It may be that some distant planet would account for certain aberrations of our orbit, but how can we confidently act on the theory of its existence unless we can point to it in our firmament, and observe its actual movements? There are records, indeed, of which the Psalms are the most conspicuous, which proclaim that men who have converted this supposition into a faith have experienced the strongest evidence of its reality; and a comparison of the presumption with the undoubted facts of human experience thus recorded should alone, perhaps, be sufficient to induce earnest minds to make, at least, practical trial of so ennobling a belief. But it must be acknowledged that there is

1 Cor. vi. 15.

force in the objection; and we may find some preliminary answer to it by a reference to the second division of this subject, as explained in the last Lecture.

What we have hitherto been considering is how Right and Wrong are to be determined. But there is a further question—namely, what is the meaning of the idea of Right and Wrong, and of the obligation under which we feel ourselves to pursue the right and avoid the wrong? As I have already said, we may easily be mistaken in our judgment of what is right in a particular case, and may still act, and be bound to act, on our erroneous judgment. It is necessary, however, to observe very carefully what it is we have to explain. It is not the mere fact that certain impressions are more permanent, or more in accordance with our nature than others; but that those impressions act on us in such an entirely different way from all others. It is the distinction between duty and desire. A variety of attempts have of late been made to explain the Moral Sense. One of the latest of them is that the greater permanence of social instincts inflicts upon us, sooner or later, a sense of dissatisfaction when we have allowed them to be over-powered by transitory individual instincts.[1] But this sense of dissatisfaction would, on the hypothesis itself, be simply one of disappointment; the sense of pain would ultimately predominate over pleasure, and we

[1] Mr. Darwin on the " Descent of Man," vol. i. ch. 3.

should feel that it would have been more desirable for us to act differently. That, however, is certainly not the feeling which provokes remorse at a bad action, or approval of a good one. Such a principle may help to explain how we judge that certain things are right and certain things are wrong; but it does not explain why, when we think them right, we feel it not merely desirable but obligatory to do them. Moreover, there are cases in which men persuade themselves that what they have done wrong will neither directly nor indirectly injure others, and in which they nevertheless suffer all the blame of an accusing conscience. The latter objection applies to the theory which would explain the growth of this sentiment by the influence of the community on the individual. That influence would cause social sentiments; but how could it create that keen sense of violated obligation which often weighs upon sensitive minds in cases where no recognized social law has been broken?

The difficulty, it may be observed, is not even fully explained by that distinction between the relative authority of Conscience and the other faculties of the soul for which we are indebted to the greatest of English Moralists. Conscience, we are shown, asserts not merely the strength, but the right to rule; it is not merely an instinct, but an authoritative one. This observation states the fact, but it does not appear to offer an explanation of it. What is the meaning and origin of this sense of obligation, this recognition of authority? Here, again, we can hardly do wrong in commencing with obvious and simple instances of obligation, and concluding from them by analogy to the nature of the higher. Is not the first idea of obligation aroused by a sense that we have been false to some person towards whom we owe certain conduct? A child's earliest idea of having done wrong is aroused by the sense of having displeased his father or mother. The feeling is quite distinct from the mere sense of having injured another ; for the injury may be entirely unintentional. It is the sense of not having recognized and fulfilled the relation in which we were placed. This becomes the more apparent if, as I think, we may further observe in this sense of wrong something quite distinct from an apprehension that we are liable to punishment. Doubtless that apprehension arises ; but it is remarkable that people often take refuge from the sense of violated obligation in welcoming the punishment which they feel must ensue upon it. It is a positive consolation to them to say that they are ready to take the consequences, and they feel a kind of pride in their submission to them. The real re-morse arises when it is felt, as it is sure to be, that the wrong is not measured by the consequences to the wrong-doer, when the sense awakens that, for our own temporary gratification, we have injured some one to whom we were bound, that we have been un-faithful to some trust, or ungrateful for some kindness. We stand in certain relations to others ; they have

claims on us, and we have disappointed them. We
are sensible that we have separated ourselves from
them; we cannot look them in the face, and we are
alone. This sense of shame, and of not having acted
worthily towards our fellows, is superior, at least in
the best minds, to the mere sense of fear.

Now why, as in the former case, should we not carry
this feeling somewhat higher, and judge by analogy of
its meaning in the one instance from its meaning in
the other? Here, also, we may employ that argument
à fortiori which I have applied to the question already
discussed in this Lecture. Nothing is more certain
than that the sense of a bad conscience is deepened,
made more acute and penetrating, in proportion to the
nearness of the personal obligation which we have
violated. There are some sins, as has been already
observed, which by the mere moralist might be regarded as almost, if not quite, against ourselves alone;
they are against the truth and the higher instincts of
our nature. But under the light of Christianity these,
sins become as much a matter for poignant repentance
as any others; and the reason is that in this fuller
light they are felt to involve the violation of that personal spiritual relationship of which I am speaking.
Without, however, assuming the force of this instance,
it will, I should think, be admitted that in the ordinary
course it is the sense of wrong done to others which
is the bitterest drop in the cup of remorse. Moreover, as we have seen, this arises in cases where no

permanent harm is believed to be done to the persons wronged. They may have been superior to
our power to injure them. It may be merely a love
unrequited or kindness abused. Now may it not be
asked, as before, whether analogy will allow us to
suppose that this keenest of all the purifying fires of
repentance is withheld from the soul in those sacred
relations in which, in its solitude, it communes with
what is within ? How much of the profoundest part
of life is passed in that solitude, I need only appeal to
poets to explain. The pathetic tones of the fifty-first
Psalm are echoed by poets like Byron in strains which
only differ in the less complete character of the consciousness they express. They, like Manfred, even
where their sin has been against one of their fellows,
still feel, above all things, alone with some power which
inflicts on them, still more bitterly, a remorse akin to
that of which they are sensible in the presence of the
wronged spirit they have called up. Now, is it not
perfectly natural—perfectly in harmony, that is, with
the facts of every-day experience I have been describing—to suppose that, as the experiences of remorse are alike in all cases, so are its causes, and
that the deep dissatisfaction we are considering arises
from a consciousness, never very far from any one, of
a spiritual Person to whom he owes obligations and
whom he has wronged ? It is one of the first rules of
philosophizing, that we ought not to admit new causes
when old ones suffice ; and if a feeling similar to that

which is caused by a violated engagement to a father, a wife, a husband, or a friend, arises in the soul when contemplating its sins, whether private or social, it is but reasonable we should accept a similar explanation.

In a word, the sense of having violated visible obligations is not sufficient to account for the facts of remorse. Pictures of human nature, like Macbeth or Manfred, reveal a further dissatisfaction. We have wronged others, but we have also wronged some power which bound us not to wrong them. It will appear hereafter that while such an apprehension quickens intensely the sensitiveness of conscience to acts of self-injury, it offers at the same time a new prospect of regeneration. All I am now urging is that the analogy of right and wrong, and of the feelings roused by a violation of duty in the cases which are confessedly within our observation, should be allowed to carry weight in those which are alleged to be beyond it. Which is more like human nature—to suppose, like the great philosopher[1] who has done such service to the cause of independent morality, that duty consists in the recognition of a " naked law " which can only be expressed in a highly philosophical phraseology, or to suppose, with the authors of the Scriptures, that it consists in a more or less conscious relation to a Being who has similar relations towards us with those of other persons ? That consciousness

---

[1] Kant.

has, indeed, been very unequally quickened in different ages and races; and except under the light of revelation it amounts only to what is described by St. Paul, when he speaks of men "as feeling after God if haply they might find Him." The revelation of right and wrong is described in the Scriptures as not less gradually developed than the rest of human knowledge. But in proportion to the awakening of conscious personal relations with a spiritual Being has been ever the keenness of remorse, the bitterness of repentance, and the fervour of amendment. If the principle which arouses the deepest moral feelings can be considered to have the strongest moral claim on our belief, the doctrine of a Personal God will ever rest on the firm support of the conscience.

LECTURE IV.

THE DIVINE PERSONALITY.

ISAIAH lv. 8, 9.

"For my thoughts are not your thoughts, neither are your ways my ways, saith the Lord. For as the heavens are higher than the earth, so are my ways higher than your ways, and my thoughts than your thoughts."

THE point to which I endeavoured to conduct this argument in the last Lecture was the presumption, afforded by analogy, that our invisible and eternal, no less than our visible and temporal, relations have reference to persons and not merely to things. It appeared that the definitions of Morality, alike in their most perfect form and in the character of their imperfections, all point to the impossibility of defining righteousness or virtue by any rule, and to the fact that the health of the soul consists in a right attitude towards persons. The sense of obligation to an unseen power, compared with the similar sense of obligation to our fellow-men, was observed to point in the same direction. The result is that the soul must be considered as part of a great system of Personalities.

You cannot decide upon its healthiness by examining it separately, as you might with an inanimate thing, or even with the inanimate part of man himself. Just as the condition of a planet does not merely consist in its internal constitution, but also in its obeying a common attraction with other planetary bodies and in its revolving round the sun, so the health or salvation of any person must depend upon his due co-ordination with other persons, and probably upon their common subordination to some central sun of the personal world. If this be the case, we find the language of Scripture at once the most simple and the most philosophical. The most exact statement of morality is the saying, " Thou shalt love thy neighbour as thyself ;" and similarly we have reason to presume that the most exact statement of our higher spiritual relations will be, " Thou shalt love the Lord thy God."

Now, such being the presumption, we are met by the fact of the existence of a nation and of a book in which the whole of life, here and hereafter, was viewed under this aspect. To the Roman the dominant influence in life may have been law, to the Greek it may have been beauty, but to the Jews it was the will and the love of an unseen Person. The first characteristic of the Scriptures is that they bring before the mind, in every page, the sense of a personal Being towards whom the writers stand in more intimate relationship than to any one or anything

else. The veil seems to be drawn aside which hangs
over the invisible world, and we see disclosed behind
it the vision of a mysterious Spirit, in whom we live
and move, towards whom our best affections are due,
and on whom we absolutely depend in body and soul.
The question which arises for our consideration in
this Lecture is whether the disclosure thus made to
us by the vision of Hebrew and Christian seers
answers those demands of which we have been speaking, and offers a worthy response to the dictates of
our moral nature.

It seems, however, necessary at the present time to
meet a preliminary objection which may be raised to
this statement of the case.   It is gravely, and even
earnestly, maintained by a writer of considerable influence,[1] that this idea of a personal God is in no way involved in the essential meaning of the Jewish Scriptures. But a short time ago such a statement would
have been deemed, at least in England, a mere paradox,
and it is in reality little else ; but it is important as
the extreme form of a tendency everywhere observable, even in religious thought, to suspect any strong
and vivid conception of the Divine Personality, to
treat the Divine nature as something so unapproach-
able as to be beyond our sympathies, and consequently
to concentrate religion almost wholly on our relations
one to another.   Infinite mockery is thrown over the
mere notion of our knowing enough of God's nature

[1] Mr. Matthew Arnold, especially in "Literature and Dogma.'

to apply the term "personal" to Him, and we are
told such language is the mere imagery of the Hebrew
writers. The statement that "The Lord our God is
one Lord," is said to be merely a "deeply-moved
way" of recommending seriousness; and trust in God
is interpreted to mean trust in the law of conduct.

The language of the Bible must have become
strangely obscured for such an explanation of it to
have received any acceptance. How do the Hebrew
Scriptures open? Is it by the revelation of a law of
life or conduct? Not at all. Their first words are,
" In the beginning God created the heaven and the
earth;" and they proceed to speak of the voice, the
will, and the design of God. To appreciate the practical significance of this language we are not concerned
with the cosmogony of the book of Genesis. The
main effect of that first chapter upon the mind is, as
was doubtless intended, to afford us a view of God,
rather than to afford us a view of nature. It is one of
the most frequent modes of argument in the Scriptures to appeal to the facts of nature for the purpose
of giving us a conception of the vast personality which
lies behind them. The most memorable instance is
that passage in the book of Job, in which, when the
patriarch and his advisers are perplexing themselves
to explain the Divine dispensations, the Lord answers
Job out of the whirlwind, and says, " Gird up now thy
loins like a man, for I will demand of thee, and
answer thou me. Where wast thou when I laid the

foundations of the earth? Declare, if thou hast understanding." The whole passage which follows might
be regarded as a poetical application of the first
chapter of the first book of Moses; and the foundations of Jewish belief were thus laid, not in mere
considerations of human conduct, but in those revelations of supreme power and wisdom which the contemplation of nature impressed, perhaps, even more
on the early thoughts of men than on our own. Is it
a mere law or an influence which is depicted in the
book of Job as creating and swaying at will every
creature in heaven and earth? Or, to take another
example, consider the 104th Psalm. What is the
effect of its opening verses? " Bless the Lord, O my
soul. O Lord my God, Thou art very great; Thou
art clothed with honour and majesty. Who coverest
Thyself with light as with a garment: who stretchest
out the heavens like a curtain: who layeth the beams
of His chambers in the waters: who maketh the
clouds His chariot: who walketh upon the wings of
the wind: who maketh His angels spirits, His minis-
ters a flaming fire." Is it not obvious that the purpose
of the poet in such passages is to reveal a personality?
The writer is not, like ordinary poets, making use of
personal imagery for the purpose of describing nature;
he is using the facts of nature for the purpose of describing a Person. These Psalms of nature alone
would suffice to vindicate the central idea of the
Hebrew prophets; but when we come to those in

which they are dealing with the inner world of the
human heart, the Personality revealed becomes clear
and intense beyond, it might have been thought, the
possibility of mistake. It may be possible, by varying
the translation, to explain " delight in the Lord " to be
" delight in the Eternal," and this again to be simply
a " deeply-moved way" of expressing the happiness
we all feel to spring from " conduct." How any cultivated, not to speak of any religious mind, can bring
itself to pare down the vivid language of the Psalms
to such common-places, is another question. But how
can the process be possibly applied to such a Psalm
as that which immediately precedes the one just
quoted—the 103rd ? " The Lord is merciful and gracious, slow to anger and plenteous in mercy. He will
not always chide : neither will He keep His anger for
ever. . . . . Like as a father pitieth his children, so the
Lord pitieth them that fear Him. For He knoweth
our frame, He remembereth that we are dust." However much imagery there may be in such language, it
is positively meaningless, alike for its author and
for ourselves, unless it be considered as consciously
addressed to a Person.

It does not seem necessary to answer very carefully
those other current objections to which I referred
against our thus speaking of the God of the universe
as a Person. Undoubtedly we are ignorant of what
personality means ; we have not sounded what the
poet calls " the abysmal depths " of even our own

personality. But does that circumstance leave us in any practical doubt as to the existence of such a characteristic in us, or as to the fact that we are distinguished by it from all inanimate and from other animate things? We could not advance a single step in science, unless we could assign things to certain classes long before we are able adequately to define them. We know it would be absurd to ascribe to a law or a force the pity of a Father, the tender thoughtfulness of a merciful Saviour, the forgiveness of a Judge. The Scripture writers, it is quite true, do not trouble themselves with our metaphysical distinctions. But they had a far keener perception than we have of the primary facts of life, and they conceived of God as at least as much a personal Being as we are ourselves. There are movements of our souls which can be called out towards persons and persons only—emotions, affections, and acts of trust—and these movements of the soul the Jews felt they could indulge to the full towards God, and be sure of a suitable response. The question of immediate practical importance is, not what God's nature is, but how we may feel towards Him, and how we may suppose Him to feel towards us. The simple and perfectly intelligible answer given to these questions by the Jews was, that they could feel towards God in a manner similar to that in which they felt towards other beings whom they considered persons, and that He felt similarly towards them. The philosophical explanation of the term, or of the reality,

may be far to seek; but, as with many other things
equally unexplained, we need have no difficulty in
our general application of the principle.

But there are other objectors who fully acknowledge
that the characteristic idea of the Scriptures is that of
a personal God, towards whom we may have personal
feelings, but who maintain that the conceptions of
His character put forward, more particularly in the
Old Testament, are unworthy and contradictory.
The Jews, it is said, did conceive of God as a Person,
but they imagined Him a Person far too like themselves—like themselves, angry, jealous, repentant,
fierce. Now, I am not concerned to defend every
expression respecting God which may be used by
every Old Testament hero. Their words are recorded
historically, not dogmatically; and they may in certain cases have thought unworthily, no less than
acted unworthily, of Him. But without descending
to special defences, I would observe that the objection,
as a whole, arises from a misconception of the spirit
of such expressions.

Recollect, for a moment, what we have already seen
respecting the manner in which the facts of nature
are employed to reveal the character of God. The
author of the book of Job, or the Psalmist, accumulates
everything that there is in nature of magnificent,
powerful, beautiful, or subtle, and treats them all as
the mere shadows of still loftier Divine lineaments.
The Psalmist disposes them as the garments which

dimly reveal, while they nevertheless shroud, His form.
But all that there is grand in natural realities is thus
regarded as having its counterpart in God Himself;
and we have to gather them all into one view, as in
the 104th Psalm, in order to gain the least conception
of His majesty.   There is scarcely any one who does
not acknowledge the grandeur of the conception thus
developed, or who does not do homage, like Job,
to this revelation of One who "can do everything."
But now let it be considered why this process of
regarding all the excellences of nature as shadows of
the Divine perfections should stop short with inanimate nature, and should not be continued into the
realm of human nature ? Fallen and imperfect as we
may be, are we alone, of all God's creatures, the beings
in whom no reflection of His attributes is to be seen ?
Marred as the human heart and the human soul may
be, are their emotions and impulses less noble than the
brute force of the leviathan ?   Or is the human reason
less worthy than the physical light to be regarded as
the garment with which the Lord covers Himself?
The authors of the Scriptures entertained too great a
reverence for human nature to permit it to be thus
excluded from the noble office of declaring the glory of
the Lord and showing His handiwork. It is true
they might, at one moment, feel their insignificance
when considering the heavens, the work of His fingers,
the moon and the stars, which He had ordained ; but
another moment's reflection recalled them to the sense

that the law of the Lord was not less perfect, which converted and restored the soul. Accordingly, just as the 104th Psalm ascribes to God all the glory of which the light and the firmament, the clouds and the wind, are the embodiments, so the Scriptures in general treat the nobler passions, capacities, and emotions of the human soul as shadows of the perfections of the Divine nature. Anger, jealousy, repentance, indignation, may indeed all be corrupt and mean passions ; but they may also be not less noble displays of the human heart than the storm or the earthquake are of the powers of nature. If, then, as is generally felt, there is no false imagery in such language as " The God of glory thundereth, the Lord is upon many waters," why should we fail to acknowledge a similar propriety in images which clothe Him for the moment in the garb of human emotions, and invest Him with the lightnings and thunders of the soul ? Neither language is strictly true ; each is as near an approximation to the truth as we can obtain ; and it is by a combination of all such images, in bold indifference to apparent contradictions, that the comprehensive and sublime conception of God in the Scriptures is created.

One of the most distinguished, for instance, of these only too rational objectors has collected from various parts of Scripture passages which ascribe to God contrary qualities and dispositions ;[1] and he draws the

[1] Mr. Greg, in the "Creed of Christendom," vol. i. p. 105.

prosaic conclusion that the Theism of the Jews was impure and progressive. In one place God declares that He will dwell in the sanctuary ; in another place it is said, "The heaven and the heaven of heavens cannot contain Thee : how much less this house that I have builded !" In one place He speaks of holding communion with His servants ; in another He is described as hidden and incapable of being seen. At one time He is entreated to repent of evil against His people ; at another time it is declared that He is not a man that He should repent. At one time He demands burnt-offerings ; at another He declares that He desires not sacrifice. But is it difficult to perceive that these daring contradictions are the very safeguard against that impure and anthropomorphic Theism of which the inspired writers are accused ? The real anthropomorphism consists in setting up an ideal which is consistent according to a human standard. There is, for instance, no anthropomorphism greater than that of some men of science, who can only conceive of God as standing in the same relation to nature as that in which they stand themselves—unable, that is, to act, except in submission to its ordinary laws. But the Scriptures take everything that is grand and beautiful, in the world without and in the world within, in the firmament or in the heart, and fuse them together into one glorious image of God. Attempt to ascribe them all to a human being, and they will be mutually destructive ; but in God the realities of

F

which they are the reflections may subsist in one
essential harmony.   It is precisely because the Scriptures are not really anthropomorphic that they venture
on such bold flights of apparent anthropomorphism.
They illustrate the Divine nature in the only way in
which it can be illustrated—by human analogies;
and then immediately add, in the words of the text,
" For my thoughts are not your thoughts, neither are
your ways my ways, saith the Lord. For as the
heavens are higher than the earth, so are my ways
higher than your ways, and my thoughts than your
thoughts."

It seemed desirable to diverge a little from the
regular course of argument to consider these objections,
because upon the reality and legitimacy of the scriptural conception of a Personal God depends the
possibility of considering aright any of the distinct
doctrines of Christianity; and when, as in the present
day, such views as I have been describing prevail
respecting that conception, it is impossible without
disputing them to advance a single step beyond the
most elementary presumptions. The doctrine of the
Atonement, for instance, as we shall see hereafter, is
indefensible except in the language of personal relations; and the perversions by which it has been dis-
credited have arisen from the fact that, even among
Christians themselves, the simple and direct language
of Scripture has been explained away into impersonal
metaphors.

These objections, however, have done us the service
of bringing before our view some of the elements of
the scriptural idea of God.   Let us now endeavour to
collect them, and consider whether they do not
correspond to the highest cravings and dictates of the
soul.   It is not necessary here to indulge our own
imaginations of what would be the effect of such a
belief.   We have it before us in utterances of the
human heart, which are as genuine records of experience as can be found in any other literature.   The
Psalms and the Prophets, for instance, are not didactic
treatises ; they reveal to us the souls of the writers :
and what do we see in them ?   We observe, in the
first place, that the double conception of a God who
unites in Himself all the majesty of nature and all the
humanity of man aroused in their minds a faith which
delivered them from all fear, and made them feel that
they possessed a superiority to all natural and spiritual
enemies, only to be measured by the superiority of
their Lord Himself.   It should be particularly observed
that it appears to be the combination of the two ideas
of loftiness and condescension, of supreme power and
of tenderness, to which this characteristic spirit of
religious courage is due.   The two are combined in
the beautiful exhortation, " But now thus saith the
Lord that created thee, O Jacob, and He that formed
thee, O Israel, Fear not : for I have redeemed thee,
I have called thee by thy name ; thou art mine.   When
thou passest through the waters, I will be with thee ;

and through the rivers, they shall not overflow thee :
when thou walkest through the fire, thou shalt not be
burned ; neither shall the flame kindle upon thee."
Other religions, indeed—or one, at least—has invested
its votaries with a spirit of unflinching courage. But
it has at the same time instilled into them a fatalism
which has been an obstacle to their waging that
incessant war with circumstances which is essential to
continued progress. . So long as God is contemplated
simply as the great and Almighty Creator, the soul
feels that it has nothing to do but to submit to His
inscrutable decrees, and bow at an infinite distance
to what may appear His will.   But once interpret the
character of God by human as well as by natural
excellences—once admit the justice of those descriptions of God as pitying and redeeming His people,
holding them by the hand and helping them, condescending to their individual needs as a father with
his children—and then all that power and overwhelming majesty, which otherwise would crush the soul,
become to it a constant spring of hope, energy, and
resource.

We are justly proud, in these days, of the courage
and calmness with which men face the mysteries and
the powers of nature.   Probably complete fearlessness
in the investigation of truth is one of the most remarkable characteristics of our time ; and it may well
be believed that much of the very scepticism against
which I am now arguing arises, not from the prevalence

of less willingness to believe, but from a habit of
looking difficulties more boldly in the face.   To a
great extent it is a scepticism of faith and not of
distrust, and we may therefore contemplate it with
the less alarm.   But shall we think it a mere accident
that the great impulse given, three centuries ago, to
this career of free thought and free speech coincided
with a religious revolution brought about by perhaps
the most fearless of all uninspired theologians ?   Deep
in the heart of Germany, I would fain believe, lies
even now the faith awakened by that master-spirit ;
and it is because he revived in the world the great
lesson of faith in God that men do not shrink from
the most unrestrained inquiries into Divine things.
At all events, this is the faith which combines in
individuals the utmost energy with the profoundest
submission, the proudest courage with the deepest
humility, and which renders possible a kind of self-
reliance utterly destitute of self-assertion.

But it is when we pass to the effect of this belief in
a Personal God upon the more spiritual excellences
of the soul, that its correspondence to our needs
becomes most apparent.   It is here that the personal
relations come chiefly into play.   What is the reason,
let me ask, for the extraordinary popularity of poems
and great works of fiction, except that, by placing us
in connection, though an imaginary one, with personal
passions and feelings, the impulses of our own nature
are called out, and our hearts are made to live and

breathe? Here again the truth has been expressed
by that great Greek philosopher I have more than
once had to quote, who says the use of tragedy is to
purify the heart by the passions of fear and pity. If
you wish to develop a human soul, you must, in
some way, rouse its feelings towards another soul;
and you cannot produce any real regenerating effect
on the heart except by means of the great affections,
such as love, indignation, anger, and scorn. The
human heart is a noble and complicated instrument,
of which the music can only be evoked by the touch
of a responsive heart. Now let us ask whether any
heart, however near, however good, however true,
among ourselves, is capable of arousing all that depth
of spiritual and moral emotion with which we know
that our hearts must be stirred, if their full music is
to be elicited. There are, indeed, some instances in
which two hearts may seem all in all, and sufficient
for each other. But rare, if even conceivable, are the
cases in which one or other of even the simpler chords
in the soul does not remain imperfectly awakened;
rarer still, alas! are the instances in which some
failing, however deeply lamented, has not marred the
response of perfect sympathy. At all events, whatever might have been, yet, taking us as we are, how
many souls are there—is there one?—which could or
would lay bare to any human being the whole of its
sins, weaknesses, and needs? Or, on the other hand,
can we, among our fellows, conceive of a soul so perfect

and so sympathetic as to be able to pour upon the heart
of another the full and adequate stream of consolation
or of rebuke ?   In one word, is it conceivable that any
imperfect human being could respond adequately to
the full revelation of the sins, the passions, the cravings
of the heart ?

To put the case in the language of Scripture, we
have a heart, a soul, a mind, and a strength, and it is
our instinct to develop that heart, soul, mind, and
strength to their utmost, to bring them all into full
play, to sound their heights and depths, their breadth
and length.   How is that satisfaction attainable ?   Is
the nature of any one of us, thus considered, capable
of being satisfied by even the most exquisite sympathy
of another like ourselves ?   Even if there were no
other imperfection, what is to be the consolation when
bereavement leaves one of two united souls to seek
its support elsewhere ?   Can you acquiesce in the
supposition that it is nothing to the Creator that
beings endowed with this intense personal consciousness should have the deepest and most permanent
energies of their souls wasted and disappointed ?
If not, do we not find at least an offer of a solution
for these enigmas in the proclamation of a Personal
Being whom we may love with all the heart, with all
the soul, with all the mind, and with all the strength ?
That is the revelation conveyed in the Psalms.   There
you have the whole permanent diapason of the human
soul aroused by the revelation of a Being towards

whom affection and sympathy, shame and regard, love for the right and hatred of the wrong, repentance and hope, joy and sorrow, fear and courage, all those passions and emotions which transcend the bounds of the present life, may have their full and complete development.   His mighty nature, His wrath, His indignation, His pity, His love—that is to say, the qualities in Him which to us have the same relation as those qualities in human beings—bring their supreme influence to bear upon our souls, and purify them with an overwhelming energy.   Add to this the record of the Gospels, in which this Divine Being is exhibited in permanent union, and consequently in sensible sympathy—in a communion which was "seen and heard and handled,"—with the soul and the body of man, and there then stands before us, complete and accessible, an all-satisfying object for the personal devotion of our souls.   If the record of the Psalms and the lives of the saints be real, this revelation has been abundantly verified by those who have trusted it. In this relationship to a Divine Person their love has been intensified, their righteousness strengthened, their courage heightened, their intellect exalted.   They have reflected the lineaments of their Divine Companion and Friend ; and it is on the witness of this supreme moral influence, not on any mere metaphysical inference, that we rest our firm faith in the doctrine of a Personal God.

LECTURE V.

THE PRACTICAL PROBLEM.

ROMANS i. 18.

" For the wrath of God is revealed from heaven against all ungodliness and unrighteousness of men."

IN resuming these Lectures,[1] permit me to remind
you of the course we have pursued. It is not
without advantage, indeed, to be thus compelled from
time to time to review the ground over which we have
passed ; for the force of any presumptions which may
be derived from man's moral nature must depend, in
great measure, upon their combination ; and it is,
moreover, essential in such an argument as the present
to assume, in its later stages, the right of using language which, at the outset, was treated as needing
vindication.

I have endeavoured, then, to show that the elementary cravings of the soul point to some other than the
present world as the goal of our life, and therefore as
affording the standard of our actions ; while all
analogy would lead us to conclude that our moral

[1] After an interval of three weeks.

relations to that world must be personal relations, as
they are in the visible world.   As in the visible world
our duties, our energies, and our happiness depend not
on mere circumstances, or even rules and laws, but on
the attitude of our hearts and souls towards individuals, and upon their attitude towards us, still more
must this be the case in those deeper and more permanent relationships in which the soul seeks its ultimate rest.   Christians, accordingly, recognize the satisfaction of their instincts in the revelation of a Personal
God, towards whom all the emotions of their souls
may have free play, and whom, in the language of the
Scriptures, they may love with all their heart, soul,
mind, and strength.   The purpose of the last Lecture
was to vindicate this conception of God from some
objections which have been recently raised against it,
particularly on the ground of its being a mere metaphysical notion, unsupported by verifiable facts, and
conveying no intelligible meaning.   We saw that,
without entering into any metaphysics, the Scriptures
simply regard as a reflection of the Divine nature
everything that is great and good in creation ; and
just as they view the mighty realities of the physical
world as voices which bespeak God's presence, or as
garments enshrouding His majesty, so they consider
the personality and all the emotions of man as still
more noble revelations of one aspect of His nature.
What He is in Himself we know not, and the Scriptures are a continual protest against the anthropo-

morphism of which they are accused. But it is by no
means so inconceivable what He may be to us ; and
the questions :—" He that planted the ear, shall He
not hear ? or He that made the eye, shall He not see ? "
may be still more forcibly applied to the spiritual
parts of our nature. He that created love, shall He
not love? or He that rendered indignation against
evil one of the noblest qualities of the soul, shall there
be nothing in His relation towards us which corresponds to it ? The possibility of further pursuing the
present argument depends upon the validity of this
presumption being admitted. In proceeding to discuss
some of the more essential Christian doctrines, it will
be necessary to speak continually of the wrath, the
love, the mercy, and the justice of God. I protest at
the outset, and may have to protest more than once,
that I am making no assumption as to the nature of
personality in ourselves—still less in God. I am
simply assuming, on the ground of a presumption
already vindicated, that the Divine nature in its relations towards us must, so to speak, assume the form of
those human emotions. Were I not speaking as an
apologist, it would be more correct to say that our
love and wrath are images of the spiritual realities of
the Divine nature.

It will be seen, however, that, so far, the points we
have been considering are, as it were, the separate elements of the problem with which the theologian, or
the philosopher, has to deal. We have been inquiring

what are the constituent parts of the spiritual world, whether they are personal or impersonal, and so on. But the far more important question remains, What is the state, as a matter of fact, in which these parts or elements are found existing in human nature? The ideas of Right and Wrong and the standard of right may indicate for us what we ought to do; the vision of our relationship to God may reveal to us the possibilities of our nature; but a religion which deals practically with human beings will take into account what is their actual condition; it will address itself, not to what men ought to do and feel, but to their real feelings and acts; and its crucial test will be the manner in which it meets the main facts of life. This is, perhaps, an observation of which the full significance may not at first be apparent; but it is the essential weakness of all mere systems of morality, and of most, if not of all other religions, that they confine themselves to pointing out what the facts of life ought to be, and make no provision whatever for dealing with facts as they are. Some physician has said that the essence of the rules of medicine may be summed up in the advice, "to keep well." It was a pointed application of the familiar maxim that "Prevention is better than cure." But what would be thought of the physician who, when brought into an hospital, had nothing but this to say to the patients whom he would see stretched before him in the various miseries and dangers of disease? It is in the latter case, not in the

former, that you have an adequate illustration of the
moral philosopher, however excellent, and of the
merely moral interpreter of the Scriptures. They can
bid us preserve our moral health ; they can define for
us in some measure in what it consists. But they do
not ask what is the actual state of our souls and what
are their consequent needs. I would not for a moment
disparage their teaching for its own purposes. It is their
main defect, not that they conflict with Christianity,
but that they fail to touch the problem with which it
most directly deals.

That problem is the actual state of human nature
from a moral point of view. Judging by individual
conscience, or by general experience, can it be disputed
that this condition is one of universal frailty, failure,
and regret ? It is not necessary to go to the theologian, it is more than sufficient to appeal to poets and
historians as witnesses to this sad reality. In a great
city like this, are there not crimes enough to sadden
the heart of any observer who can but take patent facts
into account ? Are we not continually reminded that
the Church and a number of subsidiary institutions are,
in large districts, stemming slowly and with difficulty
the tide of degradation, or struggling to overcome the
fatal lethargy of indifference to high moral aims ? But
apart from these more flagrant instances of corruption
or imperfection, how many of us are there who, when
our consciences are fully aroused, are not painfully
sensible of the lamentable failure of our own spiritual

life ? None would admit the fact more fully than those who are the best examples of human excellence. It is those who have struggled the most earnestly, and have succeeded the best, who are the most sensible of their comparative failure. In saying this I am not bringing a charge, or denying the validity of many excuses which men offer for themselves, or which are offered for them by others. I am only observing the fact of universal failure to reach the moral standard we all admit. To account for it is one thing, to recognize it is another. The higher the standard proposed, the more admirable the moral teaching considered by itself, the more conspicuous is this general and individual falling short.

As we read, in fact, some of those moralizing interpreters of the Scriptures, to whom I have more than once referred, a feeling must be continually suggested little short of despair. Take, for instance, the passage I quoted once before from a recent attack on the received interpretation of Christ's teaching. "In Christ's grand and simple creed," this author says, "expressed in His plainest words, eternal life was the assured inheritance of those who loved God with all their hearts, who loved their neighbours as themselves, and who walked purely, humbly, and beneficently while on earth."[1] Undoubtedly it was. "This do," He said on one occasion, "and thou shalt live." But it is well

---

[1] Mr. Greg, Introduction to the third edition of the "Creed of Christendom," p. xciii.

for us that this was not the whole of His creed.   Is it
not wonderful that the writer's heart did not fail him
as he was announcing this perfection as the means of
salvation?   Did salvation depend upon our having,
while on earth, loved God with all our hearts and our
neighbours as ourselves, how many of us could dare
to hope for it?   The very person to whom Christ
uttered the words, "This do, and thou shalt live,"
proceeded to "justify" himself by inquiring who was
his neighbour, and was immediately compelled, by the
parable of the Good Samaritan, to confess his failure
in the comprehension, not to speak of the fulfilment,
of the second commandment of the law.   So again
another writer proclaims his discovery " of the method
and secret and sweet reasonableness of Jesus," the
method being " inwardness," and the secret " renuncia-
tion ; "[1] and he propounds as the essence of the Gospel
that, if we will adopt these methods, we shall attain
righteousness.   But of what avail is it to tell a sick
man that if he will walk he will recover his health?
His inability to walk is of the essence of his disease.
Similarly, of what avail is it to tell men with their
natures already warped and corrupted, " betrayed too
early and beguiled too long," that all will be well with
them if they will but practise the excellences of a perfectly innocent soul?   I ask whether the most urgent
necessity of life is not left out of account in such teaching?   The Gospels, we are told, to quote once more,

Mr. Matthew Arnold in " Literature and Dogma," chap. vii.

"read in an understanding spirit . . . . contain little about which men can differ, little from which they can dissent. He is our father, we are all brethren ; . . . . this needs no Priest to teach it—no authority to indorse it. The rest is Speculation—intensely interesting, indeed, but of no practical necessity."[1] "The rest," thus dismissed as of no practical necessity, relates to the errors, the sins, the grief, the repentance of frail and struggling souls.

In the teaching of Christ and His apostles there was a method which an ordinary preacher must despair of approaching, by which they succeeded, except in the case of an especially hard-hearted class, in eliciting from men and women a frank confession of their sense of sin, and inducing in consequence an eager resort to the means offered them for deliverance from it. Yet it is only by some such appeal that the foundation for any further development of Christian truth can be laid. The point is not demonstrable by argument ; it is simply a matter of observation and experience. The axioms of geometry, it has been said, are such as no sane man can deny, while those of morality are such as no good man will deny ; and it may be added that the postulates of religion are such as no man who knows either the facts of life or his own heart dare deny. Perhaps, when we think some charge is being brought against us from the pulpit, as though its only

[1] Mr. Greg, "Creed of Christendom," third edition, vol. ii. p. 195.

object were to condemn us, it is natural to feel an impulse to repel the accusation. But let us conceive Christ standing before us, not in the attitude of a Judge, but of a Saviour, and asking us to reveal to Him the secrets of our souls, in order that He might deliver us from our evils—and which of us, who is not altogether hardened, would not respond in the tones of the penitential Psalm, " I acknowledge my transgressions, and my sin is ever before me " ? Once dismiss the notion that the Reformed Churches were enunciating a theory when they laid such stress on the doctrine of Original Sin, regard that doctrine simply as describing a fact, and can you doubt the substantial truth of its description of human nature ? Who can deny as a matter of fact the existence of such a thing as " Original or Birth sin " ?[1] Do we not observe a fault and corruption in the nature of every man, born by natural birth, from the first moment of dawning reason ? What child is there who does not betray a natural inclination towards what is practically, even when not consciously, evil, perpetually resisting other inclinations to good ? Is there not a tendency rooted in us— whether you call it "the wisdom," or "the sensuality," or " the affection," or "the desire, of the flesh "—which is not subject to the law of God ? If this is theological language, it is none the less language which describes every-day realities ; and it is with these realities that

---

[1] Article IX.

G

what is considered the technical language of theology is concerned.

Divines, it must be admitted, have been too apt to mould such facts into the shape of their own imperfect theories, and then to argue from the theories instead of from the facts; and, as a consequence, sooner or later, the theories have been found to be partial and unreal, and an air of unreality has been cast on all the language which seemed to imply them. While, however, I admit this, I cannot refrain in passing from saying that, with all their defects, there is something greater, something more true even to facts, in the spirit which has constructed schemes like that of Calvinism, than in such speculations as I have to-day been referring to, or in the whole school of moral Deism. At all events, these divines did not shut their eyes to the stupendous and distressing facts of human evil in the individual and in the race. They were not content with barely pointing out what men ought to do ; and the condition of human nature, as it actually existed, offered too terrible a problem for them to shut their eyes to it. It was to relieve their minds of a great burden that they constructed theories to account for it, and sought to elicit from the Scriptures an elaborate system of Divine Economy. They could not but fail ; and the reaction has been, in some respects, most mischievous. Yet so long as such theories, however imperfect, or even injurious, do take into account the evil of individuals and of the world, while philosophers or sceptics disregard it, so long will the theories possess, for the mass of men, a far superior attraction. Their authors were often wise and brave men who tried to look realities in the face, and to account for them; and though their schemes may have passed away, they have each contributed some point of view which assists us in gaining a full conception of the truth. But much as I respect such efforts, I am not called on to maintain the adequacy of any of them; and I must protest against that shallow criticism, which, first of all, is content to acquaint itself with their popular exaggerations, and then treats those exaggerations as Christian theology. The Christian Church has been feeling its way, from the commencement, into the full light of the revelation with which it has been entrusted. It has often advanced by means of splendid errors, and still more often through mental and spiritual agonies; and the task of true criticism would be to develop the truth of which those errors were the partial reflection, and of which those agonies were the birth-pangs.

Considerations of this nature will apply throughout these last four Lectures. It will be equally essential to vindicate ordinary theological terms from the narrow conceptions which popular theories have from time to time attributed to them, and at the same time to illustrate their profound correspondence with the realities of life. Take, for instance, in connection with the subject we are treating this afternoon, the word "Salvation." The phrase "Scheme of Salvation" has become peculiarly obnoxious, and the very ideal itself has become to many minds artificial. Men whose objections are entitled to respect continually speak as if theologians understood by it the deliverance of the soul from some mysterious, if not arbitrary, fate. The subject assumes in their thoughts a distant and unreal character; and those schemes, of which there have been, indeed, but too many, throw their artificial appearance over the whole conception. But start from the language of the Scriptures, and import the meaning thus obtained into the language of the Church, and the idea of Salvation becomes only too real and momentous. " Thou shalt call His name Jesus," it is said, " for He shall save His people from their sins." Bearing in mind those facts of life of which I have spoken, what expression can come more home to the hearts and necessities of mankind ? Doubtless, in its ultimate signification, the term Salvation is fulfilled by giving it a future meaning. It looks forward to that solemn hereafter when our souls, disembarrassed of all other interests, shall stand face to face with their eternal doom. But if we wish to know what that doom implies, we must interpret the future by its commencement in the present. To be saved is primarily to be delivered from those sins which have been our continual burden. They are not merely a weight on our conscience, they are a perpetual clog on our spiritual energies, and their

memory is an intolerable remorse to us. The very
question of life is whether we can be saved from them.
In other words, can the health of our souls be restored, so that we can breathe and live in a spiritual
atmosphere, and feel in harmony with its Divine
realities? A question of infinite perplexity to a far
greater number of souls than the external complacency of social manners might lead us to imagine!
In the business of life it may, for many a long period,
be put aside, but in some moment or other the thought
returns of what the soul might have been, of what
were its visions of everything noble, pure, and lovely ;
and the weaknesses of which we have become the
victims—the sins which, even if they have not become
habits, have left their traces in marred sympathies and
enfeebled energies, make us doubt whether we can
ever be saved from ourselves. A melancholy acqui-
escence in imperfection steals, it is to be feared, over
the souls of the majority of men and women when,
after the excitement of life is over, they begin to
realize the defeats of their spiritual struggle. They
take refuge in vague hopes of some future deliverance ;
and it is, after all, their readiness to grasp at any
consolation which lends vitality to the artificial
schemes just spoken of. To those who are conscious
of the inveterate and ingrained disease of their spirits,
it is difficult to realise the possibility of perfect
renovation; and Christianity itself, in one sense,
aggravates the difficulty by the urgency with which it

insists on the fatal effect of a lingering vice in the soul, and on the necessity of perfection as that which can alone confer peace and happiness.

I have been hitherto speaking in the ordinary language of observation and of philosophy ; but to give these considerations their full force, let us now turn upon them the light of those views of the spiritual world which I recalled at the commencement of this Lecture. We have to interpret the soul's general sense of imperfection by this further consideration—that it will have to deal directly and face to face with a Personal Being of infinite and uncompromising holiness, truth, and justice. Conscience has been but the premonitory utterance of that Divine voice which will then penetrate in its deepest tones to the recesses of the soul ; the feelings of shame have been but the foreshadowing of the utter self-abasement which a frail spirit must feel under the piercing glance of that Divine eye. Again I would urge that we must not shrink from employing these analogies. Can it be supposed for a moment that the direct introduction of the soul to those great spiritual Personalities can fail to arouse in it all the emotions of shame, fear, and self-abhorrence which it feels even in the presence of its fellows ? We have to imagine all those emotions a thousandfold intensified—a Divine light searching the inmost corners of the will, and laying bare not merely presumptuous sins but secret faults, convicting and condemning desires as well as acts, thoughts as well as words, and bringing every movement and impulse of our nature before the judgment seat. This is the first step in the revelation of Christianity.

It was a revelation of this kind, and spoken with this purpose, which Christ delivered at the outset of His ministry in the Sermon on the Mount. That Sermon is, no doubt, a proclamation of morality ; but it is strange that any one can read it in this sense, and not feel it at the same time the most terrible proclamation of judgment ever uttered. Let us conceive ourselves listening to that voice, speaking with authority, " Ye have heard that it hath been said, Thou shalt not kill ; but I say unto you that whosoever shall be angry with his brother without cause shall be in danger of the judgment." " Ye have heard that it was said by them of old time, Thou shalt not commit adultery ; but I say unto you that whosoever looketh on a woman to lust after her hath committed adultery with her already in his heart." " Till heaven and earth pass, one jot or one tittle shall in no wise pass from the law till all be fulfilled." Let us realize the penetration and inexorable severity of this voice, and which of us can contemplate unmoved its final and judicial revelation to our consciences ?

Such is the meaning of the statement from which St. Paul starts in his exposition of the gospel with which he had been entrusted—that " the wrath of God is revealed from heaven against all ungodliness and unrighteousness of men." This is a revelation which does not depend merely on external guarantees; it justifies itself. Those who heard the Sermon on the Mount felt that our Saviour spoke with authority; and when the Apostles proclaim this judgment already working in our souls, and hereafter to be fully enforced, our consciences bear witness that they are revealing realities. Just as a companion with quicker sight than ourselves will explain to us the meaning of some form approaching in the distance, and though we could not ourselves have discerned it, we recognize at once the correctness of the explanation; so, when the Scriptures interpret to us the warnings of conscience, we instinctively recognize the truth of the interpretation. If the faculties of the soul are not impenetrably dulled, it cannot but feel itself, in presence of such a revelation, surrounded by a " consuming fire " which must burn up everything base and false. Let a man interpret by these considerations, by these present facts of his conscience, the language of the Scriptures and of the Church with respect to Salvation, and he will be very far from thinking it either artificial or unworthy. Objectors have deprecated the encouragement of a mere anxiety for personal safety. But who will deprecate the anxiety to attain such a relation towards spiritual realities that the purifying fires of Divine wrath, though they may rage, shall have none but a healing influence? How can a man fail, if he have any high aims at all, to struggle perpetually for salvation from the evils he feels, and from the consequences which, both for himself and for others, he justly dreads ?

In short, the facts we have been considering embody the most marked characteristic of human life. In its external aspects that life is undoubtedly much the same as all other life. Let us, if possible, conceive an observer whose vision should be closed to the human conscience, to whom the intellect and the passions alone should be open ; and though some phenomena might perplex him, he might naturally conclude, on the whole, in favour of that scientific view of life which regards it as a mere struggle, in which the fittest survive and thus continually augment the acquisitions of their race. The progress of the whole advances with little reference to the individual. It is possible—only too possible—for a man to gain the whole world and lose his own soul ; possible, at all events, for him to contribute immeasurably to the welfare of his fellow-creatures in some important department of their existence—in war, for instance, or law, or science—and yet to remain himself with a disorganized soul, a prey to some vice, or the victim of some weakness. The work of his intellect, the labour of his hands, may remain as the heritage of his kind ; and it may matter little for their future welfare on earth what was his personal state. But what a world, my brethren, lies behind this visible manifestation of intellect and force ! It is shrouded from our view, but we cannot conceive of it adequately without recognizing it as infinitely

greater in extent and in interest than even the great
drama of history and the political and social life of
mankind. All the souls that have ever lived have had
their personal relations to that unseen Being who has
been the light, not only of Christians, but of every
man that has come into the world. Everything else
has passed away from them, as it must one day pass
from us, except the result of those relations. The
secret book which records them is not a mere detail of
isolated and private feelings ; but the influences of one
soul upon another, the temptations we have caused to
our fellows, our faithfulness or unfaithfulness to them,
have been working out, in a labyrinth only to be dis-
entangled by an omniscient eye, our several positions
in view of that final judgment. It is this which, as is
commonly said, levels all distinctions in the presence of
death ; because there remains to every soul alike the
supreme and eternal question of its relations to right
and wrong, to the law of God, and to God Himself.
This is that other world for the sake of which saints
have often wisely fled from the present, having entangled themselves too deeply with its allurements. It
has, indeed, been a part of their punishment that they
have been obliged to do so. It is the natural province
of the conscience to help us to use this world aright,
and to develop all its capacities ; and, in point of fact,
such an observer as I have imagined would be wrong
in supposing that the mere struggle of life, without
that continued elevation which the sense of duty

affords, would produce the result which he admires. But circumstances do arise in which it seems necessary that the solitude of death should be anticipated, and in which the soul is compelled to retire in order to commune alone with its Judge and its Saviour.

Now it is characteristic of the Bible and of Christianity that they deal primarily and immediately with this inner world. The charge has been raised against them that they do not concern themselves sufficiently with the visible course of human affairs, and there is a certain apparent foundation for it. What they are chiefly concerned with is that half of life which, after all, is even here the larger half, and which is the only eternal part of it—that which concerns our relations to Him in whom our conscience lives and moves and has its being. It is, therefore, a misconception of their scope to represent them, as has been lately done,[1] as dealing mainly with conduct—regarding conduct, that is, as equivalent to the regulation of our actions. They are undoubtedly concerned with it ; but their action upon it is in the main indirect. By revealing the spiritual world, or the Kingdom of Heaven, they awaken the sensibility of the soul to those spiritual principles, such as truth and love, upon which the subordinate laws of conduct depend, and in which, as St. Paul says, they are fulfilled. If, for instance, they seem to neglect, as has been alleged, such a virtue as

[1] By Mr. Matthew Arnold, in "Literature and Dogma," fourth edition, pp. 14—18.

patriotism, it is because they ascend to a higher region than that of the statesman, and are content to say that if a man be true—not to himself, but—to his God, he "cannot then be false to any man." But they would fail to touch the deepest thoughts and wants of men, if they did not deal still more with those consequences of conduct which remain fixed in the heart and the conscience—if they did not speak of a remedy for sin as well as of a correction of error. It is the revelation of "the Lamb of God, which taketh away the sin of the world"—of the world past, present, and future— which, in spite of a thousand difficulties, has retained its hold on the hearts of sinning men and women. Elsewhere you may find rules of conduct more or less satisfactory, but nowhere else will you find the wounds of the soul probed with such utter severity, while at the same time an adequate remedy for them is provided. It remains to consider the nature of that remedy, in its cause and in its operation. Its cause will be considered in the next Lecture, on the Doctrine of the Atonement, and its operation in the two last Lectures of the course, on the Doctrines of Justification and Sanctification.

LECTURE VI.

THE PRINCIPLE OF ATONEMENT.

1 JOHN ii. 1, 2.

" My little children, these things write I unto you that ye sin not. And if any man sin, we have an advocate with the Father, Jesus Christ the righteous : and He is the propitiation for our sins."

IN the last Lecture I dwelt on the nature of the problem which has to be considered by any religion or philosophy which addresses itself to the real facts of life. That problem, it appeared, was not merely the laying-down of rules for right action, but the provision of a remedy for the vast mass of moral evil, which, as a matter of fact, prevails in the world. It is not enough to show what ought to be done. That, in all the essentials of morality, we know well enough. The great problem is how to deal with the fact that men so lamentably fail to do it. If, indeed, men had no permanent conscience, their failure might be regarded as the mere inperfection of individuals incident to the process of development. The imperfection of a plant or an animal involves no such permanent consequences to the creature itself; and, perplexing as the problem of animal suffering may be, we can at least see that the struggles of individuals are working out the elevation of the race, while we know not how far there exists in the lower creatures that self-consciousness, that power of realizing their own condition, which constitutes the essential grievance, so to speak, both of pain and of imperfection. But, at all events, it is the aggravation of the problem by the permanent consciousness and conscience of man, which practically creates for us this overwhelming difficulty. A soul aroused, in bitter remorse, to a sense of what it might have been and what it ought to have done, conscious that it exists in a state which is inconsistent with its abiding relations to spiritual realities—this is the spectacle with which the physician of human nature has to deal. It is a spectacle of which the distress becomes insupportable, when we realize, as we so seldom do, the vast mass of darkened consciences and marred souls which the world contains; and it may at least be urged as an incontestable merit in Christianity, that it recognizes that dark shadow in life, and offers to enlighten it.

In considering, accordingly, in the present Lecture, how the Christian doctrine of the Atonement harmonizes with the demands of human experience, I will ask, at the outset, whether there be not an enormous presumption in its favour in the mere fact that its foundation is laid in deliberate acts of supreme

suffering and sorrow ?   Christ claims to be the representative, the head and the Lord of all mankind.
Does He not establish at least one supreme ground
for such a claim, when He commences by experi-
encing all the physical and moral agonies of the race,
when He takes upon Himself the burden of their sins
and sufferings, and, in the language of the Scriptures,
"tastes death" and all the accessories of death ? "It
became Him"—such is the bold language of the inspired writer—it was worthy of the Divine Father,
and worthy therefore of the Divine Son, that He who
claimed to be the Captain of our Salvation should be
made "perfect through sufferings."   There is nothing
for which I have been more anxious in the course of
these Lectures than to assure both myself and my
hearers that, while developing the correspondence of
Christian truths with human wants, I am at the same
time simply following the order in which those truths
are set forth in the Scriptures.   Of this the point now
before us is eminently illustrative.   The portion of the
Scriptures in which the doctrine of the Atonement is
most fully elucidated is the Epistle to the Hebrews,
and it is from the commencement of that Epistle that
the words I have just quoted are taken.   At the outset
of the argument to establish the priesthood of Christ
and the perfection of the offering He made, the writer
appeals to the fact that Jesus has identified Himself
with His brethren in all the weakness of their mortal
condition. "He is not ashamed to call them brethren";

and, "forasmuch as they are partakers of flesh and blood, He also Himself likewise took part of the same ; that through death He might destroy him that had the power of death. . . . In all things it behoved Him to be made like unto His brethren, that He might be a merciful and faithful High Priest in things pertaining to God, to make reconciliation for the sins of the people. For in that He Himself hath suffered being tempted, He is able to succour them that are tempted."

We may venture, indeed, to go still further, when we remember that the author of the Epistle has been describing the Person of whom he thus speaks as the brightness of the Father's glory, and the express image of His person ; and we may be allowed to ask whether a revelation of God which represents Him as Himself entering into and sharing the sorrows, and even in some sense the sins of the beings whom He has created, does not meet one of the profoundest difficulties involved in the belief of such a Being. It is not, at all events, a Christian who need shrink from admitting that it would be very hard to entertain trust and love towards a Person who, while Himself abiding in the imperturbed serenity of Divine existence, had created human beings to struggle alone as best they might with the laws He had established, and to suffer to all eternity the consequences of the imperfection which His will had once for all imposed upon their nature. I am very far from saying that all difficulty of this kind is removed by the Christian hypothesis. It is

not probable that, while the subordinate problems of
life and science present such innumerable perplexities,
the ultimate problem of all should offer no mystery.
But it may at least be said that, in proclaiming a God
who takes upon Himself the sins and sorrows of His
creatures in deeper measure than any of them have
themselves experienced, we obviate some of the most
urgent objections which can be raised by the human
conscience. There is an insuperable mystery in the
very idea of a suffering or of an incarnate God ; but
so far as the conscience and the heart are concerned,
the conflict between the evil of life and the goodness
of God receives an inexpressible alleviation when we
are bidden to recognize one exhibition of that goodness
in the acceptance by God Himself of the consequences
of our evil. We behold God, as it were, entering into
the experience of the creature whom He has made ;
and, from the moral point of view, His character becomes in harmony with the world of moral beings. It
is invariably kept out of sight by the opponents of
Christianity, and should be incessantly remembered
by its apologists, that it is God Himself who is revealed
as taking upon Himself the sins of the world.[1]

But from this general consideration let us pass to
the particular developments of the doctrine under discussion. The questions raised by the adversaries of
our Faith concern the necessity of any Atonement at
all, and, even if this necessity be admitted, the possi-

[1] Compare Athanasius, " De Incarnatione Verbi," 10.

bility of anything in the nature of a vicarious Atonement. As to the former question, we have to start
from the supposition of our possessing free-will and responsibility. If it could be shown that our acts were the
mere product of circumstances, if we could refer our
sins to the inevitable development of hereditary or
social influences, the idea of offering an atonement to
God for them would become unmeaning. Sin, in that
case, would cease to be a violation of law in any other
sense than that already referred to, in which the imperfection of an organism indicates that the development of the race to which it belongs is still in progress ;
and punishment would similarly be nothing more than
the inevitable consequence of imperfection. Now it is
obvious that sin and punishment have to a certain
extent this character. The sentiment to which I referred in the first of these Lectures—that free-will is
not so free as it is sometimes represented—is very true,
and we need continually to bear it in mind in pre-
suming to form any judgment of the sins and the
relative merits of our fellows. There can be no greater
injustice than to measure their personal responsibility
by the heinousness, considered in reference to society,
of the crimes they may commit. But when this argument is pressed so far as to obscure the sense of any
personal responsibility to God, it is clear that it proves
too much. It would be equally valid to disprove our
responsibility to one another, and our obligation to
make reparation and atonement for injurious conduct

We must here, in fact, revert to a class of considerations on which we have already, in great measure, based our presumptions in favour of the Christian interpretation of morality. When we have done wrong to others, do we not universally feel responsible for it—so far, at least, as they are concerned ? and do we not feel bound to make an adequate reparation ? If there were no such thing as free-will, a feeling of this nature would have no foundation, and in fact could scarcely be conceived. We might view with the utmost distress the consequences of our weaknesses, and might labour to repair them. But when the conscience is thoroughly aroused, our feeling towards those whom we have wronged is utterly different from this. It involves a sense that we are personally guilty—that we have done what we ought not to have done, what we were under no compulsion to do, and what nothing can excuse us for doing. Towards them, at least, we cannot avoid feeling and acting as though we had possessed free-will and had abused it. Now it would seem that if this feeling be valid at all, it must be valid throughout our spiritual relationships, and it becomes extremely difficult to exclude it from the highest relationship of all. All the mystery of the case must be fully admitted. It is not Christians alone who are unable to reconcile the appearances of freedom with the necessities of law. But we are dealing with the facts of conscience, and we cannot approach the ultimate problems of religion and philo-

sophy with any safety without strictly adhering to the
evidence thus afforded us.   The imperious consciousness, then, that we are personally responsible to our
fellow-men furnishes one of those facts from which
there can be no appeal, and compels us to admit
a sense of responsibility throughout our whole nature.

It indicates, indeed, a strange revolution in human
thought that it should be necessary to begin from this
consideration.   The first impulse of men, under the
dictates of nature, has almost always been to acknowledge a responsibility to a Divine Power, and to offer
some expiation for the offences they have committed.
The sacrifices of the Jews are but a more elaborate
illustration of the universal practice of mankind ; and
if the general prevalence of an instinct can be regarded as any proof of the belief it implies, there are
few cases in which experience supplies a stronger
argument than is afforded in favour of the necessity
of an atonement by the practice of expiatory sacrifices.   I do not dwell upon it, because I am not
developing an argument from history, but from the
facts of daily experience.   But I would ask, in passing, whether it be not far more natural to explain this
practice, with all its abuses, by the supposition that
it indicates an imperfect apprehension of a reality,
than by treating it as the mere dream of a timorous
imagination ?   If a sense of relationship to God was
always working in men's consciences, and if they felt
dimly that they had not been true to Him, any more

than to their fellows, their struggles to find some
expiation were inevitable. This sense has been lately
overborne by that great revolution of thought which,
for a time, has obscured the idea of personality under
the veil of a vast combination of laws. But we may
fall back on the personal relation of man to man, and
we shall there find a perpetual witness to the fact of
our responsibility, to our free-will for the purposes of
that responsibility, and to the need of Atonement
which such responsibility implies.

I need not urge that, if this consideration be admitted at all, the sense of violated duty which it
involves becomes insupportably intensified when the
person whom we recognize ourselves as having injured
and grieved is one who stands towards us in the relation of divine fatherhood, and whose voice, in whispers
of love and mercy, has been perpetually speaking to
us in our consciences. Our present concern, however,
is not with the full development of the Christian
consciousness, but with the justification of its primary
conceptions ; and I must pass to other aspects of the
doctrine. Admitting, it may be said, the truth and
reality of this sense of responsibility to God, and the
need of making atonement, how, it is asked, can that
be made by another ? What is the value of anything
in the nature of reparation which is not made by the
person who has committed the offence ? In answer
to this, it must be in the first place observed, that the
Christian doctrine of the Atonement is so far from

excluding reparation by the offender, and in a certain sense atonement by him, that it regards such atonement as essential to the moral conditions requisite for his restoration to a state of spiritual health.   Certain schemes, no doubt, have put forward the conception of a punishment so purely vicarious as to have justly shocked the consciences of thoughtful men. But such schemes will not be found by impartial inquirers to be sustained by the language of Scripture.   Atonement offered by Christ has been described under a variety of images, and it has been the temptation of divines to take one or other of these and erect it into a full account of the matter.   St. Paul compares the Atonement at one time to the payment of a ransom, and at another time to the payment of a debt.   The effects to us are the same, in many respects, as if the work accomplished had been of the nature of either of these two cases ; but the very fact of the variety of the illustrations is a proof that in neither of them is an adequate explanation of the reality to be found.

There are two points essential to the doctrine, whether enunciated by St. Paul or St. John or the author of the Epistle to the Hebrews, which, if kept in view, will be found to protect the truth from any of the unworthy conceptions just referred to.   The first is that the justice which requires to be satisfied in the matter does not concern the relationship of things, but that of persons. When I have violated some intimate relationship, I may describe myself, in a metaphor, as

having incurred a debt; but, in point of fact, the
wrong done is one of feeling and of personal regard,
and can only be fully repaired by personal acts of right
feeling. This consideration at once dissipates all such
base conceptions of the Atonement as that it consisted in the mere endurance of pain; as though the
question had been one of a bare exchange of equiva-
lents. Another point which necessarily follows from
the former, is that the value of the personal acts of
the Saviour is never contemplated apart from the
production of similar acts and feelings on our own
part. "If we walk in the light, as He is in the light,
we have fellowship one with another, and the blood of
Jesus Christ His Son cleanseth us from all sin." "If
we say that we have no sin we deceive ourselves, and
the truth is not in us; but if we confess our sins, He
is faithful and just to forgive us our sins, and to
cleanse us from all unrighteousness." In even more
urgent language, St. Paul insists that the whole virtue
of our acceptance in Christ consists in our sharing His
death, and in our entering with Him into all that
mortification of our corrupt nature, and that resurrection to a new life, of which our Baptism is the pledge.
"Know ye not that so many of us as were baptized
into Jesus Christ were baptized into His death?
Therefore we are buried with Him by baptism into
death, that like as Christ was raised up from the dead
by the glory of the Father, even so we also should
walk in newness of life." It is to the Apostle incon-

ceivable, and a contradiction in terms, that men
should claim freedom from the consequences of sin
by Christ's death without possessing union with His
Spirit.   It is here that those fundamental doctrines in
Christianity, which render it possible for us to conceive of Christ as united with all Christians, and as
bestowing His Spirit and His nature on them, become
essentially involved in the idea of the Atonement.   It
is assumed that, by His Divine nature, He can bring
us into deeper union with Himself than with any
other influence or person, and can thus infuse into us
His own Spirit and make us partakers in His own
disposition.

Let us dismiss, then, as unworthy of serious notice,
such objections as that, punishment being the result
of sin, its ordinary and logical consequences must needs
be borne by the sinner.   When, indeed, objectors go
on to say, as they do, that it cannot be borne by any
other than the sinner, they contradict, as has often
been pointed out, one of the most obvious facts of
life.   The effects of sin are continually borne, often in
a very severe degree, by the innocent ; and it will be
shown presently that it is not unreasonable to speak
of such effects, even when thus borne, as a penalty.
But it is no part of the Christian doctrine that the
Christian does not bear the punishment of his sin.
That its total consequences, as they would ensue if no
Divine hand interposed, are averted, is, indeed, the
blessing promised by the doctrine.   But the sinner is

expressly called on to bear, in what the Apostle describes as a death to his old nature—as a kind of life-long mortification—results of his evil which often amount to a very bitter penalty. He is delivered from it at last; but not without a repentance, an anguish of spirit, and a painful struggle, which is proportionate to his fall. I must repeat what I said in the last Lecture, that Christianity is not to be made responsible for popular exaggerations of artificial systems. On one point of fact important to this argument, a verdict may be safely challenged. There is a deeper sense of repentance for evil, a more profound self-abasement, in those books of the New Testament from which the doctrine of the Atonement has been derived than in any other human writings. The proclamation that Christ made Atonement for us intensified infinitely, if it did not practically create, the repentance for which it has been alleged to be a substitute.

In fact, the force of the argument for the necessity of an Atonement can only be realized in proportion as this personal repentance is developed. Men may argue, so to speak, in cold blood that such remorse and amendment as I have been speaking of are an adequate atonement for their faults. But let their consciences be fully touched, and the whole springs of their nature aroused, and they are sure to feel overwhelmed with a sense of the miserable disproportion which exists between the evils they have done, the wrongs they have inflicted, and the reparation they have made or can make. Some, alas! of the commonest sins are of a nature for which no effectual reparation can be made by the offender. A thief may restore the money he has stolen ; but who is to replace the innocence, the purity, the peace of mind, which, even in mere recklessness if in nothing worse, a man may have marred in others? Looking back upon mischievous words and suggestions and deeds, who can estimate the illimitable stretch of those ever-expanding spheres of evil influence which he has set on foot? Is it not to be feared that all of us would tremble if we could catch a glance of the evil, in its ultimate development, for which in its germination we are responsible, and that we should need no Divine message to assure us that we could never make atonement for it? Look, moreover, at that vast mass of iniquity to which I have more than once referred, and ask what mere human repentance can be an adequate acknowledgment of its vileness? It is by the consciences of men, and not by the schemes of divines, that the demand for an Atoning Sacrifice has been created.

But after disposing of these misconceptions, we return to the question which often creates the greatest difficulty. How, it is said, is it possible for a vicarious satisfaction to be offered for us? How can another in any degree fulfil that work of repentance for which we are ourselves incompetent? Let us, however,

consider whether it would not be more true to nature
to invert the inquiry, and to ask how satisfaction can
ever be rendered for evil except by the intervention of
others? The Scriptures assume one fact with reference to human nature which it is a peculiar danger
of modern speculation to overlook. The tendency of
our civilization has been to individualize life. Men
are contemplated as standing alone, and as independent persons. In legal phrase, the hypothesis of
"status" has given place to that of "contract." But
among the legal fictions which are sometimes de-
nounced in reference to this subject, there can hardly
be a more flagrant fiction than this. There is not one
important element in their lives in respect to which
men stand alone. In all their acts they are inseparably bound up together; their characters, their excellences and vices are the result of mutual actions
incessantly accumulated. The case is inconceivable
in which one man alone is responsible for the condition,
whether of vice or virtue, in which he exists. His
parents, his family, his friends have all co-operated to
make him what he is. He has, indeed, his own
responsibility; but they too have a responsibility for
him, and if we would estimate the responsibility of
each aright, we must view them as parts of a whole.
In practical life we are compelled to act on this
principle. We treat countries and similar communities as being jointly responsible for the acts of
the individuals composing them; and similarly we

constantly accept reparation from the whole body for
the wrong done by one member of it. Such con-
ventions may, indeed, all be imperfect ; but their
validity is derived from the fact that they are imperfect applications of a reality. The arrangement is
not artificial; but it is felt that all have their share, to
some extent, in the act of the individual, and that
they must therefore hold themselves responsible for
him. He, in his turn, may be regarded as representing
them, and may be called upon to act and suffer on
their behalf, in pursuance of the consequences of their
collective character and conduct.

Now extend this principle to the whole human
race, and you have the foundation of the idea under
which Christ is treated as the Head of mankind, and
under which His merits are attributed to us. The
first step, as we have seen, in His atoning work is
that He makes Himself one with us—partaker of
our flesh and blood. So far as that is the case,
He shares with all of us the consequences of our
evil, while we share His spirit and His excellences.
It cannot be otherwise. If in a family there are good
and bad members, it is impossible, in proportion to
the intimacy of their union, to separate the one from
the other ; the bad are sheltered by the merits of the
good, and, on the other hand, the good suffer for the
bad. If the ordinary course of life thus requires that
the human race should be viewed as a whole, the
language of the Scriptures, and even much of the

language which at first may startle us in Christian
divines, becomes natural. Would it be possible for
a perfectly good man, if a member of a wicked family,
to avoid feeling, with intense grief and bitterness,
their sin and evil, and labouring to make reparation
in every possible way for the harm they had done,
while endeavouring, with equal devotion, to win them
back by example and influence? Conceive this, and
then further consider whether it would not be in strict
conformity with the dictates of natural justice for a
third person, whom that family had wronged, to accept
the grief and the efforts at repentance of such a man
as a kind of atonement, and to be disposed to forgive,
if possible, the whole family for his sake. All would,
indeed, be fruitless unless the mediating person were
able ultimately to win back his fellows to repentance
and to justice; but the possibility of this is, as we
have seen, what Christianity supposes.

The case as thus stated corresponds, perhaps, more
closely to the language of the Scriptures than any
other illustration. It is the fact of Christ personally
acting and having acted for us and among us which
is described as constituting the operative virtue of
His Atonement. "If any man sin we have an advocate with the Father, Jesus Christ the righteous; and
He is the propitiation for our sins." The Apostle
does not merely say He makes propitiation for our
sins, but that He Himself, in His perfect nature, is
the propitiation. Our whole family must henceforth

be contemplated as inseparably bound up with Him; and He refuses, in the Divine self-sacrifice of His will, to let us be judged or regarded apart from Himself. In this sense what is more natural than to say that He fulfils the law for us, and that He bears our sins? Not, as has been abundantly said, that we escape from fulfiling the law ourselves; but that it is His complete obedience which, in the sight of One who views us as a whole body, constitutes the justification of our nature, and that He expresses on our behalf and as the earnest of feelings He will awaken within us, a due repentance for our sins. The virtue of the cross is not its mere suffering, but the fact that, by means of it, Christ tasted to the very dregs the evil of man, and uttered towards God the deep grief and sorrow which such evil demands.[1] In one word, transfer the whole question from the region of laws to that of persons, conceive those storms which in the Divine nature correspond to wrath and judgment, mercy and love in human beings evoked, as they must be, towards the human race, by the spectacle of its evil, conceive Christ standing like Moses of old, and praying "Forgive now this people—but if not, blot me, I pray Thee, out of the book which Thou hast written," and we have a conception of personal relations which is at least perfectly consistent with the justest impulses of the heart.

[1] It is, I hope, almost superflous to mention that I am deeply indebted in the course of this argument to the work of the late Dr. McLeod Campbell upon the "Atonement."

It may be well to add, without intruding too far
upon peculiarly sacred ground, that this spiritual
aspect of Christ's sacrifice must ever be borne in mind
in interpreting the solemn language in which the
sacred writers speak of the shedding of His blood,
and of its atoning efficacy. The supreme value of
His Atonement depends upon His spiritual and
voluntary sacrifice of Himself on our behalf to the
will of God ; and in order that this sacrifice might be
perfected, it was carried out even to the shedding of
His blood and the offering of His body. The Captain
of our Salvation, we read, had to be made perfect
through sufferings. "The blood," it is said, "is the
life," and the life of the soul, no less than of the body,
was drawn forth in the sufferings of the Cross. The
last mortal agony was needed in order to put that
holy soul to its final proof, to evoke from its inmost
depths its sorrow and its love, and to inspire with full
meaning that final utterance of the whole life, and
will, and mind of Christ, "Father, into Thy hands I
commend my spirit." The blood of Christ, willingly
and patiently yielded, was the sign and seal, to heaven
and earth, that this commendation of the spirit was
finished and perfect. It offered to God a complete
propitiation, and at the same time it imposed upon
man the strongest and most affecting of all obligations
towards the Son of God. This, as is observed by
ancient interpreters, is one reason why the blood of
Christ is said to cleanse us from all sin, original or
actual. It has this effect " not merely in the sense of

removing the guilt of our former sins, but also because it purges the will from sinful affections, causing a true conversion of heart, a love of righteousness and work of virtue."[1] It purges the conscience from dead works to serve the living God, to whom that complete surrender of soul and body was made.

But it must be sufficient in a controversial argument to have thus indicated, with reverent reserve, the intense moral and spiritual force enshrined in the inner recesses of Christian faith on this subject. We commenced by considering Christ in His suffering as representing God to us. We have concluded by regarding Him as representing us to God; and thus, by His mediation, God and man are bound together in one bond of mutual sympathy and confidence. He does and He feels, in the first place, all that it becomes us to do and to feel, and in the second place He infuses into us the power of growing like Him. As evil spreads from person to person, so does good ; and the Divine and human personality of Christ renders possible an union and a communion with Him which impart a new hope and a new life to the human race. But the mode in which that union is effected must be the subject of the next two Lectures.

[1] Estius, "Com. in Ep. 1 Joan." c. 1, v. 7.

LECTURE VII.

THE MEANING OF JUSTIFICATION.

ROMANS v. I.

"Therefore being justified by faith, we have peace with God through our Lord Jesus Christ."

IT would seem evident that a religion which, like Christianity, offers the means of redemption for the whole nature of man, must enter into definite statements respecting the manner in which that redemption operates. It must make distinctions, it must observe the various actions, relations, and demands of man's spiritual being, and it must exhibit its application to them in detail. But however obvious such an observation may be, the neglect of it seems at the root of many of the presumptive objections raised against Christian theology. The very language of such theology provokes in many minds a kind of uneasiness. They appear to resent being troubled with what they are inclined to call mere metaphysical distinctions, and it may be desirable to meet this difficulty in entering on the discussion of such terms as Justification and Sanctification.

Now it does undoubtedly require some concentration

I

of thought and some sustained reflection to apprehend Christian truths. I am, indeed, far from saying that a man cannot receive the benefits of Christianity without mental ability and intellectual training. The case is in some measure parallel with that of our physical nature. A man may be perfectly healthy, his body may respond to all the life-giving influences of air, of light, of food, and yet, like a child, he may be perfectly ignorant of the structure of his body, or of its physiological relations. But if the laws which govern his health are to be known, still more if means are to be found of relieving him from disease, it is necessary to develop a most elaborate science ; and for the purposes of the general health of the community we are beginning to realize the necessity of the wide diffusion of a sound knowledge of the main elements and relations of our physical nature. Similarly, in religion, the Christian theologian will be the last to deny the truth of the sentiment, which has now become so popular, that a very simple faith is sufficient for salvation. It is sufficient in a similar sense to that in which very simple rules of life are sufficient for health. Happy indeed, in one way, are those who have no need to go further. Multitudes of simple souls have passed a pure and tranquil spiritual existence, breathing an untroubled atmosphere of faith in God and love to Christ, and quickened by that faith and love to a perpetual growth in the graces of the Christian character. These are, as it were, the

pastoral lives of the spiritual sphere, unshadowed by
the clouds of doubt, and but lightly ruffled by the
storms of temptation.   But the health of the soul—or,
in other words, salvation—is not, as a rule, thus easily
preserved ;   and when once lost, it needs a science at
least as profound as that of the body to guide us to
its restoration.   It might be asked, indeed, whether
this craving for simplicity in religion be not very
similar to the fancy of the poets for the charms of a
simple and pastoral existence.   Taking life as a whole
we find ourselves destined for a rougher and less
placid career ;   and after all, what soul of any worth
would exchange for an unconscious serenity the
struggle of battle and the experience of life ?

If, in short, we regard the constitution of the soul
as not less complex and delicate than that of the
body, we cannot dream of rejecting, as either unin-
teresting or unimportant, the detailed development of
its laws and its relations.   It is not worthy of intelligent beings, with a heart and a conscience, to live in
any respect an unconscious spiritual life.   If we could
be content to neglect that life entirely, and to fall
back on the mere development of our physical and
intellectual powers, the reluctance to entertain such
considerations as theology involves would be intelligible.   But if, as the practical experience of mankind
indicates, our deepest interests lie in the relations of
our souls to the spiritual world, the reluctance in
question is equally unreasonable and faint-hearted.

Is it, in fact, conceivable that questions which relate to the very dividing asunder of the soul and body, which deal with the secret thoughts and intents of the heart and with the springs of the conscience, should be capable of discussion without careful and even laborious discrimination of terms and facts? It is the office of a Lecturer in this science, as in all others, to render its results plain and comprehensible; but, like other sciences, it has its laws and its terminology, and none can understand it but those who will have the patience to learn what these mean.

If, then, I were lecturing on Natural Science, I should be compelled to use such terms as Gravitation, Conservation of Force, Oxidation, and the like; and it would be felt that the acquisition of the truth depended on understanding them. They are simply brief designations of facts, and they serve to guide us to the results of recorded experience. It is from this point of view that we should consider such theological terms as Justification and Sanctification. They also are terms which guide us to the results of recorded experience. Justification, for instance, might be regarded as holding towards the spiritual life a similar position to that which Gravitation occupies towards natural life. It is a theological abstraction, in the sense in which Gravitation is a scientific abstraction. It is doubtless sufficient for many ordinary purposes to know that bodies fall to the earth; but that is no reason for disregarding the more exact and scientific statement that "every portion of matter attracts every other portion, and the attraction between them is proportional to the product of their masses divided by the square of their distance." Similarly, it may be enough for many purposes to say that men are saved by faith and truth; but this is no reason for neglecting the more complete revelation that "we are accounted righteous before God, only for the merit of our Lord and Saviour Jesus Christ by Faith, and not for our own works or deservings." Both in natural and in religious matters the simple statements have hitherto sufficed, more or less, for the great majority of men; but it is no less reasonable in the one case than in the other that the advancement of mankind should depend upon our fuller comprehension of the truth. By means of the law of Gravitation, we have multiplied our physical powers and transformed our natural life; and not less certainly by the development of Christian truths have we quickened our spiritual conscience, and transformed the moral and spiritual character both of individuals and of communities. In proportion as men have realized the truths of the Gospel and have acted on them, have they developed a new world of spiritual excellences; and if we would share the experiences of the holiest members of our race, we must appreciate the revelation which illuminated their spirits.

The previous Lectures of this course ought to have supplied us with the necessary materials for appre-

hending the doctrines now in question. It may not
be superfluous to observe, in the first place, that the
two theological terms it remains to discuss have perfectly distinct and definite significations. A far too
careless employment of them among religious writers
and preachers offers some excuse for that inability to
recognize the meaning of Christian doctrines which,
as I observed in the first Lecture, characterizes much
of the sceptical writing of the day. The words Salvation, Justification, and Sanctification, have been used
without any adequate discrimination, until a vague
confusion has obscured the whole subject. I trust,
however, that those who have followed me thus far
will find no difficulty in perceiving to what very distinct realities in the spiritual life they refer. Salvation, let me repeat, is not to be confined to some
mysterious future deliverance from doom ; it means
the restoration of the soul—a restoration to be commenced here and completed hereafter—to its true
relations and its perfect health. It is beyond all
question diseased ; and we need no revelation to tell
us that, at all events with vast numbers of men and
women, the disease is incurable by any natural process, and tends, with an increasing acceleration, to
issue in the moral dissolution of the whole being.
Conscience duly awakened has, indeed, borne testimony to the presence of this corruption even in men
of the highest aims and efforts. The problem which
Christianity offers to solve is to remedy this fatal

disorganization, and in Justification and Salvation we consider two successive processes in the application of this remedy.

We have seen, then, the light which the Gospel throws on the conditions of our spiritual existence, and the harmony which it introduces into our perceptions of the other world. We observed that the whole health of the soul consists in the soundness of its personal relations. You cannot isolate a man, as you may a plant or an animal, and judge of his condition by independent tests. You have to consider in what relation he stands with other persons; and Christianity reveals an extension of this personal relation towards God. Whatever may be the meaning of the Divine Personality, we have, at all events, personal relations towards it; and if so, it can only be by rectifying these that the salvation of our nature can be procured. We have further seen that since, in our relations with our fellow-men, we cannot escape the sense of guilt and responsibility, a similar sense must needs weigh upon the soul in its deeper spiritual relationship; and that we may recognize here the full interpretation of that remorse which burdens the soul in its solitude. Contemplating mankind also as one family, bound together by a common evil, and a common responsibility, we saw that if the favour and love of a righteous Being were to rest upon them without restriction, it was essential that some Atonement should be made for their sins, and that a source of perfect holiness should be established to counteract the prevalent evil. That Christ should have taken upon Himself our nature and borne our sins must, to put the case no higher, necessarily confer new powers and higher dignity upon mankind ; and if He refuses to be separated from us, if we have in Him an Advocate with the Father, who is the propitiation for our sins, we may be sure we cannot be excluded from that Divine fellowship. What reasons we have for believing that Jesus Christ was such a person as this, and that He stands in this relation to God and to us, it has not, indeed, been within the scope of my present subject to inquire, and that question must be reserved to a future occasion.[1] What I have been endeavouring to show is that these suppositions answer certain imperious demands of our consciousness, and are in no way inconsistent with the dictates of our conscience. We have now to advance a step further, and consider the manner in which the redeeming influence operates.

Now the first requisite on these suppositions must be to restore or to raise the soul to conscious communion with God. The ultimate aim is that we should love the Lord our God with all our heart, soul, mind, and strength, and our neighbour as ourselves. The attainment of that end would be our complete Sanctification, and the manner in which this is fully wrought out in us will be the subject of my next and

[1] See the second course of these Lectures.

last Lecture.   But there must needs be a first step in
this restoration, a preliminary deliverance from the
state of ignorance or alienation in which the soul has
been existing ; and it is this first step, this original
act of reconciliation, which the Church, following St.
Paul, designates by the term Justification.   The
primary meaning of the term will serve to connect it,
from another point of view, with our previous inquiries,
and to show how deep a necessity of human nature it
touches.   It implies acquittal from guilt.   Even so
far as that involves what is called a forensic meaning,
it is very far from being the mere image it has sometimes been considered ; and no one will be disposed
to disparage its significance in this respect who bears in
mind how natural and how real a thing it seems to us
to speak of our final judgment.   The Divine judgment-
seat, both here and hereafter, is a terrible reality.   It
is ever present to the mind of St. Paul ; and he starts
from it in announcing to the Romans the Justification
offered by his Gospel.   If, under the sanction of other
apostolic language, I endeavour to exhibit the more
personal meaning which the word involves, it is only
as more in accordance with the general course of this
argument.   I would, indeed, nowhere be understood
as limiting the meaning of Christian doctrine to the
interpretation which it bears from the particular point
of view under our consideration.   But apart from any
such judicial sense, the word may be considered as
appealing to that personal and private sense of guilt

which we have been contemplating as one of the great burdens of the soul. Poets have asked more than once, how we should bear the revelation if our hearts were suddenly laid bare to all our fellows, and have depicted the keen and overpowering distress we should feel in the sense of shame and of unworthiness to claim friendship with them. Need we even have recourse to this supposition? Who has not felt, at least at times, a sense of inconsistency between the regard in which others may hold him, and the reality of which he is conscious within himself? Who has not sometimes felt that a perfect confession might separate him from hearts which repose in his own, or on which he himself would fain repose? It is not merely that our nature, or that theirs, is injured; there is something which keeps us apart and mars all confidence. "If we walk in the light as He is in the light," says St. John, "we have fellowship one with another." Lack of fellowship is the inseparable consequence of any darkness in our thoughts or deeds.

Now to recognize, from our present point of view, the reasonableness of the theological idea of Justification, we have only to extend this analogy, as in former instances, to our relation towards God. We have to conceive ourselves brought into full conscious relationship with a Being to whom every evil thought, word, and deed of our lives lie open, and whose eye penetrates to the very depths of our conscience. What is the natural result of such a revelation? Is it to

establish a feeling of fellowship between the soul and
its God ? Experience has sufficiently supplied the
answer. The attitude of the human conscience towards God is expressed in every natural religion as
one of fear, and that fear is inseparably blended with
a confused sense of guilt. Wherever the idea of a
superior being is realized, it arouses a dim apprehension of failure in some duty required by him—an
apprehension distorted in proportion to the distortion
of the prevalent morality, but deriving its force and its
inextinguishable vitality from the germs of the moral
sense. The consciousness of contact with a Divine
Spirit awakens, in however low a degree, a feeling of
imperfection ; and a feeling of imperfection is inseparably associated with a conviction of some degree or
other of responsibility. "Enter not into judgment
with thy servant" is the utterance at once of the
highest and of the lowest religious consciousness. I
need not, indeed, appeal only to natural religions.
The experience of a large part of Christendom is
unhappily of the same character. It has been the
essential influence of Christianity to deepen men's
sense of sin and evil. Christ declared that He would
send a Spirit who should convince the world of sin ;
and He has certainly established an influence of that
character, which has been working on the conscience
of Christians ever since, and which cannot be eradicated. One consequence is that a Christian people
are liable, under an imperfect apprehension of the
Gospel, to become even more cowardly and super-

stitious than others ; and Christianity itself has too
often been perverted into a mere satisfaction of such
superstitions.   If, however, on calm reflection, or in
some moments of sudden revelation, we realize the
full meaning of our whole soul lying open before the
Divine eye, there can be few but must involuntarily
utter the cry, " Depart from me, for I am a sinful
man, O Lord."   So long as this sense of guilt and
fear remain, peace with God and love towards Him
is impossible, and our free communion with Him is
fatally obstructed.   It is not that we shrink from the
punishments He may see necessary for us.   With Him,
as with our fellows, what we most crave for is the
assurance of the oblivion of our sin, and of our complete admission to His favour.

In other words, there is an essential distinction, even
in our private relation towards God, between guilt and
punishment ; and though the consciousness of guilt
is the bitterest of all punishments, the discipline of
punishment may exist apart from a sense of guilt.   If
we be capable of such relationship to God as we have
been supposing, the remission of guilt, and the knowledge of that remission, must be the first and deepest
needs of the soul.   With that, every punishment is
bearable ; without that, every blessing becomes intolerable.   Hell has been described as " punishment
with guilt remaining " :—

> " The mind is its own place, and in itself
> Can make a heaven of hell, a hell of heaven."

As though a man with a keen sense of his personal
relationship to God, and who does not believe himself
forgiven, might be in hell in heaven ; and such a man,
if he does believe himself forgiven, might be in heaven
in hell.   What theology invites us to do in this matter
is, not to imagine " forensic fictions," but to raise our
conceptions of our own capacities, and to seek our
ultimate perfection and happiness in fellowship with a
perfect Being, and in indulging the profoundest emotions of our souls towards Him.   Realize, for a moment, all that it would involve for sinful beings like
ourselves to live in complete light, and at the same
time in complete confidence, with our fellow-creatures ;
and it will then be apparent how vast a blessing is involved in the supposition of our being able to claim
perfect confidence towards God.   St. Paul's original
motive may have been a craving for righteousness ; but
for that very reason, believing, as he did, that he was
in personal relation with a righteous God, peace
with that God became the most imperious necessity of
his nature.   He had formerly sought satisfaction in
conformity with a righteous law, but in proportion as
the conception of a righteous God laid hold of his
conscience, he could be satisfied with nothing less than
peace with Him.   His ideal of the Christian life is
therefore in substance identical with that of St. John :
" Beloved, if our hearts condemn us not, then have we
confidence towards God ; and whatsoever we ask we
receive of Him, because we keep His commandments,

and do those things that are pleasing in His sight."
But who can say of himself that his heart condemns
him not ?

Now consider how this difficulty is met among ourselves when it happens to arise. If a violated relation
between two persons is to be re-established, must it not
necessarily be by an act of forgiveness, which, in its
result, would have the effect of imputing to the offend-
ing person a character he does not deserve ? When the
prodigal son exclaimed, " I am not worthy to be called
thy son," was he not speaking the literal truth ? When,
again, his father treated him as if he were worthy, was
he not, strictly speaking, imputing to him what he did
not deserve ?   If you treat the relation of man to God
as that of a mere creature to his Creator, if you regard
the soul as a mere subject for the operation of certain
laws, the language of Scripture respecting Imputation
and accounting righteous may become unreal.   But if,
as I have shown in former Lectures, the primary aspect
of God's relations to us may be considered as that of a
Person to persons, if we may assume, so to speak, that
a play of personal feeling may be as justly attributed
to Him as we may attribute to Him the reflections of
other excellences in His creatures, then we at once
introduce between Him and ourselves the element of
moral acceptance, or that of the imputation of moral
characteristics.

This, moreover, becomes, not the accidental, but the
essential element of the relationship.   Consider, for
instance, more in detail, the illustration just quoted

from our Lord's own teaching. The physical relation
between father and son constitutes the least part of
their mutual relations. The son's enjoyment of the
benefits his father can bestow upon him must, if they
are to act as responsible beings, depend in a great degree on his moral attitude towards his father. It is perfectly possible for a son so to act that his father, though
still feeling towards him as a father, is compelled to
treat him as if he were not his son. Now in such a
case, suppose the father to send a message to his son,
who had left his house, to the following effect : —
Although you have acted unworthily of yourself and
of me, my love towards you is unchanged, and I
entreat you to return to my protection. I will forgive you the past, and say not one word about it. I
will treat you in all respects as my son. I will im-
pute to you the full character of a true son of mine ;
and though I fear you may not be able at once to
shake off your inveterate bad habits and false ways
of thought, I will not allow your failures to alter my
manner of regarding you. Would any one feel that this
language was unnatural ?[1] Would not the son feel that
this imputation on his father's part of a character he
had not deserved constituted the very essence and
sweetness of his father's goodness ? If such a message
aroused once more in his heart the true feelings of filial
affection, would he not feel that so long as his father's
love were assured him, he could cheerfully bear all

---

[1] Compare Newman's " Lectures on Justification," Lect. iii.
p. 74, ed. 1840.

things and endure all things which might be thought
necessary for him?   This is but the story of the
Prodigal Son, with the simple addition of the father
sending after his son, as God does after His wandering
children in the Gospel.   What constitutes the chief
blessedness of the son's return to the father's house?
Not certainly that the fatted calf was killed, that the
best robe was put on him, not even that he had a new
career before him, and an opportunity of shaking off
his bad habits.   In proportion to the depth of personal affection still subsisting between father and son,
it would be the sweetest element in that reception
that the father ran to meet him, fell on his neck, and
kissed him, that the son felt he was completely forgiven, that the past was forgotten, that a character
was imputed to him which he had not deserved, and
that, prodigal though he had been, he could nevertheless live in his father's house as his father's son.
That moral imputation would constitute the first, the
deepest, the most essential element in his future life.
Similarly, a man who is awake to the personal relation of his soul with a personal God must feel that
the question of God's perfect forgiveness and acceptance of him is the most imperious question of his life;
and a man who is sensible of his own inveterate sin-
fulness must feel that such forgiveness and acceptance
involves an inputation of a character he does not deserve.   It is this forgiveness and acceptance, with the
imputation they involve, which constitute Justification,

in that personal rather than judicial sense in which
we are now considering it.

But it may be said that such an imputation, even
thus understood, is inconceivable, unless the person
who exercises this forgiveness has the assurance that
he whom he pardons and accepts has really repented,
and is in a right disposition of mind for the future.
That is unquestionable; and it is this consideration
which introduces us to the further element in the
statement of this doctrine, that it is on condition of
faith in Jesus Christ that we are thus accounted righteous by God. I need not dwell long upon the term
Faith. Though there have been many disputes about
it, its ordinary meaning is, I believe, sufficiently clear,
and we need only take it as it is commonly understood. No one supposes it to mean mere belief. It
involves the idea of trust in a person; and the better,
the more powerful and more benevolent the person,
the more absolute will be the faith. Faith in Jesus
Christ, therefore, will imply that we yield to the claim
which He asserts in His Gospel, and by His Church,
to be our Lord and our Saviour, that we surrender
ourselves to His hands, to obey Him, to follow Him,
to be as He was, and to be dealt with by Him according to His will. Now bearing in mind what has
been said respecting the character of the health of
our souls, is it not evident that, supposing Christ to
be what we proclaim Him, we are, by such an act of
faith, taking the one step which is necessary to bring

K

us into a true and sound condition ? He accepts us
as a part of Himself, He undertakes to answer for us,
and becomes our representative ; and, on the other
hand, He moulds us continually after His own character and excellences. A man thus attached, or
united, to Christ cannot be regarded by God as existing only in his own sinful individuality. It is not
merely the power and the good-will, but the spirit
and very nature of Christ under which he becomes
sheltered. There may be discerned in him, thenceforth, all the possibilities of a Christ-like nature. The
Apostle's language elsewhere alone describes the case ;
such a man is a new creature, old things have passed
away ; behold ! all things are become new. That
spirit of grief and repentance for evil which Christ
displayed in his behalf becomes, in an increasing
degree, his own ; and the Atonement, in its spirit as
well as in its independent action, becomes the means
of reconciling the man to God, as well as God to the
man. The act of faith places the man in a new relation ; and that relation involves a complete transfor-
mation in his nature and capacities. He is like a
branch grafted into a vine, which thenceforth partakes
of the life of the vine itself.

Now it is evident, as in former instances, how much
all this assumes respecting the nature and the power
of Christ ; but admit the possibility of such a personal relation between Christ and the soul, and then I
ask whether the doctrine of Justification, with its

imputation to the sinner of a new character and his reception into a new position, does not become in perfect harmony with a just view of the relations which persons may hold towards each other. Does it not supply, indeed, a necessity which is inherent in any bare doctrine of forgiveness ? It has been sometimes asked why God cannot forgive unconditionally, and without this requirement of faith ? The answer depends on what you mean by forgiveness. It does not always, between man and man, imply a re-acceptance of the offender to his old position in your heart and your confidence. You may, in one sense, forgive a man an injury he has done you ; but can you, without condition, receive him again into the position in which he inflicted it ? Certainly not, unless you have a guarantee. not merely of his repentance, but of his repentance being of such a character that he is not likely to commit such an injury again. Now Justification is not bare forgiveness, but forgiveness and re-acceptance combined. Before this can be fully granted, some guarantee of the future is essential ; and it is just this assurance which is afforded by that requirement of faith in Jesus Christ, which is attached by St. Paul to Justification. Let it only be made clear that a man is placed in his true relation, under a regenerating influence, and he may then be accepted or justified without hesitation.

It will be seen, then, that it can only be due to an utter misconception of this doctrine if it appears to

any mind to impose an arbitrary condition of salvation.
What it requires is that the soul should recognize the
truth.   If Christ be the Guide and Saviour of men—
the one Person through whose personality our own
can be purified—it becomes almost a truism that there
is no salvation save through faith in Him.   Neither
here, nor hereafter, can that be possible. By some
means or other, the soul must be reconciled with truth,
if it is to be made true ; and it must be made true,
if it is to be saved.   A distinguished man of science
not long ago spoke of Justification by Verification.
All we ask, as theologians, by such a doctrine as this,
is that men should verify by their consciences the
moral claims of Christ, and then render Him the trust
which is His due.   Faith, as the great theologians of
the Reformation were never weary of insisting, is not
a mere belief respecting Christ—still less, as it has
been perversely misrepresented, a belief respecting
one's own condition.   It is the response of the heart
to the words of Christ ; and from the life and spirit
inherent in those words it derives its whole value and
vitality.   Hence, too, they insisted that Justification
must be not only by faith, but by faith alone ; because
everything is involved in submission to that truth and
life, and every subsequent righteous action can be
but a consequence of its efficacy, and not an addition
to it.

But the greatest of all misconceptions of the doctrine is that which represents it as disparaging the

value and necessity of moral amendment, of repentance, and of chastisement. On the contrary, it
simply declares the indispensable means of amendment, the primary and most essential element in
repentance, and the only condition under which chastisement can be morally beneficial. If, indeed, the
moral aspect of God's nature be left out of view, if
Justification be confused with Salvation, and if it be
regarded, as perhaps it too often has been, as simply
implying deliverance from some future doom, the sus-
picions in question would be warranted. But if Justification be simply regarded, as it was by St. Paul and
by the great Reformers, as the establishment of confidence and fellowship between the soul and a God of
all righteousness, it must then be regarded as bringing
to bear upon the soul the whole moral influence of the
Divine will and energy. What, in a word, is the proclamation of the doctrine? Is it that a man may
escape the punishment of his sin when he pleases?
On the contrary, that is the very falsehood against
which it was a protest. What it proclaims is that a
pure and just God offers His pardon, His purity, His
justice, His truth, to every soul that will accept them
from Him, and that will unite itself to Jesus Christ in
His faith, His sorrow for sin, and His patient submission to its penalties. It declares that this God, in
the love He bears to every such soul, will purge it
from its iniquity, its injustice, its impurity, by any
discipline that may be necessary. The soul that

desires this blessing can have it for the asking; but
they are not antinomian souls that ask it.

You are well aware what an immense moral influence this doctrine exerted over the mind of Europe
when it was revived at the Reformation; and there
is no historical fact which affords a more striking
testimony to the vast power inherent in theological
truths. Many influences, doubtless, were co-operating
in the same direction; but it was not till Luther had
spoken, and had set free the consciences of priests
and people, that those influences could produce their
full effect. If I have at all succeeded in explaining the meaning of the doctrine, it will not seem
wonderful that it should have had such an influence.
Its very object, as we have seen, is to remove from
the soul every fear, to banish those shadows of guilt
which render it timorous in action and in thought,
and to restore it to perfect confidence in a just and
an almighty God. This is the Protestantism which,
in the mouth of Luther, gave a new life to the world.
The proclamation of the Reformer was that "it is the
design of God to have dauntless, calm, and generous
sons, in all eternity and perfection, who fear absolutely
nothing, but by confidence in His grace triumph over
and despise all things, and treat punishments and
deaths as sport. The rest He hates as cowards, who
are confounded by the fear of everything, even by the
sound of a rustling leaf."[1] Unhappily this was too

[1] "Deus autem proposuit habere filios impavidos, securos,

soon transformed into a rigid statement of impersonal transactions; and in that form it deserves much of the severe criticism it has recently received.[1]   But that is not the form in which the principle was proclaimed at the Reformation, and in which it is embodied in the formularies of the Church of England; and it is a matter of some patience that men who ought to be capable of appreciating the magnificent utterances of that new birthday of Christianity should be content to seek the living among the dead in the controversial statements of a smaller age.   If they would go back to those utterances, they would find that, in its essential and vital form, the doctrine was the republication of the two cardinal truths of Christianity—that the human soul is summoned to direct relationship with a Personal God of all righteousness and of all power; and that this relationship may be accepted, or claimed, in perfect confidence, peace, and fearlessness, on the sole condition of absolute submission to the will and the spirit of Jesus Christ.   If that be not an ennobling,

generosos, æternaliter et perfectè, qui prorsus nihil timeant, sed per gratiæ suæ fiduciam omnia triumphent atque contemnant, pœnasque et mortes pro ludibrio habeant; ceteros ignavos odit, qui omnium timore confunduntur, etiam a sonitu folii volantis." (Luther, " Resolutiones Disputationum." *Conclusio* xix. An endeavour was made three or four years ago, in a contribution I furnished to " Present Day Papers," to exhibit the form in which this doctrine arose in Luther's mind; and I have ventured in this Lecture to use some expressions from that paper.

[1] Especially at the hand of Mr. Matthew Arnold in " St. Paul and Protestantism."

purifying, and elevating doctrine, none such has ever been proclaimed.

Luther accordingly called this doctrine the article of a standing or a falling Church. We may do well to reflect whether, in a country which has once been illuminated by the light of Christianity, it be not also the article of a standing or a falling civilization. In such a country the conception of a righteous and almighty God will not easily be eradicated; and in that conception there are elements which, if they be not counterbalanced, are apt to render it the most terrible of all ideas to the human mind. Unless, in conjunction with a Divine Judge, a Divine Redeemer be also upheld in His due office, unless God be represented as the giver, no less than as the exactor, of righteousness, the way is open for all the devices of priestcraft and all the inventions of superstition. Those fears and apprehensions from an unseen world are not to be conjured away by declaring they are mere phantoms, and that the material world is all with which we are concerned. But they may be mastered, as they have been mastered before, by belief in a Saviour who has triumphed over them, and who, if we obey Him, will deliver us from them. There can be little doubt that the course of history and of human thought since the Reformation has been marked by a peculiar freedom and courage, and that the " dauntless, calm, and generous " spirit, of which Luther spoke, has in fact been promoted by the

proclamation of his great doctrine. Even where it
has not been explicitly recognized, its influence has
been felt in a stronger confidence in God and God's
laws, and in a readiness to pursue the truth at all
hazards of error and of its inevitable punishment,
secure that all was well with us in His hands. Of the
two, God is certainly less dishonoured by an undue
confidence than by an unworthy fear. But a confidence based on a false foundation, or on an imperfect
foundation, is with a large proportion of men liable
at any moment to be overthrown. Living trust in a
justifying and saving God is the only permanent and
universal security for manly courage, for womanly
confidence, or for love of truth. But that trust alone
is sure which rests on a definite faith; and faith can
only endure all its possible trials when it is quickened
by the life, the death, and the resurrection of Christ.
If the Clergy are anywhere suspected as the enemies
of freedom, they must have utterly perverted their
message. They are charged with a Gospel from God
of deliverance from all fear, of peace to all consciences,
of salvation from every evil, by converting every evil
into good. In this great doctrine of Justification by
Faith in Christ, they hold the charter of the freedom
of the world; in this sense, at all events, the power
to Bind and Loose has been conferred upon the
Church; and in proportion as she preaches this truth
aright will her mission be recognized and her power
acknowledged.

LECTURE VIII.

THE METHOD OF SANCTIFICATION.

ROMANS viii. 22-23.

" For we know that the whole creation groaneth and travaileth
in pain together until now. And not only they, but ourselves
also which have the firstfruits of the Spirit, even we ourselves
groan within ourselves, waiting for the adoption, to wit, the
redemption of our body."

MY task in this last Lecture of the present course
would be comparatively easy, if I could confine myself to developing the natural results of the
principles I have hitherto been vindicating. I am to
speak of the second great element in the Christian
doctrine of the practical life of the soul—that, namely,
which is embodied in the theological term " Sanctification." If, in accordance with the truths already
vindicated, we may assume that our deepest life consists in our relations with a spiritual world ; that that
world is a world of persons ; that the highest of all
such relations is with a personal God, in whom every
movement of righteousness, truth, and beauty, of which
we are conscious, finds its origin and its perfection ;
if, in order to render it even conceivable that such a

Being should be in harmonious relation with moral natures so evil as our own, it be necessary to introduce the mediation of some holy Person with whom we may be personally united ; if the first step in the regeneration of our spirits must consist in entering, through union with such a mediator, into a life of confidence and of freedom of conscience towards God —if, in a word, we may thus recognize at once the necessity and the possibility of fellowship with the Father and with His Son Jesus Christ as the ultimate aim and the sole completion of our lives—what remains but to crave, with equal yearning and hope, from His Divine influence, for that holiness, that Sanctification, which alone is compatible with such a communion ?　"If we say that we have fellowship with Him, and walk in darkness, we lie, and do not the truth ; but if we walk in the light as He is in the light, we have fellowship one with another, and the blood of Jesus Christ His Son cleanseth us from all sin."　Such is the introduction to the comprehensive epistle of St. John ; and no one starting from Christian premises can fail to echo the simple words which follow, "My little children, these things write I unto you that ye sin not."　Moreover, this Divine fellowship, if it creates the necessity for such holiness, must be at the same time its only adequate source, and only in communion with the Spirit of the Father and the Son can we look for an influence equal to the miracle of re-creating us in Their image.

Such is the inevitable course of Christian thought, as it is embodied in the simplest symbols of our faith. The creed begins with Creation; it leads us through the mystery and the agony of Redemption, but it culminates in the confession of a Holy Spirit, who sanctifies all the people of God. It may be, as is implied in some recent speculations to which I referred at the outset of these Lectures, and as I have already admitted, that this final aim of the Christian revelation has been obscured; that men have spoken of Salvation without duly remembering that it means deliverance, not merely from punishment, but from sin; and that the life which the Creed ends by proclaiming has been too often interpreted as a mere future existence of imaginary beatitude, rather than as the actual life, both present and future, of spiritual peace and holiness. But the Scriptures and the Creeds have always provided the means of rectifying any such distortion of the true proportions of our Faith; and the deliverance both of the soul from its iniquity and of the body from its corruption, by union with Christ, has been the hope in which the Christian Church has lived. So far from our theological premises obscuring such an aim, they on the contrary bring it into vivid prominence; and on the basis of the presumptions hitherto vindicated, we differ from the moralists, not in rendering righteousness an imperative pursuit of the soul, but in offering to render it a practicable pursuit. But though it is within the

purpose of these Lectures thus to point out the internal coherence of Christian doctrine, and the manner
in which its primary assumptions lead necessarily to
its practical conclusions, it has been my constant
object to consider each truth as far as possible by
itself, and to exhibit its harmony with the indisputable facts and necessities of human nature. Leaving,
therefore, the mere logical deduction from Christian
premises, we have to consider whether the main principles of the doctrine of Sanctification correspond
with the general facts of human nature. That doctrine, briefly explained, is this—that holiness is created
and developed in us by the influence of a personal
Spirit on our souls : that this Spirit operates not
merely upon individuals directly, but through the
agency of the Christian Church ; and that its ultimate
work is the complete renovation both of our souls
and of our bodies. This is what is implied in the
confession that we believe in the Holy Ghost, the
holy Catholic Church, the Communion of Saints, the
Forgiveness of Sins, the Resurrection of the Body,
and the Life Everlasting.

Now this is, in part, a statement of the method of
human development; and it encounters, no doubt,
some prejudice at the outset, so far as certain scientific theories of physical development have taken possession of men's minds. It is alleged that the various
forms of natural life may be explained, without assuming the constant influence of any designing and

controlling intelligence, by the natural action of circumstances on certain organisms. Animals, for instance, in the struggle for life, find certain qualities or organic developments serviceable ; and the individuals in whom these developments are most strongly marked survive and reproduce their peculiarities. How far this hypothesis corresponds to the facts of natural history it would be beyond my scope to inquire. But a decided attempt is made to extend the same hypothesis to human life, and to explain by the operation of a similar mutual struggle the whole growth of human morality and civilization. Human nature, according to this view, is not moulded from within, but from without ; and the very idea of a permanent central influence directing and controlling its development becomes inadmissible.

Now I would first observe that this is another of those instances, already noticed in these Lectures, in which the conditions of mere physical life are entirely distinct from those of human life. We have seen, for example, how the personal character of human relationships distinguishes them from all others ; and this consideration will be found to be of force in respect to the present subject. But it would seem equally apparent that we should disregard one of the most prominent characteristics of the course of human thought and feeling by attempting to explain it on the principle of natural development. It is an essential part of such a theory that a given result should

be produced by the action either of present circumstances or of inherited tendencies. It is by this
gradual accumulation of present influences that the
successive development of plants and animals must
be determined. In human development, however,
whether Christian or Pagan, there is an element entirely distinct from this. It is the direct influence of
one spirit upon another by means which are comparatively independent of external circumstances. Take,
for example, the case of Mahommedanism or Buddhism. It may be that the circumstances of national
or social existence predispose men to accept such religions. But this is clearly far from being the whole
of the matter. In addition to this, the ideas and impulses of Mahommed and Buddha themselves are
living and generative forces in the minds of their
adherents. At this moment those ideas and impulses
are powerful instruments in gathering new followers
and in animating the existing votaries of such faiths.
There is enshrined in the Koran the spirit of one of
the greatest masters of the human heart, and in India
that spirit is at this moment a power which acts from
within outwardly, which is continually modifying circumstances, and moulding the intellectual and moral
growth of generation after generation. It would seem
obviously contrary to such facts to urge that it is the
mere force either of present or of inherited circumstances which has made particular nations Mahom-
medan or which keeps them so. The immediate

cause, at all events, has been the action of a personal influence which arose long ago in Arabia, and which has ever since been acting upon human spirits directly by the force of an inherent vitality.

In a still higher degree is this apparent in the case of Christianity. Whatever may be urged with respect to the preparation of society in the time of the Roman Empire for such a religion, the supposition that the society itself gave birth to it could only be maintained by disregarding the immense moral innovation which the Gospel introduced. The contrast between the two principles of human development we are now considering is forcibly stated by St. Paul at the commencement of the twelfth chapter of the Epistle to the Romans, and is illustrated by the exhortations which follow. "Be not," he says, "conformed to this world; but be ye transformed by the renewing of your mind;" and he proceeds to describe the transfiguration of the whole of human life under the force of the spiritual influence of which, in the previous part of the Epistle, he had been explaining the character. It will be observed how comprehensively he surveys the whole range of human action and conduct. He starts from the consideration of men as constituting many members in one body, and he proceeds to direct them in their various offices. He passes in review the private and public duties to which they might be called—ministering, teaching, exhorting, giving, ruling and obeying; he depicts the spirit of the Christian in business and

in rest, in joy and in sorrow, in hope and in tribulation, towards friends and towards enemies, in peace
and in wrath ; and he lays down the Christian principles of civil government and civil obedience.   It is a
picture of life in its length and breadth, and even in
all its lights and shadows, transfigured, as the landscape
by the sun, under the renovating influence of those
spiritual rays of love which illuminated and warmed
the Apostle's soul.   "The night," he concludes, "is
far spent, the day is at hand ; " and we can only appreciate the justice of the image by endeavouring to
realize the moral condition of the age on which this
new day was dawning.   The New Testament is of
necessity regarded by us to a great extent as detached
from its original surroundings.   Its revelation claims
an eternal character, and it is destined to find a con-
genial home in every country and in every age.   But
for our present purpose it is most instructive to contemplate it as embedded, so to speak, in its original
associations, and to imagine ourselves reading it, or
rather listening to its authors, amidst the life of the
Roman Empire and of Pagan civilization.   The contrast between the surrounding night and the emerging
dawn gives a novel force to the vivid imagery of the
Apostle.   Conceive, for instance, this portion of the
Epistle to the Romans coming upon us for the first
time amidst the Annals of Tacitus, as a description of
the teaching of a Jew who arrived in Rome under the
reign of Nero.   This is only to suppose what would

have been the case if the annalist had been able to
record for us a complete review of the circumstances
and movements of his age.   But what an inconceivable
contrast would be apparent !   Thus viewed, the rise of
the day-star of Christian love and light would probably impress us as being at least as marvellous in
character as the physical miracles of the Gospels.   It
was nothing less than a moral miracle—the sudden
appearance, amidst a corrupted society, of men " be-
holding as in a glass the glory of the Lord," and
transfigured into the same image in all their thoughts
and words.

Now the Apostle, in the words I have just quoted,
expresses exactly the nature of the two principles of
development exhibited in this contrast.   " Be not," he
says, " conformed to this world," or this age.   There
could hardly be an apter description of the process of
civilization by the pressure of circumstances.   But the
very essence of the Apostle's mind was to renounce
conformity with his age and his circumstances, and to
reveal in himself and in others an entirely new form
and conception of life.   The Christian life as exhibited
by him burst into existence and into full perfection in
Christ and in His disciples.   St. Paul's explanation of
it alone answers to the historical reality.   They had
been " transfigured by the renewing of their minds."
Such is the vital method of human progress.   A new
internal influence arises in the soul, like a hidden
spring bursting from a rock, or like fire descending

from heaven. Instead of the mind of a man being
developed by the form and fashion of his age, he receives within himself the source of a new life, and
becomes the originating germ of a transformed age.
From within and not from without, from the mind
and not from the world, by the birth of what is new
and not by the growth of what is old, the whole
aspect of human nature is transfigured. This conception lies at the root of the teaching of the Apostle.
Baptism, with its associated images of new birth and
of resurrection, embodies the cardinal Christian idea.
The words, "Except a man be born again he cannot
see the kingdom of God," are the most pregnant
statement of the main principle of the Gospel.

The subsequent history of Christianity is in no less
remarkable a degree the history of the modification of
the external by the internal. The words and deeds of
Jesus of Nazareth become a perennial source of life,
modifying, by direct as well as by indirect influence,
the whole current of men's thoughts and lives, and
transforming their civilization. It is the words of
Christ which seize on the heart of an Augustine and
render him in his turn the dominant power in a great
period of European thought. The great saints and
masters of our Christian civilization have cherished
and have enforced principles of domestic and of social
life entirely independent of the circumstances in which
they lived. The Christian idea of marriage, for instance, lives in the New Testament. Its spirit is there

as that of a living force fashioning in men's minds a model to be imitated and a law to be obeyed. For eighteen centuries it has been continually modifying the circumstances, the passions, the interests, the social tendencies of mankind. The idea of man's relation to a Personal God lives similarly in those Scriptures, and has had a not less potent influence. Time after time in history—in the history of our own country— have the ideas of Prophets and Apostles burst upon men's minds from those ancient pages, and have evoked movements which have overturned thrones and re-organized national life. They are seeds which need, no doubt, a favourable soil in which to grow ; but which have in them a fertilizing power of perennial vitality. There is a spirit in them which quickeneth, in comparison with which the flesh profiteth nothing. The material is dead and formless until this spiritual influence moves within, and calls it into life and order. In a word, circumstances are an unquestionable element in human development ; but its most characteristic and important factor is the influence of personal and spiritual agencies in controlling circumstances.

So far, then, as the Christian doctrine of the Spirit supposes a central spiritual influence as the operative power in the growth of the soul, it is in harmony with the facts of human experience. The Apostle accordingly draws a close parallel between the operation of evil and the operation of good in this respect. "As by one man's disobedience many were made sinners, so by the obedience of one shall many be made

righteous." Whether or not the story of the fall to
which the Apostle refers is to be taken as an historical narrative, the principle it embodies is equally a
fact of human nature. The sin of one man, who is
the father, or the leader, or the teacher, will multiply
itself indefinitely, by the force both of example and of
inheritance, among those who become subject to his
influence. St. Paul represents this evil influence as
encountered by one of precisely the same character
in the revelation of a Person who shall be a central
source of righteousness, truth, and spiritual health ;
"that as sin hath reigned unto death, even so might
grace reign through righteousness unto eternal life by
Jesus Christ our Lord."

Now the Christian doctrine of the Holy Spirit pro-
vides for the extension of this central and personal
influence to each individual soul in every age. It
rests, not upon deductions from particular texts, but
upon the whole burden of the last discourses of our
Lord as recorded in the Gospel of St. John. It
would be out of place, for the immediate purposes
of this argument, to consider the objections which
have been raised to the authenticity of those discourses. They have, in fact, generated the Christian
doctrine ; and the question is whether that doctrine
corresponds with the legitimate demands of human
nature. It is at the same time a point of extreme
interest, even with reference to the collateral controversy of the authenticity of St. John's Gospel, to observe the intimate correspondence between the strong

human interest with which those discourses are replete and the doctrine which has grown out of them ; and a brief consideration of them from this point of view will throw a strong light upon the point more especially under our notice. Our Lord is contemplating His speedy departure from His disciples, and He, concentrates in these final words the guidance and consolation on which they would have to rest when He was gone.   There is something inexpressibly touching in the tender concern which breathes in almost every word at the thought of the distress and perplexity they were about to feel. He begins with the exhortation, " Let not your heart be troubled," and He ends with the words, " These things I have spoken unto you that in me ye might have peace. In the world ye shall have tribulation, but be of good cheer, I have overcome the world."   More than once He exhorts them, " Let not your heart be troubled, neither let it be afraid." He knew better than they did themselves how entirely they had been dependent on Him, how utterly incapable they would be at first of maintaining their faith and their loyalty without Him ; and even at the close of His gracious assurances He is forced to utter the exclamation, " Do ye now believe ? Behold, the hour cometh, yea, is now come, that ye shall be scattered every man to his own, and shall leave me alone."

Our Lord recognized, in short, the fact that it had been His personal influence to which all the allegiance

of His disciples had been hitherto rendered. He had
lived with them day by day, ever at hand to enlighten
their ignorance, to sustain their faith, to correct their
errors. They had been able to appeal to Him in all
the perplexities of their thoughts and the confusions
of their hearts, and they had learned that He was a
guide who could lead them safely through every
labyrinth. It was this they were about to lose, and
accordingly His encouragements are immediately
directed to meet this want. He assures them that
His place would be taken in that very personal relationship in which, at first, He would be so grievously
missed. " I will pray the Father, and He shall give
you another Comforter, that He may abide with you
for ever." He obviously implies a Comforter like the
One who was about to leave them—another such as
Himself for all purposes of consolation and of guidance.
Nay, the new Comforter would be equivalent to Himself : " I will not leave you comfortless, I will come to
you." Again, " These things have I spoken unto you,
being yet present with you ; but the Comforter, which
is the Holy Ghost, whom the Father will send in my
name, He shall teach you all things, and bring all
things to your remembrance, whatsoever I have said
unto you."

It is when we thus compare the assurances of our
Lord with the circumstances under which, and the
purposes for which, they were given, that we discern
the full practical significance of the Christian belief

in the Personality of the Holy Spirit. The habits of
thought in the present day and its chief intellectual
movements incline many minds to contemplate the
Holy Spirit in the character of some divine influence
or impersonal power. But without at present entering
into the strictly dogmatic aspect of the doctrine, thus
much, at least, is apparent from the language just
quoted, considered in connection with the occasion on
which it was used. The promised Comforter was to
be as much a Person as Christ Himself, and was to
exercise over the disciples precisely the influence
which Christ had Himself exerted while He was with
them. This was to be the very source of the peace
He left with them. They were to lose His visible
companionship, but they were to gain a companion
even more intimately present with them. How intensely personal His own influence had been need not
be insisted on. It is one of the most marked characteristics of His ministry that, instead of consisting
chiefly in the declaration of general laws or rules of
conduct, it is adapted to every shade of thought and
feeling in the characters with whom He has to deal.
He constantly has in view the secret thoughts and
inward dispositions of the individuals whom He is
addressing, and touches the particular weakness of
their souls. It was all this of which the disciples
were about to be deprived ; and it was this they were
assured would be bestowed upon them in the gift of
the Spirit.

Now if the previous argument of these Lectures has been valid, it will be seen how deep and essential a need of human nature is met by such a revelation. If, as I have endeavoured to show, the human soul breathes, as it were, in an atmosphere of personal relations ; if laws, to be thoroughly efficient, need to be applied, interpreted, modified with the delicate variations which only personal feeling and apprehension can afford ; if, in short, the fellowship of Christ with His disciples illustrates the sole conditions under which the perfect training and development of the soul is possible, it is evident that the mission of a Holy Spirit, whose personal influences, when faithfully followed, guide us into all truth, supplies the necessary supplement to all moral teaching and discipline. We have only to consider the infinite boon it was to the Apostles to live in the society of One who, like our Lord, exerted this influence upon them, in order to appreciate the intense force and reality which the doctrine has possessed for the Christian conscience. They were subject in His presence to the sure and delicate touch of one who had a Divine knowledge of all the movements of their souls, and whose every word and look brought them into contact with a Divine life. This is the blessing which, in an even more penetrating form, and in a manner which touches the secrets of our souls, if possible, more profoundly, is offered to the world in the revelation of the Holy Spirit. No soul, we are assured, need be desti-

tute of a Divine companionship; none need resort to
a human authority for infallible guidance. The guid
ance, indeed, is addressed to the conscience rather
than to the intellect; and it is consequently enjoyed
only so far as the conscience is true to its Divine
monitor. In proportion, however, as this moral and
spiritual authority is consulted and obeyed, do the perplexities both of thought and of practice disappear.

But the summary of Christian doctrine proceeds to
indicate another point in which this personal character
of the spiritual life is recognized and satisfied by the
Gospel. The immediate sequel to the acknowledgment of the Holy Spirit is a belief in the Holy Catholic Church and in the Communion of Saints. In other
words, even the inward spiritual influence of a Divine
Person is not independent of that constitution of
human nature which renders it impossible that man
should live alone. Our personal life can only be fully
developed in an environment of personal relations;
and the order of our moral universe depends not
merely on the central attraction of a spiritual sun, but
upon the mutual attractions and pressures of its
numerous constituent bodies. The true life of Christians is not that of individual and separate Saints, but
that of a society of Saints. Bound to their common
Head and to each other by means of sacraments,
worship, and discipline, their life is that of one entire
organism, and the vitality of each member is intimately dependent upon the closeness of his fellowship

with the rest. The law of the Church's existence is that laid down by Christ, "Where two or three are gathered together in my name, there," in a special manner, "am I in the midst of them." It was in the days when this communion of saints was most conspicuous, and when the discipline involved in it was most efficient, that the life of the Church was more vigorous than at any subsequent period. The secret, probably, of the success of many sectarian movements has lain in their partial resuscitation of this mutual influence at times when it had been neglected by the Church at large; and it has been the weakness of all philosophical and moral systems that they have failed to provide for this indispensable necessity of human nature.

But I must pass to the last point in which the Creed exhibits the method of Christian Sanctification—" The Forgiveness of Sins, the Resurrection of the Body, and the Life Everlasting." It is here, perhaps, that the ultimate, if not the innermost, essence of Christian doctrine is reached. Sanctification and Resurrection, as has of late been justly observed by an author whose objections I have had to controvert,[1] are, in apostolic language, almost synonymous terms; and it is only to the negative side of the interpretation which this author has placed on such language that exception must be taken. I must invite those who have been good enough to follow me thus far to turn at this

[1] Mr. Matthew Arnold, in "St. Paul and Protes

point to the comprehensive exposition of Christian
doctrine which is contained in the Epistle to the
Romans. In the course of these Lectures I have for
the most part followed the order of the Apostle's
argument, and the value of the discussion will depend
on whether I have succeeded in elucidating that order
and illustrating its correspondence with facts. The
writer just referred to is of opinion that St. Paul did
not understand what were really the leading thoughts
and principles of his own mind, and, as though possessing an intelligence superior to that of the Apostle,
he has offered to re-arrange the Epistle to the Romans
in the order of the real importance of its truths. That,
however, is not the way in which great writers are
ordinarily interpreted ; and if we wish to understand
the Gospel which St. Paul preached, we must be able to
place ourselves in harmony with his language and with
his method of development. Now it will be perceived
that, in the course of thought pursued in the previous
Lectures, we have reached the close of the fifth chapter, in which the Apostle proclaims the universality of
the grace and forgiveness of God. He then, in the
three following chapters, proceeds to develop the consequences of this grace and forgiveness in the complete deliverance of both our souls and bodies from
the dominion of corruption. Of that series of chapters
Death and Resurrection are, as has been truly observed, the key-notes. " Christ," says the Apostle,
" being raised from the dead dieth no more ; death

hath no more dominion over Him. For in that He
died, He died unto sin once : but in that He liveth,
He liveth unto God. Likewise reckon ye also yourselves to be dead indeed unto sin, but alive unto God
through Jesus Christ our Lord."

Now it is perfectly true that it is impossible to interpret such words as these of mere physical life and
death, but, on the other hand, it requires no less a
strain to suppose that physical life and death are not
included in their meaning ; and it is impossible, consequently, to regard them as mere figures of speech. If
St. Paul declares that "the spirit is life because of
righteousness," he immediately adds that " if the Spirit
of Him that raised up Jesus from the dead dwell in
you, He that raised up Christ from the dead shall
also quicken your mortal bodies by His Spirit that
dwelleth in you." The Apostle describes in these
chapters, with intense power, the bitter sense he felt
of a tendency, which of his own strength he could not
resist, to spiritual, moral, mental, and physical corruption. In the Resurrection he saw a pledge that this
tendency could be stayed and overcome ; and he assures us, from his own experience, that the Christian
who has been baptized into Jesus Christ, and who lives
by faith in Him, is already in possession, at least in the
inner man, of this power of revivification. He could
not, indeed, anticipate the law of God's operation in
finally revealing that changed, that glorious and in-
corruptible existence reserved for the whole man in

body and soul. But we have the firstfruits of the Spirit in the purification of our affections and desires. It is a purification which cannot be complete so long as the old man remains. But in heart, and soul, and spirit, we may already experience the life of the new man, who, after God, is created in righteousness and true holiness. Here, accordingly, the strong yearnings of the Apostle for a new life and for holier powers are for the present mainly directed ; and he concentrates the energy of his spirit upon the realization of this life and peace in the soul. "Therefore we are buried with Him by baptism into death, that like as Christ was raised up from the dead by the glory of the Father, even so we also should walk in newness of life."

In a word, the doctrine of Sanctification, as taught by the Apostle, appears to imply that our whole nature, in body and in soul, is liable to a kind of dissolution, and that our deliverance can only be effected by a process of restoration similar to that which we associate with the idea of the resurrection of the body. An attempt, however, as I have said, has been made to interpret him as referring merely, in strong figures of speech, to the renovation of our desires by the force of sympathy with Christ. Now, so far as concerns the mere reference of his language to the desires of the soul, it is not for a minister of our Church, especially at this season,[1] to raise any

[1] The Boyle Lectures are, under present arrangements, preached in the season following Easter Day.

objection to such an interpretation. The Collect for
Easter Day expressly adopts it in principle. "Almighty God," it says, "who through Thy only-begot-
ten Son Jesus Christ hast overcome death and opened
unto us the gate of everlasting life, we humbly beseech
Thee that, as by Thy special grace preventing us
Thou dost put into our minds good desires, so by
Thy continual help we may bring the same to good
effect." I would only ask those who for this reason
are disposed to eliminate from the essence of the
Apostle's teaching the apparent literal meaning of his
words, to consider a little more carefully all that is
involved in such a word as " desire."

Need, then, any of us look beyond our own hearts
to discern what a world of weal or woe, of order or
disorder, of internal peace or internal war, is covered
by that simple word? Have not desires of one kind
or another been the very elements of our life? Are
they not, at this moment, the elements upon the due
regulation of which our own happiness, and the happiness of all connected with us, depends? Looking
back on life, does it not seem like a long war of
desires? Noble impulses and high aspirations have
at one time incited us to all that was lovely and of
good report. At another time, or even simultaneously, the desire of the flesh, the desire of the eyes,
and the pride of life have diverted us from those high
aims. There are none but have been more or less thus
led astray; none in whom the war of the desires has

been a continual victory for one side alone. To pursue the image, who is not conscious that there have been killed and wounded in this lifelong struggle? In some unhappy cases the evil desires seem all but to exterminate the good; in some most blessed instances the good have so nearly exterminated the evil, that nothing but a desultory warfare remains. But to many of us the issue is a sadly chequered one. Many a good desire, if not killed, has been maimed and marred. The better side holds its own, but we know we are not the men we might have been, and not even the men we desired to be. To how many a life, and to how much of individual lives, does not the famous saying apply that, next to a defeat, there is nothing so sad as a victory? We have won the day, it may be, in our conflict with Apollyon; but what a wreck, for all that, has he made of many a fine impulse and bright hope; and how melancholy often is that humility, scarcely to be distinguished from humiliation, with which the chastened spirit of many a truly repentant soul awaits the forgiveness of a merciful God! How many there are who,

> "Day by day and year by year,
>   Survey the past with deepening fear,
>   Yet hourly, with more hopeful ear,
> To the dim future turn, the absolving voice abide."[1]

All this world of conflict, of passions struggling with principles, of impulses and faculties marred or

[1] Keble, "Lyra Innocentium."

made, is covered by that prayer that, as God by His special grace preventing us, puts into our minds good desires, so by His continual help we may bring the same to good effect. It is the whole length and breadth, and depth and height, of human life which is involved in that simple phrase.

Consider further, in reference to the Apostle's application of the truth of the Resurrection to these desires of the soul of man, that the idea of resurrection, whether applied to the soul or to the body, is obviously a very different thing from the mere idea of immortality. The latter is by no means a characteristically Christian idea. On the contrary, the conviction of immortality in some form or other, seems, with rare exceptions, part of the birthright of humanity. Nor, again, is the belief in future rewards and punishments peculiar to our own religion. On the contrary, it is, in one form or another, the dominant motive in the principal religions of the world. But it is something far greater which is involved in the Christian idea of the Resurrection. It is one thing to suppose that the soul lives on after death, whether to be re-united to the body or not, and another thing, altogether, to suppose that it is to be re-organized, revivified, and re-generated. Mere immortality might imply no more than our continuing to live as we were here, carrying with us to all eternity the characters into which we had moulded ourselves, the imperfections, the ill-regulated desires, of which many of us must to the last be conscious. Alas! not a few persons die in true Christian faith and practice who, if they continued hereafter as they were in this world, would live but a maimed immortality. It is, however, more than mere immortality, it is life and incorruption,[1] which Christ brought to light by His victory. His Resurrection is the assurance that we shall not merely exist hereafter, but that we shall be endued with a newness of life. Of the soul, no less than of the body, is it in measure true that " it is sown in corruption, it is raised in incorruption ; it is sown in dishonour, it is raised in glory ; it is sown in weakness, it is raised in power."

In this, indeed, even more than in the resurrection of the body, consist the wonder and the mystery of the doctrine. It is, perhaps, comparatively conceivable that a vital spark which has been clothed with flesh and blood once should be clothed with flesh and blood again. But there is something which might well seem indestructible in the fibres of which the soul is composed. There are impressions, habits, tendencies of heart and mind, from which it might appear almost impossible that we should be emancipated. It cannot, surely, be in scientific days, when the permanence of impressions on the body is so keenly appreciated, and when it is also recognized in a higher degree than ever how closely the soul and the body are united, that this difficulty can be made light of, or that we can be supposed to overcome the effects of

[1] ζωὴν καὶ ἀφθαρσίαν.—2 Tim. i 10.

past sin by the mere ameliorating influence of sympathy or example. He who knows the struggle against some besetting sin, and is conscious of the scar and stain which even victory leaves, will understand the blessing of the declaration that, when Christ shall appear, we shall be like Him ; and that as we have been planted together in the likeness of His death, we shall be also in the likeness of His resurrection—in the likeness of that glorious form which supplanted His marred visage and tortured frame. But such is the meaning of the Apostle ; this is the blessing which He promises to the sons of God.

It is indeed impossible, on the basis of mere morality, to break the stern law of continuity. Leave men to the operation of their natural powers, and it is inconceivable how desires and impulses once marred and mutilated can ever acquire that life, that completeness, that purity, for which they were designed. The doctrine, accordingly, has been actually propounded, and with perfect consistency, by a writer who stands on this basis, that sin cannot be forgiven ; [1] an awful proclamation, to be explained, we may well believe, on the supposition that the soul that utters it has been spared, by a life of comparative innocence, from knowing the misery, not merely of guilt, but of the sense of irreparable self-injury. But it is a form of despair to which the soul is often tempted, when, after some great lapse, it remembers from whence it

Mr. Greg, in " The Creed of Christendom," vol. ii. p. 222.

fell, and is sensible once more of the good desires it
has failed so lamentably to bring to good effect. The
evil does seem irreparable ; and even though we may
stop short of complete self-abandonment, it seems to
us impossible that we can recover the full vigour of
our spiritual faculties. Which, then, is the truest to
human nature—moral writers who discourse to you
without anxiety on the possibility of recovering yourselves by sympathy with an example ; or an Apostle
who cries out in the agony of his own struggle, "Who
shall deliver me from the body of this death ?" and
who points to nothing less than a miracle similar to
that of Christ's physical resurrection for his own final
deliverance, and for ours ? It is this, in the Apostle's
mind, which is the final blessing of the Gospel he
proclaimed. "They that are in the flesh cannot please
God ;" they cannot attain that holiness, that fulfilment of their good desires, which alone can answer
God's high aim for them. "But ye are not in the
flesh, but in the Spirit, if so be that the Spirit of God
dwell in you. Now if any man have not the Spirit of
Christ, he is none of His. And if Christ be in you,
the body is dead because of sin, but the Spirit is life
because of righteousness. But if the Spirit of Him
that raised up Jesus from the dead dwell in you, He
that raised up Christ from the dead shall also quicken
your mortal bodies by His Spirit that dwelleth in
you." By a mysterious process, though not, perhaps,
more essentially mysterious than some processes of

our natural life, the old man must die, and the new
man will be renewed after the image of Him that
created Him.   "So when this corruptible shall have
put on incorruption, and this mortal shall have put
on immortality, then shall be brought to pass the
saying that is written, Death is swallowed up in
victory."

In conclusion, there is perhaps nothing which in
moments of religious doubt and perplexity is more
fitted, so to speak, to rally our thoughts, than to compare the intense sympathy with the ordinary struggling life of humanity which breathes in every page of
the New Testament with the placidity with which
that life is reviewed and interpreted by most of those
who would provide us with a profounder philosophy.
In the last page, for instance, of the last book of this
kind which has been published among us,[1] I find the
writer congratulating himself that by abandoning a
Supernatural Revelation "we exchange a Jewish
anthropomorphic Divinity for an omnipresent God,
from whose serene reign of Law disorder and anarchy
are absolutely excluded."   What was the world, one
wonders, which the writer had in mind in penning this
description ?   Was it that world of storm and passion,

---

[1] "Supernatural Religion," 1st Edition, 1874, vol. ii. p. 492.
The author has in subsequent editions suppressed this admiration of the serenity of the world ; but his original statement is
a memorable illustration of the point of view from which the
problem of religion is often approached in such speculations.

of moral and mental disorganization, amidst which we labour, and to which each of us, alas! contributes some element of disorder and anarchy? An Apostle speaks to our hearts with very different force when he declares in the text, "We know that the whole creation groaneth and travaileth in pain together until now; and not only they, but ourselves also, which have the firstfruits of the Spirit, even we ourselves groan within ourselves, waiting for the adoption, to wit, the redemption of our body." Had St. Paul left no other utterance than this, he would have established an inalienable claim on the hearts of mankind; and it is alone enough to show how deeply the great doctrines of Christian theology touch the life and the necessities of our race.

With this attempt to illustrate the practical significance of the Christian doctrine of Sanctification, my duty for this year is ended; and it only remains for me to ask pardon from God and indulgence from my hearers for the imperfection with which it has been accomplished.

BOYLE LECTURES

SECOND COURSE

1875.

LECTURE I.

THE PROVINCE OF FAITH.

ROMANS i. 17.

" For therein is the righteousness of God revealed from faith to
faith : as it is written, The just shall live by faith."

IN commencing the second course of these Lectures
let me recall the point of view from which they
are written. Unbelief at the present day appears to
be distinguished from that of most previous periods,
and particularly from that of the last century, by one
marked characteristic. That characteristic is that it
heartily recognizes the obligation of morality ; and
that it hesitates to accept the Christian Revelation,
not in consequence of any reluctance to follow, on the
whole, its moral guidance, but simply on the ground
of the demand which it makes on our faith. This
change in the position is, as I observed last year, only
to be appreciated by reference to the greatest apologists of the last century, who seem quite as much
concerned to defend the cause of Virtue as that of

Religion.   Now taking men in general, and not speaking individually, it can hardly be doubted by a Christian
mind that the cause of Virtue is involved in that of
Religion ; and that if the Christian Faith were generally abandoned, the source and support of the highest
morality would be lost.   It would at least be perilous
to underrate the gravity of a lapse from that high
spiritual ground which the Christian Church has attained.   But, nevertheless, if, as we believe, Christian
faith is the culmination of the long and toilsome
ascent, imposed upon mankind, of the " strong moun-
tains " of the Divine righteousness, it is a matter for
infinite thankfulness and hope that the most dan-
gerous relapses at the present moment are, so to
speak, no further than to the last ridge or pla-
teau below the summit.   While we are struggling, as
we believe, to the highest peak, our companions, who
for the time are holding back, are not beyond the
reach of our voices, and we have not parted fellowship.
Righteousness, for ourselves and for others, is our
common aim and pursuit.   To the Christian, indeed,
this pursuit is ultimately merged in a still higher one
—that of a divine and eternal love.   But whatever
that final blessing, righteousness is its essential con_
dition ; and to a great extent, therefore, the contest
of the apologist with the modern sceptic concerns the
means rather than the end.   St. Paul, in the words
which precede the text, declares that he is not ashamed
of the Gospel of Christ, " for it is the power of God

unto salvation to every one that believeth ;" and for
this reason, that "therein is the righteousness of God
revealed." If that be so—if the Christian Faith be
really a power unto salvation by virtue of its revelation of righteousness—the main difficulties in the way
of its acceptance are overcome, and we may assume
that, with most of those to whom a defence of Christianity need in these days be addressed, there is an
end of the question. At all events, if the truths of
that Gospel which St. Paul proclaimed are found to
reveal the deep foundations of morality, to complete
its structure, and to answer the profoundest cravings
of those who hunger and thirst after righteousness, we
obtain a presumptive evidence which in the present
day ought to carry a most powerful weight.

If, to those who are acquainted with the writings of
the leaders of thought among us, any confirmation of
this view of the case were needed, it might be supplied
by a remarkable appeal addressed to the public and
its teachers in a periodical of last month by the heir
of a distinguished name.[1] It is a kind of despairing
cry for light and help, amidst what is described as the
"maddening and disheartening uncertainty," which
now weighs upon the minds of numbers who have lost
their hold on Christian faith. We are told that "they
would do the right thing, many of them, if they could
be sure what the right thing is; they would devote

[1] The Earl of Pembroke, in "The Contemporary Review,"
April, 1875.

their lives to doing good to others, if they could be
sure that they were doing good.   But they cannot,
and so drift on unsatisfactorily enough, without any
consistent principle or fixed purpose in living."   "It
is the curse," the writer adds, "and it is to be feared,
the growing curse, of our so-called enlightened age.
An age which might be bitterly described as one in
which every one acknowledged the obligations of duty,
but in which no one was certain what duty consisted
in."   A more robust or less scrupulous temperament
might, indeed, overcome these uncertainties by active
work ; but, in various degrees, this ingenuous confession is, it may be feared, only too true a descriptio
of a very prevalent disposition in the present day—a
disposition not unlike that which, at the time when
Christianity was first proclaimed, was sapping the
energies of the Roman world.   To such a temper of
mind, a Gospel which can be described in these words
of St. Paul at least offers, as it offered then, the very
remedy which is needed ; and if modern writers reject
it, the rejection should be with melancholy and with
hesitation, and not, as in more than one conspicuous
instance, with an easy confidence or an inopportune
raillery and humour.

In accordance with this view, I endeavoured in the
Lectures of last year to show how profoundly some of
the cardinal doctrines of the Christian Faith—in particular, those which relate to the character of sin and
the need and means of redemption—meet the neces-

sities of our craving for righteousness, and answer the
demands of the heart.   The foundation of the argument was laid in a discussion of the essential character
of human righteousness, as consisting in a relationship
between persons.   It was observed that moral righteousness does not consist, like physical soundness, in
a mere condition of the individual organism, but in
the right relation of the individual towards other
individuals, of the person towards other persons ; so
that, in a word, it is love which includes righteousness,
rather than righteousness which includes love. I shall
have occasion further to illustrate this principle, which
appears to offer a key to many of the difficulties of
the day ; but it would be evading the main problem
to overlook the fact that, whether or not such a principle be true in respect to Morality, the very possibility
of its application to Theology is disputed.   The tree
of Christian life is struck at its very root, by throwing
doubt over the reality and possibility of our personal
relations with a personal God, and by charging Christian Theology with mere metaphysical and baseless
speculations.   Some explanation was, indeed, offered
last year of Christian belief on this subject ; but the
denial is so strenuously reiterated, and so confidently
advanced, it appears to be in so large a measure the
source of the prevalent doubt, that it demands a
closer consideration.

The complete definition of Christian righteousness
is to love God with all our heart, soul, mind, and

strength, and our neighbours as ourselves; that is, it implies the existence of a spiritual Being towards whom we may entertain feelings similar to those we entertain towards each other, only vastly intensified; and the main problem of religion is to attain to the knowledge of this Being and to communion with Him. The address, accordingly, of St. Paul to the Athenians would, with a slight variation, be almost as appropriate among ourselves at the present hour. If he came at this day, and observed the most prominent of the writings now referred to, he might say, as he said then, that he beheld a homage offered to " The Unknown God." To many a recent speculation no more appropriate motto could be prefixed than the old inscription on the Athenian altar. Again would the Apostle have reason to exclaim, " Whom therefore ye reverence in ignorance, Him declare I unto you;" and the modern apologist must needs attempt to follow his example. It may be well to observe, indeed, that while it is perfectly true, as one of the most popular of the writers in question has observed,[1] that the desire for righteousness is the dominant impulse in St. Paul's mind, it is a complete mistake to represent it as the sole operative principle of his teaching. He, in fact, no less than St. John, recognizes the final supremacy of love; but whatever his goal, it is from principles of theology, from God and our relations to God, that he starts. Adapting himself, indeed, with

[1] Mr. Matthew Arnold, in " St. Paul and Protestantism."

his inspired skill, to the various dispositions of the
people whom he addressed, he dwells with special
force upon the righteousness revealed in the Gospel
when he writes to the Romans, by whom law, justice,
and righteousness were held in special honour.   But
even to the Romans, while promising, at the outset,
a satisfaction of their love of righteousness, he commences his argument, as we shall have further occasion to observe, by a statement respecting the relation
of man to God ; and on the memorable occasion when
he is confronted by the life and thought of Greece, his
address is founded on the proclamation of the Divine
nature and will.

I purpose, then, while supplementing in some other
respects the course of last year, to consider particularly
the ground and the nature of this elementary principle
of our Religion, and as far as possible to do so historically, and with reference not to mere speculative
possibilities, but to the actual facts of religious life
and faith.   The only safe method of judging of what
can be is to endeavour to understand what has been ;
and the Scriptures, without being treated as authori-
ties, may and must be regarded as records of facts of
human experience and consciousness.   The whole
inquiry, indeed, so far as one prominent objector is
concerned,[1] might be reduced to the question of what
those records really mean, and whether they can be
taken in their full natural sense, or must be reduced

[1] Mr. Matthew Arnold.

to a more purely moral mould.   Is it the case that
their Theology, no less than their Morality, is justified
by the Nature of Man ?   Such will be the main purpose of our inquiry this year.

But there is one difficulty which it may be as well
to face at the outset.   We find ourselves met by a
preliminary claim which, if admitted, would place our
inquiries in an entirely erroneous light and would
subject us to an unfair disadvantage.   The claim is
often made almost unconsciously, and as a natural
result of the main course of modern thought.   That
course is a scientific one ; and accordingly we seem
expected to offer a scientific justification of our creed.
The very foundation of that cry of almost despairing
uncertainty which I have quoted is that no solutions
of our moral difficulties seem attainable such as those
on which we act in other matters.   The growth of
knowledge has, in an extraordinary degree, made men
sensible of the " enigmas of life," while at the same
time it creates a very rigid conception of the sort of
answer which ought to be given to them.   The development of experimental science has deeply influenced
the mental habits of the day ; and the truths of Religion
are expected to be submitted to tests similar to those
of Physics or Chemistry.   We are loudly told that we
must be prepared to verify our assertions, and to verify
them by plain, experimental proofs, such as that fire
burns us if we touch it.[1]   This demand, indeed, as we

---

[1] Mr. Matthew Arnold, " Literature and Dogma," ch. x. p.
320, 4th ed.

shall subsequently have occasion to observe, can be met in a greater degree than the objector supposes. But still, when we are asked to verify, in this sense, the allegation that there exists and rules a Being whom we may, for some practical purposes, describe as a great personal First Cause, and as the moral and intelligent Governor of the universe, it is no doubt true that we can make no such simple answer as if we were asked to verify the fact that fire burns; and if we cannot verify this preliminary assumption, we are told our whole creed is baseless. That of which we cannot thus ascertain the scientific certainty, may, it is said, be a harmless hypothesis; but it must not be treated as affording any serious basis for life and action. The posthumous Essays of one of the most distinguished of recent English philosophers[1] afford a melancholy illustration of this principle, carried to an extreme. At the close of an Essay in which the existence of God and our own immortality are reduced, on grounds of rational evidence, to mere possibilities, the writer makes the pathetic inquiry, whether, in accordance with his own principles, he may be permitted some slight solace of hope. He asks himself "whether the indulgence of hope, in a region of imagination merely, . . is irrational, and ought to be discarded, as a departure from the rational principle of regulating our feelings, as well as opinions, strictly by evidence." He defends this last resource of human

---

[1] Mr. J. S. Mill.

N

aspirations; and for doing so he has been severely taken to task by some of his more rigid or less sensitive followers.

Now, the Christian preacher or apologist must repudiate at once this view of life, and must refuse to be judged by any such scientific standard. He will not treat scientific reasoning with the least disrespect, and he may be capable of fully appreciating it within its own province ; but that province is not moral action, and still less spiritual devotion. The words of my text embody the opposite principle, in its most explicit form ; and St. Paul, at the outset of his argument, has concentrated in them the essence of his subsequent teaching. The modern philosopher might not inappropriately express his principle by saying that righteousness is revealed "from science to science." That is to say, he would regard it as based on facts scientifically established, and advancing as science advances. But St. Paul's idea is that righteousness is revealed from faith to faith ; that is to say, it begins by acts of faith, it advances by acts of faith, and, in this life, its highest attainment consists in further and larger acts of faith. Let these words be considered apart from any references to special controversies with which they may have become entangled, and they may be found, I think, to reveal to us the essential principle of moral and spiritual action. I would not be thought to limit their meaning to the particular application I am now making of them ; and indeed, if these Lectures have any value, they will suggest still further and further depths of meaning in the words. But taking them in their first and simplest significance, let us see whether they do not correspond to the facts of life and history better than that principle of scientific righteousness just described.

Look at the course of the world's history, and consider how, as a matter of fact, the advances of the human race in righteousness have been gained. I put aside for the present the theological aspect of Faith, as involving the principle which it is the ultimate object of the argument to establish ; but take Faith in its simplest meaning, as trust in another, and observe whether it has not been the uniform instrument of moral education. That which history reveals is the appearance of a succession of men possessing higher conceptions of righteousness than their fellows, and either by example, or precept, or law, or all combined, inducing others to trust and follow them. Be it Moses or Socrates, Buddha or Confucius, these men have not made experiments in Morality, and demonstrated scientifically to their nation, or their followers, the righteousness of this or that course of action. They have felt ; they have trusted ; they have hoped ; they have acted : the souls of other men have been inspired by their influence, or overawed by their authority, and, willingly or reluctantly, have followed their guidance. This view of the matter becomes the more remarkable, if we consider what immense steps

in advance have been taken by some of these reformers of our race.   Buddha, for example, propounds
principles of morality of which the loftiness is amazing ;
and he must have been as much above the conceptions
of the mass of the people of his country and time as
the Himalayas are above the plains of India.   He
gathers adherents, not because his assurances can be
verified and the value of his exhortations tested.   His
followers are for ever below him, and neither do, nor
can, put to the test his highest and most characteristic
counsels.   But they have faith in him, and by that
faith they are lifted above themselves, beyond the
region of their experience, and are by this personal
trust elevated to a higher level of life.

The best, however, and most conspicuous of all
examples, even when considered merely from a natural
point of view, is afforded by the history of the Christian Church, and by the creation of Christian Morality.
That Morality, whatever previous approaches to it
had been made, started in its completeness full born
from the words of Christ and from the teaching of
the Apostles.   We have before us, in the Greek and
Roman writers, and in the pages of the New Testament itself, an account of the moral state of the Pagan
world ; and we know that Christianity effected a
revolution in some of the primary conditions and relations of life.   Undoubtedly the growing weight of
experience, in attestation of the excellence of Christian lives, acquired year by year an accumulating

force. But was it by men and women who waited for
that experience that the victory was gained? No:
the experience was created by men who were not
careful to ask for verification; who heard, who loved,
who trusted; and who followed, not the precepts
which they could verify, but those which the leaders
and teachers to whom they attached themselves imposed. The most characteristic feature of the early
Christian Church is the earnestness and warmth with
which men attached themselves to personal guides,
and accepted personal assurances, in matters which
involved the utter overthrow of their previous hopes
and their ordinary lives. It is for this reason, among
others, that the history of the Church is essentially
the history of a Society, growing, like other societies,
by the attraction of mutual trust and fellowship—not
that of a Scientific School, receiving the more or less
qualified intellectual assent of its adherents.

It would seem, in fact, that if this were not the
dominant law in human nature, the very experience
and verification which the objection demands would
remain impossible, even in respect to the most important principles of practical morality. If the question concerns the health of my body, I can try a
remedy and abide by the result; because the action
of the remedy in no way depends upon me. It is
ordinarily no matter whether I try it with utter distrust, or with credulous faith; if it has any definite
action at all, it will produce the result without any

reference to my feeling or my will. But a moral remedy, or the acquirement of a new moral habit, requires, as the very condition of its operation, the assent and consent of the heart, the co-operation of the will, the sympathy of the feelings. I cannot love experimentally, be truthful on hypothesis, chaste provisionally, or unselfish with a careful observation of the consequences. The very notions are self-contradictory. My whole will and heart must be engaged in the effort, and I must resist all temptation to look back or hesitate. Now doubtless there are souls whose pure and true intuitions discern, even at a distance, the blessedness of these righteous dispositions of heart ; but the Epistles of the New Testament are alone sufficient to show that, with Christians in general, this influence could not be relied on. St. Paul, for example—to mention only one conspicuous instance—regenerated among his converts the marriage relation ; but it is abundantly evident that he does so by virtue of his authority, and that it is by means of that authority, in the final resort, that the new relation is organized and maintained. Moreover, it should be remembered that the effects of moral habits and social customs are infinitely more subtle and distant than those of physical conditions. It is in moral, far more than in physical diseases, that the sins of the fathers are visited on the children ; and history is the record of vicious national habits or tendencies working themselves out to their fatal re-

sults in the course of long generations. Where would
have been the progress of our race, if men had waited
to verify the comparative effects of polygamy or
monogamy, instead of adopting the latter in faith, on
the authority of the first Christian teachers, and in
that faith resolutely turning their backs upon everything inconsistent with the Christian standard of
purity? It is one thing to speak of verifying the
effects of righteousness in general, and a very different
thing to verify it in particulars; but it is on the re-
form of moral habits in particulars that the moral
salvation of men and of communities depends.

From this point of view Faith may, in fact, be
regarded as the form which is assumed in practice
by the principle of probability as a guide to action.
That principle has, indeed, been very unduly disparaged of late in consequence of a neglect to observe
that peculiar characteristic of moral action which has
just been pointed out. It is made an objection to the
great argument of Bishop Butler that it reduces us to
rest on "mere probabilities,"[1] and it is urged that this
is a very insufficient basis for such momentous decisions as religion and morality demand. In actual
life, however, the most momentous decisions have
frequently to be made on grounds of this doubtful
character. A statesman may feel the greatest uncertainty respecting the policy he ought to adopt in a
great crisis; he may hesitate months before deciding;

Mr. Matthew Arnold, "Literature and Dogma," pp. 320-21.

but when the decision has been made, he will, if he be
a wise man, devote his whole energies and all the
power he wields to carry it into effect. In a matter,
indeed, in which no immediate moral issue is involved, it may be admitted that a wise man would
often abstain as long as possible from acting on a low
degree of probability; and that when he does act, he
would do so with great caution and reserve. But a
moral decision can rarely be thus evaded; and when
made it involves, as a rule, an absolute and unreserved
adoption of the course of action which is chosen.
The conduct of a friend or of a child often renders it
imperative for a man to interpose and to act; and he
may find it a most difficult matter, needing the anxious
consultation of friends, to decide what course it is
his duty to take. But he must decide, and decide
promptly; and having decided, he must do what he
considers his duty without hesitation. For the purposes of our moral responsibility, whether in great
matters or in small, Butler's statement is impregnable
that "to us probability is the very guide of life."

But it is none the less very true that the mass
of men are most imperfectly capable of estimating
the balance of evidence on so profound a subject as
the truth of a new religion, or even the claim of a
new code of morality. If there were no other obstacle,
it is enough that they have no time for it. They
cannot put aside the business of life to prosecute a
scientific inquiry into comparative religion. Now it

is this difficulty which is met by that tendency of
human nature, which the Scriptures treat as its ultimate law, that in matters of spiritual and moral action
men should attach themselves to those who seem to
them their natural leaders, and should trust and follow
them with a heartiness and devotion proportionate to
the love, the faith, and the hope they arouse. It is
this which kindles the real fire of life that runs from
soul to soul, and which elevates generation after generation towards the level of its best men. The strong,
the truthful, the clear-sighted, the pure, arouse the
trust of the weak, the faith of the uncertain, the hopes
of the defiled, and thus induce them to believe before
they see, and to act on grounds of the sureness of
which they could never have satisfied themselves. If
we look historically at the cause which first induced
men to become Christians, and which converted the
Roman world, we find that it was in the form of this
imperious personal attraction that the principle of
probability operated, and acquired its motive power.
That which is often adduced as a taunt against the
early Christians is perfectly true as a matter of fact ;
they did not act on the rational principle advocated
by the philosopher just referred to—that of regulating our feelings, as well as our opinions, strictly by
evidence—understanding by evidence, as is clearly
implied, judicial and intellectual evidence. But the
feelings have their own evidence, and their own laws
of action ; and the Christians acted on those dictates

of the heart which impelled them, as they impel all
men in proportion to the healthiness of their moral
and spiritual condition, to recognize those who are
wiser and better than themselves, and to follow their
guidance in the obscurities and uncertainties of moral
action.   Faith, hope, and love are not mere theological
virtues; they are the three cardinal functions, so to
speak, of man's nature regarded as a whole ; and it is
in their operation that the principles of human development and of moral and spiritual salvation are to
be discerned.

It will be seen, therefore, that when we are asked to
submit our faith, as the first condition of its acceptance,
to " plain, experimental" verification, we are, in fact,
asked to abandon the process by which the chief
moral and spiritual advances of mankind have been
gained.   No person who has any interest in this argument would deny that the operation of the Christian
Church has elevated both the standard and the
practice of morality more than any influence yet seen.
The analogous, though imperfect, operation of faith in
other religions may, in varying degrees, be similarly
justified.   But with respect to our own religion,
the blessings conferred by it upon the world are
indisputable ; and I would ask whether it is reasonable to suppose that the action of human beings,
for centuries, on so vast and beneficial a scale,
can have been—I do not say erroneous in particulars
—but that it can have been due to an entirely false

and mischievous process ? That which we are called on to do by this demand, and which we must decline doing, is nothing less than to reject the intuitions of the noblest members of our race as a warrant for our moral and spiritual convictions. The example of Columbus has, with justice, been often quoted as an illustration of faith ; and even now what we are called on to do is, no doubt, in great measure, to sail over mysterious seas in search of the eternal shores, under the guidance of Captains of our Salvation, who appeal, in the first instance, less to our power of verification than to our love and our trust. Life, in fact, is not a laboratory of social experiments, but a field of action and of conflict ; and the men who win the day, both for themselves and for their fellows, are those who, amidst all the din and confusion of the struggle, know their leaders and follow them.

Such is the course of life in matters of morality ; and the first axiom of the Christian apologist must be that an analogous course should be followed in Theology. His efforts will be directed to the vindication of the moral authority, rather than of the scientific truth, of revelation. That truth, indeed, can only be scientifically established, like all other truth, by experience ; and experience can in this matter only be afforded by an obedience which rests upon faith. According to the saying of Augustine, we must believe in order that we may understand, and faith must precede sight. The object, in short, of such a course

of Lectures as the present must be to exhibit the
moral claim upon our consciences possessed by the
primary assumptions of the Gospel, by the inspired
writers who have enforced them, and, above all, by the
Lord Jesus Christ.   Any one who believes that in the
Gospel lies the true key to "the mystery hid from
ages and generations," must acknowledge, at the outset of such an argument, that there are difficulties,
mysteries—contradictions, if you will—which nothing
but the meditation and the spiritual experience of many
generations can suffice to explain.   It will be enough if
he himself feels, and can make it felt, that amidst all
these struggles and confusions the voice of Christ and
of His Apostles is heard speaking with a moral authority which commands our faith and love, and which
inspires in us an enduring hope of ultimate illumination and deliverance.   His invitation to those perplexed souls of whom he has spoken will be that they
should make a moral instead of a merely intellectual
decision, and should cast in their lot with that noble
army of Saints who—amidst all their ignorance, all
their sin, and all their doubts—have recognized in the
Lord Jesus Christ, and in His Gospel, the true rest fo
their souls and the sure guide of their life.

LECTURE II.

WITNESS OF CONSCIENCE TO A
PERSONAL GOD.

PSALM cxxxix. I.

"O Lord, Thou hast searched me, and known me."

IN the first Lecture of this course, I entered a
preliminary protest against that demand for the
scientific verification of the principles of our religion
which is now so often pressed upon us. I endeavoured
to show that the law of the life of religion and of
righteousness is that which is announced by St. Paul,
when he says that, in the Gospel, "the righteousness
of God is revealed from faith to faith." In other
words, the moral and religious growth of mankind
has arisen, and, by the nature of the case, must arise,
from their trust and love, from their instinctive impulse
to follow the guidance of the best and wisest of their
fellows, and thus, so to speak, to be continually reach-
ing out beyond their own experience to higher truths

and nobler lives. Faith, indeed, in its highest acceptation, is directed towards a Monitor and Guide far
higher, and more worthy of trust, than any saint or
prophet. But this is the point to be established ; and,
without assuming it, the general principle of human
action in moral and religious matters is sufficiently
evident. If moral and religious truths are ever to
receive a verification, we must act on them in faith
before they are verified.

But, in making this protest, it is by no means implied that no experimental evidence can be afforded in
justification of our faith. On the contrary, we may be
sure that, unless the foundations of faith were laid
deep in human experience, they would be unable to
bear any lofty superstructure. It is most reasonable
to believe that Prophets and Apostles have seen more,
felt more, and understood more, than ourselves ; but
it would be most unreasonable to trust them, if their
primary principles had no response in our consciences,
and were not justified by our experience, so far as that
reaches. It would be most unreasonable to assume
that a man's most intimate friend cannot know more
of him than I do ; but I should justly distrust his
friend's report, if it did not agree with what I knew of
him, so far as my opportunities extended. Religious
faith is thus a matter of combined experience and
trust ; and with this qualification we can heartily
respond to the demand that we should offer some
verifiable evidence of our first principles. We refuse

to restrict our creed to that which can be scientifically established; but we ought to be able, and we are confident we are able, to base its claims on the evidence of the human Conscience and Reason.

Let us approach, then, from this point of view the question now raised : whether we have sufficient grounds of evidence and experience for the first postulate of religion—that of the existence of a Personal God. Certainly, if it be true, it is a truth so momentous, and of such intimate concern to us, that we cannot but crave for some plain, direct, and experimental assurance of it. In respect to a belief of such supreme import, there is, no doubt, great justice in the objections of late so vigorously urged against our trusting to metaphysical arguments and mere logical deductions. Human reason, however cultivated, is a perilous instrument to be solely relied on in regions beyond our direct experience ; and it needs at least to be perpetually tested by plain facts. At all events, it would be vain to rely upon mere abstract proof in appealing to men in general. If religion were only the concern of philosophers, or if simple men could be asked to surrender themselves, in such a matter, to the guidance of philosophers, a belief in a Personal God might, perhaps, be rested on such arguments as those which have been elaborated to prove the existence of a First Cause. But looking at human nature in history and in life, those arguments appear rather of the nature of valuable auxiliaries for the defence of a position once gained, than forces capable of gaining it. As has been urged with perfect truth by one of the principal objectors now in view,[1] it was not by means of any such logical speculations that the people of Israel acquired those firm and vivid religious conceptions which have been a revelation to the rest of the world. If this belief is to be a practical one, and is to lay hold of men in general as the starting-point of their religious thought, it must appeal to some nearer, simpler, and more moving evidence.

Important, moreover, as these arguments are for the intellectual justification of the Christian position, there is another consideration which renders them less valuable for the practical purpose of these Lectures. They may demonstrate the existence of a personal First Cause; but, if we are to consider the correspondence of the Gospel with the Moral Nature of Man, what we are chiefly concerned with is the character of that Divine Person. We want evidence, not merely that there is such a Being, but that we are directly concerned with Him in the moral and spiritual part of our nature. It is this which, we are so confidently told, is beyond our power of verification. We can satisfy ourselves, by observation and personal experience, that there is an eternal power in the world, external to ourselves, which maintains righteousness; but that this power is personal, and that its value to us depends in any degree on the fact of its personality,

---

[1] Mr. Matthew Arnold, in "Literature and Dogma;" *passim.*

these are said to be gratuitous assumptions.[1] Similarly,
the distinguished philosopher to whose posthumous
Essays I referred last Sunday, dismisses as comparatively unimportant the argument for the belief in God to
be derived from Conscience ; and treating the argument
from Design as that which alone possesses a scientific
value, concludes that the belief is no more than an
admissible hope, which possesses, consequently, no
essential moral significance.[2] We ought then, I admit,
if this belief is to be a reality, to adduce some cogent
moral evidence for it ; and this evidence we shall,
I think, readily find if we follow the guidance of the
Scriptures. If the true character and justification of
belief in God is to be discovered anywhere, it must be
there. Let us ask then, as a matter of fact, what was
the motive which gave this belief so overwhelming a
power over the Hebrew mind ?

In answer to this question, we find admitted, or
rather asserted, by objectors that which, if duly considered, is sufficient for our purpose. It is urged with
truth that the people of Israel were distinguished from
other nations by the intensity with which they apprehended the supremacy of righteousness. It was given
to them to discern, in the whole course of human life,
the steadfast, unchanging, invincible operation of a
righteous power. Now as this conviction was, as a
matter of fact, associated with an equally vivid per-

[1] "Literature and Dogma," ch. x.
[2] Mr. Mill's Essay on "Theism."

ception of the Divine personality, it is reasonable to
surmise that the two conceptions may be indissolubly
connected ; and that connection will be rendered
apparent, if we consider more carefully what was the
nature of the righteous influence which the Israelites
thus discerned.

We may observe, then, that it is wholly inadequate
to represent this influence as a mere law, or power,
which asserted the supremacy of righteousness in
matters of human conduct. It was something nearer,
something much more practical, something much more
verifiable than that. The experience of mankind in
such a matter is, indeed, a somewhat vague and
distant kind of evidence to appeal to. As the Scriptures themselves witness, it is an experience which
has often perplexed, rather than re-assured, those who
have relied upon it. Even prophets, animated by the
deepest faith, have nevertheless been so baffled and
disturbed by the general course of things around them,
as to exclaim that "the law is slacked, and judgment
doth never go forth." To the rule, as stated above,
life presents, and has always presented, such great
and distressing exceptions, that the scientific verification which is claimed for it might well be disputed.
The book of Job, which is the record of the earliest
and most natural experience on this subject, is practically a confession that the relation between the claims
of righteousness and the actual facts of life presents
insoluble mysteries, and that if a righteous man, like

Job, is to retain his faith, it can only be under a conviction of his utter ignorance. Moreover, this is another instance of an argument which, however powerful it may become with the support of the increasing experience of mankind, is far too much of a generalization to have been the source of faith in simpler times, and to simpler hearts. The Jewish conviction of righteousness comes much more closely home. That which impressed them was not merely a law, or stream of tendency, which asserted righteousness in human conduct; it was an influence which asserted the claims of righteousness, and its supremacy, in each individual. They felt not merely, nor perhaps so much, that righteousness was the greatest authority and power in the world, as that it was the greatest authority and power in the heart of every one of them. That sense of Right and Wrong, which we are taking as the starting-point of our considerations, had a profound and vivid reality for them in their innermost consciences; and they felt that some power beyond themselves was perpetually working within them to support the Right and to defeat the Wrong. That is a verifiable conception, indeed. It is a fact of Conscience which every man may verify for himself; and if this justifies and demands belief in a Personal God, it is an evidence which comes home to every heart.

But to appreciate its bearings, consider the vivid expression of it which is afforded in the Psalm from which the text is taken. "O Lord," says David,

"Thou hast searched me and known me. Thou
knowest my downsitting, and mine uprising; Thou
understandest my thought afar off. Thou compassest
my path and my lying down, and art acquainted with
all my ways. For there is not a word in my tongue,
but, lo! O Lord, Thou knowest it altogether. Thou
hast beset me behind and before, and laid Thine hand
upon me." Now, in what particular way does the man
feel himself thus beset? What is the faculty in his
nature which apprehends this wonderful presence so
vividly? The last verses of the Psalm reveal it:
" Search me, O God, and know my heart; try me, and
know my thoughts; and see if there be any wicked
way in me, and lead me in the way everlasting."
The writer is not speaking of any mere intellectual
apprehension of a spiritual presence; he is not merely
describing the ubiquity and omniscience of the Divine
nature. That of which he has an almost distressing
consciousness—that which awes his weakness, though
it finally fascinates his trust—is the sense of a
presence which is searching his heart, trying his
thoughts, and seeing whether there be any wicked way
in him. It is a process, as the word implies, as keen
in its operation as the searching fire of a refiner.
" The fining pot is for silver, and the furnace for gold,
but the Lord trieth the hearts." It is from this witness and judgment of right and wrong within him that
the man knows he cannot escape. " Whither shall I
go from Thy spirit? or whither shall I flee from Thy

presence? If I ascend up into heaven, Thou art there;
if I make my bed in hell, behold, Thou art there. If I
take the wings of the morning, and dwell in the uttermost parts of the sea, even there shall Thy hand lead
me, and Thy right hand shall hold me. If I say,
Surely the darkness shall cover me, even the night
shall be light about me. Yea, the darkness hideth not
from Thee; but the night shineth as the day: the
darkness and the light are both alike to Thee." What
remains for him, but to surrender himself to this per-
sistent, ever-present power, to obey it, and unite himself with it? "Do not I hate them, O Lord, that hate
Thee? and am not I grieved with those that rise up
against Thee? I hate them with perfect hatred; I
count them mine enemies. Search me, O God, and
know my heart; try me, and know my thoughts: and
see if there be any wicked way in me, and lead me in
the way everlasting."

I appeal to the Psalm, not as a dogmatic authority,
but as a record of the experience of the human heart
and conscience; and I ask whether every heart among
us does not, at one time or another, feel the profound
truth of the description? Conscience may for a time
be dulled and deadened; but is it not on the whole the
one presence which you cannot get rid of? Does it
not beset you in your path and in your bed, abroad
or at home, by night or by day? If you count its
suggestions, are they not more in number than the
sand? If you forget it in your sleep, when you awake

is it not still with you ?   And what is the operation of
its voice ?   Is it content with proclaiming to you the
general supremacy of a righteous law ?   Does it not, on
the contrary, search your heart and try your thoughts,
and see if there be any wicked way in you ?   Does it
not, with a mysterious justice, deal with your personal
character, your private, individual, and peculiar re-
sponsibilities, making allowance for your weaknesses,
condemning you in proportion to the wilfulness of
your sin, but above all things meeting you at every
turn and in every instant of your lives with the particular warning and guidance you need ?

On the answer which may be made to these questions depends the force of the considerations now
suggested.   But this Psalm is sufficient to show the
intense vividness with which this operation of Conscience was apprehended by the Jew ; and let us now
ask further whether he was not justified in the instinctive interpretation which he put upon it ?   He felt,
indeed, in the first place, that this authority was not
himself.   It was an influence independent of him,
stronger than he was ; controlling him, and enforcing
its dictates upon him.   So far he commands the
approval of our modern objector.   But, in addition to
this, he felt that an influence which acted upon him
individually and personally must be individual and
personal itself.   Probably he had no speculative ideas
as to what Personality meant.   But he knew that his
Conscience dealt with him in a way to which there was

nothing analogous, except the way in which living persons dealt with him. It praised and it blamed ; it was not like a law, acting without reference to his special peculiarities, but it adapted its operation with infinite variety to all the varying shades of right and wrong, of error or of weakness, within him. In a word, it was just as personal as he was. As heart answers to heart, and the face of man to man, so did that power which was felt in his Conscience correspond to his own nature.

Such appears, as a matter of fact, to be the connection in the Psalms between the two ideas of the Personality and the Righteousness of God ; and it is here that we may lay the firm basis of that verifying experience for which we are asked. It is far too easily assumed, in most of the objections to which I am referring, that the only evidences for the existence of a Personal God are Physical, Metaphysical, of Supernatural. The strongest of all, and those which appeal to every soul, are the Moral. This sense of Right and Wrong, with the searching and abiding responsibility which it entails, is probably a far more distinctive and essential human attribute than any other. In all the exercises of the intellect there is a certain impersonality ; in some of its highest exercises, the more complete the impersonal character of the operation the greater its excellence. But in the sense of Right and Wrong, the personality, or the distinct existence of the individual, is the primary element of

Conscience. Much has been written on the famous argument, *Cogito, ergo sum*—" I think, and therefore I exist"; and again, "As I have a clear idea of God, therefore He exists"; and it is an argument which at least deserved more respect than to be treated, as it has lately been, as either unmeaning or a truism.[1] There is nothing unintelligible in the argument that in the act of thinking I exercise an individualizing action on the things around me, and am, as it were, a separate centre of life and action. It seems, however, a far stronger argument to say, "I have a sense of Right and Wrong, and therefore I am an individual, personal being." Whatever foreshadowings of this sense may be discerned, as is sometimes alleged, in the higher animals, there is at least one thing of which there is no trace among them : and that is, a feeling of continuous responsibility for the whole of life and for its successive actions. But each man feels that all his acts constitute an abiding element of his personal and individual being, and that he has a living and abiding responsibility for them. Similarly, it is far more forcible, at least for practical purposes, to argue from the moral than from the intellectual idea of God ; and instead of saying, " I have the idea of God, and there must be an object to correspond to it," to say, " I feel within my soul at every moment a righteous voice dealing with me individually ; and I conclude that I am in contact with a righteous Person." Appeal to

[1] " God and the Bible," by Mr. Matthew Arnold, ch. ii.

this sense in men, and you are touching the keenest and most vital of their experiences ; you are verifying your message by the most indestructible and unalterable part of their consciousness.   Here, too, it may be observed, lies an irrefragable proof of the unity of God, if His existence be once admitted.   Contemplate Him primarily in Nature, and the absurdity is not perhaps so evident, on the face of it, of supposing the existence of co-ordinate deities with distinct spheres of action.   But contemplate Him as revealed in that moral law which, in a continually increasing degree, asserts its one unique supremacy over every human conscience, and we then hear reiterated, with an ever-growing unanimity, " Hear, O Israel : the Lord our God is one Lord."   It must be one Being, and only one, who speaks in the same tones to millions of separate hearts, who searches and tries them all by a similar test, and who guides them all, from whatever wanderings, in one direction.

Consider, in fact, whether the case may not be put even more simply and strongly.   May we not say that a power which, in individuals and in the world at large, " makes for righteousness," must be a righteous power ; and a righteous power, or a power which acts righteously, must in some sense or other be a Person who exercises towards us acts of will, love, and reason? If a man admits the sense of Right and Wrong, and the existence of righteous government, but denies that this involves the personality of the governing force, all we have to ask of him is to observe with more thoroughness the operation of this righteous influence; and when an objector insists that the personification by the Jews of "an eternal power which makes for righteousness" was a mere instance of the anthropomorphic tendency of mankind, we have again only to ask him to observe more closely the operation of that power as described by the Jews themselves. He is quite right as far as he goes; but he does not go far enough. The people of Israel had a still more deep and penetrating apprehension of that righteous influence than even he claims for them. Assume that the only or the main action of that influence is in enforcing the practical supremacy of righteousness in human conduct, and it may be possible to regard it as a law, or "stream of tendency." But once recognize it as a power dealing with your own soul, in the depths of your conscience, and dealing similarly with every individual soul; and then, if I mistake not, it becomes impossible to regard it as impersonal. A law, by its very nature, takes no account of individuals. It inflicts itself upon them, and passes by, and takes no note of consequences to them. But a power which is striving to make me, in my personality, righteous, must adjust its action to my sins, my infirmities, and my necessities, and must, in a word, act righteously towards me.

Take, for instance, another expression of the manner in which Israel apprehended the action of this eternal

power. "Out of the depths have I cried unto Thee,
O Lord: Lord, hear my voice; let Thine ears be
attentive to the voice of my supplications. If Thou,
Lord, shouldest mark iniquities, O Lord, who shall
stand? But there is forgiveness with Thee, that Thou
mayest be feared." Is not this language, like that of
the Psalm previously quoted, a simple transcript of
the moral consciousness when keenly aroused? While
the voice of that consciousness convicts us of sin, does
it not also speak both of the need and of the possibility
of forgiveness? But what forgiveness can there be in
a law? The natural method by which a person is
recovered from his evil, and is made righteous, is by
the combined operation on his soul of condemnation
and of forgiveness, of censure and of encouragement,
such as are more or less imperfectly administered by
his fellows. If he is to be made perfectly righteous,
if his repentance and his regeneration are to be complete, these influences must be brought to bear on
him in perfection. The right and the wrong of the
soul must be confronted with that righteous action
which is their test, and their controlling influence;
and this righteous action requires a Spiritual and
Righteous Person.

In short, we might, perhaps, venture to describe
Conscience as that sixth sense by which God is apprehended. How we are to speak of Him, or regard
Him intellectually, is another matter; and I hope to
show, in the sequel, how this moral apprehension of

Him connects itself with other beliefs respecting Him. But it is to this that we may most safely appeal when we are asked for some experimental proof that there exists a Divine and Spiritual Person, who lives and acts with righteousness and with reason. It is not indeed a demonstrative proof. It does not establish the fact once and for all, beyond the possibility of dispute. But perhaps it is something better than that; it is a witness which addresses itself to each individual soul, and which appeals to it with the force of a personal and of a moral obligation

LECTURE III.

WITNESS OF CONSCIENCE TO A MORAL CREATOR.

PSALM cxxxix. 14.

" I will praise Thee ; for I am fearfully and wonderfully made : marvellous are Thy works ; and that my soul knoweth right well."

IN the previous Lecture I endeavoured to point out what was the experience in human nature to which our belief in a personal God appeals. It becomes us to recognize, in the fullest manner, the justice of the demand made upon us, that we should not be content with adducing logical arguments or probabilities in defence of this belief, but that we should feel for ourselves, and show to others, that the necessity lies deep in the commonest and most essential feelings of our nature. The claim of Christianity, and not of Christianity alone, but of the prophets before the appearance of Christ, is not merely that we should believe in the existence of God, but that we should love Him, and love Him with all the heart, soul, mind, and strength— love Him, that is, as we can only love the most

personal, the most wise, the most holy, of all beings.
The demand is addressed not only to the intelligent
and the acute, but to the simplest heart, and the most
unlearned soul. "Hear, O heavens," says the prophet,
"and give ear, O earth; for the Lord hath spoken, I
have nourished and brought up children, and they
have rebelled against me. The ox knoweth his owner,
and the ass his master's crib: but Israel doth not
know, my people doth not consider." Similarly,
St. Paul declares that "the invisible things of Him
from the creation of the world are clearly seen, being
understood by the things that are made, even His
eternal power and Godhead; so that they are without
excuse." If this language is to be justified—if, as it
implies, a belief in a Personal God, and a love of Him,
is the true instinct of every soul—its basis must be
sought in the commonest and most imperious of
human experiences. Looking to faith in a Personal
God as an historical fact, we do not find it arising out
of a process of ratiocination. It springs up in the
hearts of comparatively uncultivated people; and it
spreads by a contagion of feeling rather than by a con-
secution of argument. That it should be defensible
on logical and metaphysical grounds is, indeed, essential to its validity; but for our present purpose we
are not so much concerned with that aspect of the
subject. We are simply endeavouring to trace, in
history and in experience, the actual grounds of the
belief, and to estimate their practical force.

We have observed, then, in the hundred and thirty-ninth Psalm—regarded not as an authority, but as the record of experience—an appeal to the Conscience rather than to the Intellect. If we wish to estimate the force of this appeal, we must ask ourselves whether the picture be not true of a power which not only maintains righteousness in the world at large, and punishes evil, but which besets us individually in the depths of our conscience, which compasses our path and our lying down, and is acquainted with all our ways. This power does not correspond in character with a law which inflicts itself on us, and which we must either obey or endure. It deals with us as persons, and adapts itself, in its judgments and in its encouragements, to our individual personalities, with all their variations of guilt and weakness, of wilfulness or ignorance. It answers, in short, to our own personality ; and it is personal, at all events, in its relations to us. Dealing with us righteously, it cannot be deemed other than a righteous influence ; and an influence acting righteously upon our personal wills cannot be deemed otherwise than as, in relation to us, a personal and righteous will. We should observe that this inference is something more than the logical deduction, forcible as it is, that the law implies a law-giver, that the " categorical imperative " of the conscience implies some one who has a right to command. It is more than an inference ; it amounts, in each individual, to an immediate consciousness of a moral

will acting upon his will ; and its verification lies, not
in the clearness with which it can be demonstrated,
but in the force with which it is felt. Such, as the
Psalmist declares, was the nature of that Power which
the people of Israel discerned to be exercising judgment and righteousness in the earth—a power which
is, indeed, "not ourselves," but which is the nearest
thing to ourselves in the world, the most intimate and
the most personal of the guests of our souls.

Such seem to be the experiences on which the belief
in a righteous and personal God may be made to rest
in every human soul, as they were those on which it
rested in the Psalmist. But if we would justify the
full conception of the Scriptures and of the Gospel, we
must go much further ; and the next step appears
again to be indicated by the Psalm under our consideration. We have to rise, in the first instance, to the
conception of this personal and righteous being as
our Creator, and we have to seek for the individual
experience which justifies the magnificent conceptions
in the Scriptures of the power, wisdom, and love of
God. The voice in the conscience, it might be said,
speaks of the presence of a righteous Person ; but how
does it enable us to identify Him with that omni-
potent and omnipresent Being whose operations we
believe we discern in nature ? Again, I apprehend,
the practical answer lies in the conscience ; and is
furnished by the most simple and imperative of infer-
ences. It will be observed that in this Psalm, in

addition to the keen sense we have noticed of a
righteous Power besetting the conscience, there is a
not less vivid apprehension of the cognizance, by the
same Power, of the whole frame of the man in body
and soul.   It is not merely that God understands his
thoughts afar off; but he exclaims: "Thou hast
possessed my reins; Thou hast covered me in my
mother's womb.   I will praise Thee, for I am fearfully and wonderfully made: marvellous are Thy
works; and that my soul knoweth right well.   My
substance was not hid from Thee, when I was made
in secret, and curiously wrought in the lowest parts of
the earth.   Thine eyes did see my substance, yet
being unperfect; and in Thy book all my members
were written, which in continuance were fashioned,
when as yet there was none of them."   The writer
seems, so to speak, to pass to and fro between these
two conceptions.   "How precious," he continues, "are
Thy thoughts unto me, O God! how great is the sum
of them!"   A God who searches him and knows his
heart, who tries him and knows his thoughts, cannot,
in his mind, be separated from a God who possessed
his reins and covered him in his mother's womb.

Now I would ask whether the course of thought
thus expressed be not, both to individuals and on
a large scale, natural and inevitable.   The Psalmist is
conscious that in every particular action, no matter
how small, there is a voice which tells him what he
ought to do, and what he ought not to do; or what

he ought to have done, and what he ought not to have done. He does not merely discern, by experience and reflection, that such and such a course of conduct would have been more satisfactory to himself and others. But he is beset behind and before ; there is not a word in his tongue—or rather, before there is a word in his tongue, this Power knows it altogether. It checks him before action, and in action, and after action ; it searches him and knows his heart, and is capable, not merely of rewarding and punishing him, but of leading him in the way everlasting. How can he avoid the conclusion that a Power which asserts this authority over him in body and soul, and in every part of his nature, is the very Power by which that nature was constituted, and its parts and their general functions established ? The body and its several parts, the mind and its numberless faculties, can be used in a variety of ways. I need not ask by what right a particular authority within me commands that each faculty should be used in a certain way and in no other ; it is a much more pertinent question to ask by what means, by what capacity, it asserts this command ? Go, like the Psalmist, to the very recesses of your bodily constitution ; view it in its elements, in its germs, in its primary members ; and then consider that every man who attains to consciousness and conscience has a sense that, though these members may be used in so many ways, they ought only to be used in one. It cannot be replied—at least, not by the objectors whom we now have in view—that no such distinct and permanent consciousness exists. To say so would be to abandon the whole ground on which we are standing—that of a sense of right and wrong. That this sense, indeed, can be perverted is obvious in every-day life ; and if it can be perverted at all, no limits can well be placed to the possible extent of the perversion. But to acknowledge the existence of a sense of right and wrong is to acknowledge that on the whole, and as the general result of their constitution, men have a natural apprehension that some things, in particular, are right, and some things, in particular, are wrong. Whether that apprehension be perfect or imperfect, partial or full, how can it be dictated or imposed on me, except by the power which rendered particular things conformable to my nature, and particular things not conformable ?

To appreciate, moreover, the bearing of this consideration, it must be remembered that many actions which Conscience commands or forbids are commanded or forbidden with direct reference to their moral, as distinguished from their natural, aspect. Physically speaking, the members of the body might appear to be capable of a variety of uses, but morally speaking they are adapted only for one ; and that one, when duly tested, proves also to be the best for their physical perfection. There may, indeed, be cases in which the moral perfection and the physical do not coincide, and in which a man is compelled to dwarf the

lower part of his nature in obedience to the moral.
In that case, it may be urged, the consideration of the
general good of the race comes into play; and the
general experience dictates the conduct in question.
But there seem many cases to which this explanation
would not apply; and these seem, moreover, the most
characteristic of all. When Christian morality was
created, as I observed in the first Lecture, the sense
of obligation, in numberless instances, preceded experience of the result.   Conscience, responding to
Revelation, dictated obedience to a law which is now
acknowledged to be the best guide of life.   Can any
conviction be conceived adequate either to create or to
sustain this sense of obligation, but that of the Psalmist.
" My reins are Thine "? " Thou," that is, " hadst both
the power and the right to create me for certain purposes and for certain capacities; and I am bound to
fulfil those purposes and to carry out those capacities,
because they are those for which my nature was
curiously wrought and made in secret.   I will praise
Thee," and obey Thee, " for I am fearfully and wonderfully made.   Marvellous are Thy works; and that my
soul knoweth right well."   The soul knows right well
that the power which asserts this right to command it,
which besets it behind and before, with this antecedent
and subsequent claim, must be a power in whose book,
in whose deliberate wisdom, all its members were
written, which in continuance were fashioned, when as
yet there were none of them.

It is the most simple and direct aspect of this consideration which seems revealed in the Psalm ; and it is upon its strength, thus viewed, that, as I have said, our appeal to the convictions of men in general must rely. But the consideration appears to gain force when it is viewed more generally, as involving a considerable extension of the usual argument from design. That argument is acknowledged in the posthumous Essays of Mr. Mill to be one of a really scientific character ; and though he scrutinizes it with jealousy, he admits that it affords a large balance of probability in favour of creation by intelligence.[1] This admission is based, however, upon a survey of the argument from a purely physical point of view. But accepting, for the purpose of this discussion, the mode in which it is presented, I would observe that it acquires an immensely enhanced force when moral considerations are taken into account. Mr. Mill takes the case of the eye. The parts of which the eye is composed, and the arrangement of those parts, have this very remarkable character—that they all conduce to enable the animal to see. "These things being as they are, the animal sees ; if any one of them were different from what it is, the animal, for the most part, would not see, or would not see equally well." It must be supposed, therefore, that the purpose of enabling the animal to see was the final cause of the structure of the eye ; and that structure, consequently, must have proceeded from an intelligent will.

[1] Essay on "Theism."

The plea which is at present advanced to meet the force of this argument is that which attributes the growth of all physical organizations, however complicated, to the gradual operation, through countless ages, of the law of the survival of the fittest; so that in the struggle for life, out of an infinite number of successive adaptations, the most beneficial on the whole survived.   Now, there are great difficulties, as Mr. Mill admits, in accepting this explanation of such an elaborate structure as the eye, even from a merely physical point of view; but regard the body and some of its most vital functions from a moral point of view, and the difficulty will become infinitely greater.

I mean to observe that the structure of the human frame is not merely calculated to produce certain physical results, such as sight.   It is also calculated to produce, and does in fact produce, certain moral results, of the highest beauty and delicacy.   The most beautiful, the most elevating, the most sacred of all human feelings spring from the relations of marriage and fatherhood, and are inseparably bound up with the physical constitution of human nature.   No antagonist with whom it would be worth while to dispute regards the obligations of those relationships as having a merely natural and physical bearing. They touch the soul in its innermost recesses.   They call out, for weal or woe, its truth, its honour, its patience, its gentleness, its purity—in a word, its love. In proportion as they have been faithfully observed.

have they revealed, to generation after generation,
new heavens and a new earth of noble and inspiring
emotions, and have suggested the most sublime of all
the conceptions under which the Supreme Being can
be imagined.   It is not merely the material welfare
of states which is dependent on these laws of morality ;
it is not merely any general social results whatever.
It is the grace of your homes, the purity of your hearts,
the refinement of your love ; it is all the poetry and
sublimity of your lives, which is at stake in them.
The constitution of the human frame, therefore, in
such a matter, for instance, as the relation of the
sexes, has not merely, like the structure of the eye, a
physical end ; but it has a moral end.   It is directly
adapted to produce the highest spiritual excellences ;
and it is not fully developed or properly used except
in relation to them.   Now if the production of a
structure with reference to a physical end be an argument of its having proceeded from an intelligent will,
how much more is the adaptation of a structure to a
moral end an argument of its proceeding from a
moral will?   History and experience appear to show,
in an increasing degree, that the highest perfection of
man's physical nature is only possible on the whole,
and in the course of generations, in harmony with the
development of his moral nature ; and in proportion
as this becomes apparent, the evidence of moral design
becomes overwhelming. So far, at all events, as human
nature goes, we discern a pregnant significance in the

verse, " The Lord is righteous in all His ways, and holy in all His works." In other words, He has a righteous object and a holy aim in all the ways and works of that fearful and wonderful structure of our frame. This moral view of the argument from design would seem not merely to strengthen, but to comprehend, the other. For a moral purpose is, in its nature, inseparable from an intelligent purpose, as righteousness is inseparable from reason ; and if the human body and the human race bear witness to their adaptation to a moral purpose by a moral will, it becomes superfluous to argue that they are adapted to an intelligent purpose by an intelligent will.

In fact, any doctrine which assumes the development of nature by the mere operation of physical and material struggles, can only carry any appearance of truth by the exclusion of the moral character and capacities of man from the field of contemplation—an exclusion very natural in an age when the mind has been intensely absorbed in the contemplation of physical nature. Bring the moral nature of man— using the word " moral" in its most comprehensive signification—into the field of view, and observe what the assumption supposes. It is not merely that a certain physical perfection was elaborated, in the course of ages, by the struggle for life ; but that a struggle for a purely physical life elaborated a constitution of man, adapted not merely to the perfection of physical existence, but to the perfection of an existence of

which the highest excellence may often consist in an
absolute disregard for everything physical and temporal. The greater, moreover, the amount of truth
allowed to be present in this theory, considered as a
summary of a certain class of observations of natural
facts, the more weighty does the consideration now
suggested become. Such theories, whether true or
not in their full extent, rest undoubtedly upon one of
the most remarkable revelations which Science has
yet afforded—I mean, the close and intimate association of the whole of nature with the condition of
every part and member of its organization. Whether
it be the doctrine of the Conservation of Force, or the
principle of Continuity, or the theory of Natural
Selection, all combine in recognizing one fact—that
all the various parts of nature—all its elements, all its
forces, and the whole of its history—co-operate in the
constitution of each particular part. St. Paul's image
applied to the human frame affords an exact description of this relation :—"The body is not one member,
but many. If the foot shall say, Because I am not
the hand, I am not of the body ; is it therefore not of
the body ? . . . God hath set the members every one
of them in the body, as it hath pleased Him ; . . . but
now are they many members, yet but one body. And
the eye cannot say unto the hand, I have no need of
thee ; nor again the head to the feet, I have no need
of you. Nay, much more those members of the body,
which seem to be more feeble, are necessary ; and

those members of the body, which we think to be less
honourable, upon these we bestow more abundant
honour; and our uncomely parts have more abundant
comeliness. For . . . God hath tempered the body
together, having given more abundant honour to that
part which lacked. That there should be no schism in
the body; but . . . whether one member suffer, all the
members suffer with it; or one member be honoured,
all the members rejoice with it."

"That there should be no schism in the body:"
could there be a more forcible expression of that intense sense of continuity and conservation which has
of late absorbed the contemplation of the observers of
nature? For the defence of the Christian faith, and
for the purposes of this argument, no truth could be
of greater value. It is only necessary—and on the
very hypothesis itself it is essential—that moral considerations should also be brought into the field of
observation. You tell me that every chemical element,
however insignificant, that every star, however distant,
that every stage of geological development, however
remote, that every fossil, however buried in the depths
of the earth, that every force, however slight and im-
perceptible, have all been co-operating—and for what?
For what final and ultimate cause it is neither necessary
nor possible to consider. But at all events, among
other things, for this: that your Conscience might be
what it is now; that you might have that sense of
Right and Wrong; that you might have that idea of

a life, a virtue, and a beauty eternal in the heavens ;
that your little child might have that gentleness and
trustfulness, that your wife or your husband might
have that devotion, that faith, hope, and love towards
you, which are to you eternal and imperishable posses-
sions ; that men might develop self-sacrificing bravery
and truth, and women a self-abandoning patience and
an unearthly purity—nay, it was for the production of
the Sermon on the Mount, and of the character, viewed
merely as a human character, of Christ.   As a matter
of fact, on the mere basis of this scientific observation, the Apostle's conclusion from the image I have
quoted is in a certain sense literally true—true not
merely of individual Christians, but of that whole
concatenation of forces of which the universe is composed : " Now ye are the body of Christ, and members
in particular."

Now, is it not incredible—far more incredible than
that which may seem at first sight the most abstruse
speculation of theology—that the most exquisite and
most delicate, the most moral of spiritual characters, a
character which finds its apotheosis in death, and its
life in the invisible, should thus have all nature co-
operating towards its realization, and yet that no
moral or spiritual will should have been the agent in
that infinite and endless co-ordination of cause and
effect ? If righteousness and holiness exist at all,
they exist as essential constituents of the universe ;
and they extort from us the exclamation already

quoted :—" The Lord is righteous in all His ways, and holy in all His works."

It is this which, in its bearing on the individual conscience, the Psalmist reveals ; and the consideration appears a direct answer to the demand, which I commenced by admitting, that we should show some urgent and intimate dictate of our nature, as the foundation of that intense belief in a Personal God, Who, whatever He be in Himself, is to us reason and love, which our Religion prescribes. This is the spirit in which the Psalmist, and every human soul whose conscience is quickened by such words, is carried from his sense of the presence of God in his conscience to a conviction that the same moral power, the same reasonable will, is also the Author of every element of his body and of his existence. In one way, perhaps, the inference is even more forcible to the individual conscience than to the general reason ; for it is to the individual soul that Conscience dictates its commands. But whether in regard to the general reason of men or to the individual, it is of the essence of Conscience that it claims, with respect to every action and every element of the human frame, to be both a final cause and a final moral cause.

LECTURE IV.

WITNESS OF CONSCIENCE TO A MORAL GOVERNOR

PSALM cxxxix. 8-10.

" If I ascend up into heaven, Thou art there : If I make my bed in hell, behold, Thou art there. If I take the wings of the morning, and dwell in the uttermost parts of the sea ; even there shall Thy hand lead me, and Thy right hand shall hold me."

IN our endeavour to trace in the Conscience, and in the personal experience of individuals, the roots of our faith in a God of infinite power, wisdom, and goodness, we have now advanced two considerable steps beyond our first and simplest sense of Right and Wrong. We have seen that this sense, when allowed to speak with its full imperative and personal force, arouses in us, as it aroused in the Psalmist, a conviction of our being in contact with a personal and righteous Will. This conviction necessarily involves, as it involved in the writer of the hundred and thirty-ninth Psalm, the further belief that an authority which has this claim upon our obedience in every particular of our conduct, in all our thoughts and acts, must at the same time be the author and source of our whole constitution ; that the righteous eyes which now penetrate, whether through darkness or through light, to the very depths of our souls, must also have seen our "substance, yet being imperfect," and that in their book must all our members have been written. If it be the imperative and paramount law of our nature to obey our Conscience, and to make moral perfection, or spiritual excellence, our ultimate aim, we cannot but conclude that our whole nature, and the whole order of things in which we are placed, is in the hands of a moral power ; and that, as we are fearfully and wonderfully made for righteous and reasonable ends, it must be by a righteous and reasonable Will that we are made. The Conscience of man must never be omitted from our view of the design of man ; and it is only when we contemplate the adjustment of his whole nature to the purposes of the loftiest moral development that the argument from design acquires its full strength. So far, therefore, our belief in a personal God who exerts reason and love is not a mere logical deduction from abstract premises ; it is the imperative dictate of the Conscience. We are led to it, not merely by reason, but by practical reason—by the reason, that is, on which the whole conduct of our life is based.

But another step is necessary before we fully identify this God of the Conscience and of Human

Nature with the God of the Scriptures and of the
Creeds,—the step, namely, which enables us to contemplate Him as that Almighty Being by whose
direct will the whole creation, and every particular
occurrence in it, is governed and guided. That which
is implied in the Scriptures, and in the language of
Christian devotion, is something much more than a
conviction that we ourselves, and the whole world,
have been created by a moral and intelligent Will.
It implies further, that that Will is ever and everywhere directly operative ; so that in every particular
of our lives we are dealing, not merely with an order
such as Science reveals, but with an order controlled
for moral purposes. The Psalmist cannot contemplate any part or appearance of nature except as the
immediate act of God. Alike in great things and in
small, in the vast operations of nature and in its
minutest adjustments, an individual agency is discerned. On the one hand, it is the God of glory who
thundereth ; it is the Lord who is upon many waters.
On the other hand, He satisfies the desire of every
living thing. He has not merely laid the foundations
of the earth, that it should not be moved for ever ; but
He feeds the young ravens which call upon Him.

It is an unworthy and injurious representation of
this idea, to describe it as that of a "magnified man."
The grandeur and infinity of the vision raise it above
any mere anthropomorphism. If there should appear
at first to be only a difference of degree, yet the

degrees are so innumerable, and the difference so
infinite, as to constitute an absolute diversity in kind.
A Being so Almighty that "in His hands are the
deep places of the earth, and the strength of the hills
is His also," and at the same time condescending to
the slightest and most secret feelings of the human
heart, is elevated infinitely above every conception of
humanity. "Great is our Lord, and of great power;
His understanding is infinite: the Lord lifteth up the
meek; He casteth the wicked down to the ground."
But the conception is undoubtedly, so to speak, even
more than human in the intensity and vividness with
which personal agency is apprehended, alike in every
detail and in the whole order of the universe. Without doing violence to the language, whether of the
Psalms, of the Prophets, or of our Lord, we cannot
escape from the presence, in every natural phenomenon, as well as in the recesses of our own hearts, of
a personal eye and hand and will. "If I ascend into
heaven, Thou art there. If I make my bed in hell,
behold, Thou art there. If I take the wings of the
morning, and dwell in the uttermost parts of the sea,
even there shall Thy hand lead me, and Thy right
hand shall hold me."

It is obvious that this conviction offers the strongest
possible contrast to that impersonal view of Nature
which Science has rendered familiar to us in the
present day. There we see nothing but a complicated
mechanism of laws, the operation of which appears to

be independent of any individual agency, and to
have, in fact, no reference to any individual needs.
Accordingly, in proportion as the scientific view is
exclusively contemplated, it inexorably represses those
aspirations of personal trust towards an ever-present
person, which are the most essential element in the
Christian life. It is not merely miracles which are
thus excluded ; but, as is clearly and boldly avowed,
prayer—so far, at least, as it appeals for personal aid
—becomes not less inadmissible. It becomes impossible to utter the deep conviction of the Psalmist:
" The Lord is nigh unto all them that call upon Him,
to all that call upon Him in truth. He will fulfil the
desire of them that fear Him ; He also will hear their
cry, and will save them."

It will be observed that we do not escape from the
deadening influence of this purely scientific view by
the mere admission of the existence of a First Cause.
The First Cause, if He be only the first, cannot enter
into the daily life and thought of the soul in the
manner in which the God of the Psalms enters into it.
He may be admitted as a scientific hypothesis ; and
yet Science may pursue its course, and continue its
analysis, in comparative disregard of Him. That
which religious life demands is a cause which is not
merely the first, but at the same time the last—which
is " Alpha and Omega, the beginning and the end ;
which is, and which was, and which is to come, the
Almighty." It is perilous to attempt any compromise

whatever on this point.   On the first advance of
Science there was a disposition on the part of the
advocates of Christian principles to allow of the direct
agency of God being, so to speak, pushed only a little
further back ; to permit just one and another secondary
cause to be interposed between ourselves and Him.
But the course of Science has shown the imprac-
ticableness of any such mode of defence, even if it
were not essentially erroneous.   For Science has been
truly described as " a philosophy which never rests ;
whose law is progress : a point which yesterday was
invisible is its goal to-day, and will be its starting-post
to-morrow."   Step by step it extends its domain over
every region of Nature, and step by step does it
dislodge the theologian who attempts to satisfy it by
a mere division of territory.   What we have before us
in the Scriptures and in Science are two distinct and
separate claims to the whole domain of Nature.   If
they are antagonistic claims, one or other must be
completely suppressed.   But it will, I hope, appear,
upon consideration, that they are not thus antagonistic ; but that they are simply distinct apprehensions of the same reality from different points of view ;
and that the one is as justifiable and necessary as the
other.

For this purpose, let us consider, in the first place,
what is the experience upon which the Psalmist and
the prophets base their intense conviction of a personal agency in Nature.   Here, again, the root of their

convictions is to be discerned in the Conscience, and in the demands of Right and Wrong. The appre-hension of a Power which establishes Righteousness as the law of life involves also the conviction that it is able to enforce that law, and to render it finally and everywhere supreme. The conviction, indeed, is one of faith and not of demonstration ; and the Scriptures, no less than life, are full of instances in which this faith is tried by the bitterest experience. Even pro-phets, as I have before observed, are at times driven to the cry that " the law is slacked, and that judg-ment doth never go forth." But the deepest instincts and necessities of Conscience forbid the toleration of any such impulse of despair. If Right were not essentially and ultimately Might, I do not say—God forbid—that it would not still claim the supreme allegiance of the soul ; but life would be a bitter mockery and an inexplicable cruelty. Not merely to be under an imperative law to pursue that which cannot be realized, but to be bound to the fruitless pursuit by every noble and lovely influence—to be condemned in moral and spiritual realities to the torments of a Tantalus—this is a conception of human life against which the whole soul rebels. Accordingly, a God of all Righteousness must of necessity be re-garded as a God of all Power ; and it is invariably with this moral aspect that the power of God is contem-plated in the Psalms. Transitions which, except from this point of view, might seem abrupt, constantly

connect descriptions of God in nature with His righteousness and judgment.   Thus, the hundred and
fourth Psalm is mainly devoted to the celebration of
the grandeur and infinity of God as displayed in the
world of Nature.   He is revealed as clothed with
honour and majesty, covering Himself with light as
with a garment, and stretching out the heavens like a
curtain.   "O Lord!" the Psalmist exclaims, "how
wonderful are Thy works!—the earth is full of Thy
riches;" but after being wrapped and absorbed in
this meditation, he concludes with a sudden outburst
of moral indignation : "Let the sinners be consumed
out of the earth, and let the wicked be no more.
Bless thou the Lord, O my soul."   Magnificent as are
all these powers of the Creator, they are directed to
this ultimate purpose—that sin and wickedness
should be consumed out of the earth.   That "categorical imperative" of the Conscience, on which the
German philosopher insisted, is imperative in demanding not only a God, but an Almighty God.

But a precisely similar conviction compels the Conscience to demand an equal supremacy of moral agency
in all the details of life.   If righteousness be the paramount law, it must be regarded as everywhere, no less
than finally, operative.   If, whether I ascend into
heaven, the voice of Conscience is there; if, though
I make my bed in hell, it is there also ; and though I
dwell in the uttermost parts of the sea, even there that
mysterious voice pursues me: if, that is, under all

circumstances and in all positions I am under moral
obligations, I must suppose, as a mere matter of justice,
that the power which makes the demand upon me is
present to adjust the circumstances to my moral capacities or deserts.   A world in which everything is
regulated by purely physical circumstances, and in
which moral intervention can have no place, may
possibly be consistent with the final infliction of justice,
considered as an external rule; but it is certainly
inconsistent with any just treatment of individuals, as
such.   Even if compatible with the moral education
of the race, it is not compatible with the moral education of each individual soul; and this, as we have seen,
is an essential element in that voice of the Conscience
to which the Psalms respond.   Is it, or is it not, in
accordance with the dictates of justice, that the Lord
should uphold all that fall and raise up all those that
are bowed down?   The physical law is that the
stronger should crush the weaker, and that there
should be no place for repentance.   Regarding men
as personal beings, can such a rule be equitably
applied to them in moral and spiritual concerns?
"God," says the Apostle, "is just, who will not suffer
you to be tempted above that ye are able, but will,
with the temptation, also make a way to escape, that ye
may be able to bear it."   In other words, God would
not be just, unless, in the case of those who are honestly
struggling with temptation, He interposed sufficiently
to compensate for the inequality of their several trials.

That, in short, which is vividly present in the consciousness of the Scripture writers, is the distinction between justice in dealing with acts and justice in dealing with persons. Justice in dealing with acts may mainly consist in the enactment and enforcement of unbending laws ; but no father who has to deal with children could be considered as treating them justly, if, in his treatment of all of them, he were rigidly to enforce precisely the same rules. The law of fatherly and personal government is that of the Psalmist : "Like as a father pitieth his children, so the Lord pitieth them that fear Him. He will not always chide, neither will He keep His anger for ever. He hath not dealt with us after our sins, nor rewarded us according to our iniquities."

There is, therefore, a grave fallacy in an assumption which, in the present day, is so frequently advanced by such writers as I am considering as to be evidently regarded by them in the nature of an axiom—the assumption, namely, that there is something unworthy of a perfect Being in supposing that He interferes to modify the natural operation of circumstances, and that the highest conception of God is that of a Being governing the world by invariable laws. Certainly, if it be assumed that the world is a machine, of which we are nothing but parts, there is something unworthy of a perfect Designer in the idea of His having perpetually to interpose to check its action. But if we include persons, with a sense of right and wrong—a

claim, therefore, to righteous treatment, a claim to pity,
mercy, and aid from the Father of their spirits—it becomes utterly unworthy of such a Father and Creator
that He should not interpose for moral purposes.
The spectacle of a world of moral beings governed by
invariable laws would only afford a stupendous instance of the truth of the maxim, "*Summum jus,
summa injuria.*" Just as you have to modify human
law by human equity, so is it essential to the idea of
justice between God and man that Divine law should
be modified by Divine equity. The fallacy of the
principle thus asserted lies in the assumption that all
exercise of power which is not according to strict rule
is arbitrary. On the contrary, the highest kind of
justice is that which proceeds from the free moral
determination of a just person, adapting itself to all
the varying shades of personal needs, merits, and
demerits. A God, in fact, governing human beings
by invariable natural laws would be a God who exerted once for all one gigantic act of arbitrariness, and
who mercilessly left all the personal beings whom He
had created to bear the consequences. The invari-
ableness which is the great attribute of God consists
in the eternal permanence of His righteousness and
truth—or, to quote the highest form of expression, of
His love. The Psalmist thus binds together indissolubly His righteousness and His mercy. "Men
shall abundantly utter the memory of Thy great goodness, and shall sing of Thy righteousness. The Lord

is gracious and full of compassion ; slow to anger, and
of great mercy." Such is the ideal of a just God
which has ever commended itself to the hearts of true
Israelites. Next to a conviction that right is might,
and that a Righteous God must be an Almighty God,
comes the conviction that the same Righteous Being,
by virtue of His righteousness, must be ever present
to every soul, alike in heaven, in hell, or in the uttermost parts of the sea, able to act upon it, at every
moment, with variations adapted to its moral needs
and claims.

This being the demand of the Conscience, the
question remains whether the scientific revelation of
uniform sequence be incompatible with it. If the two
conceptions cover the same ground and deal with the
same subject-matter, there is undoubtedly an absolute
incompatibility between them. The assumption that
they do thus coincide is too frequently made on both
sides, and, so far as it is admitted, occasions a real anta-
gonism. Theologians were formerly wont to suppose
that moral and final causes occupied the whole realm
of Nature ; and now, in their turn, men of Science are
apt to suppose that physical causes have an equal
extent of operation. But, in the first place, it would
probably be admitted on all hands to be an assumption of great rashness, that because we trace a regular
order in the manifestation of natural functions, that
order expresses the whole reality and truth of their
action. A cone cut by a plane produces four different

kinds of surfaces, according to the angle at which the plane crosses it. Each of those surfaces—as, for instance, the circle and the ellipse—has its definite laws of construction, and is perfectly complete in itself. Now suppose a being inside the cone, whose field of vision was entirely confined to a circular section. If he argued as we are sometimes apt to do in scientific matters, he would regard the whole region of his existence as circular in its construction; while another being, with his vision confined to another plane, would regard it as elliptic. We have no right to assume that the human senses are in any other position than that of one of these imaginary beings—confined, namely, to a particular plane of observation; and although all their observations on that plane may exhibit a complete regularity, it does not follow that the appearances observed may not have an entirely distinct relationship. In other words, Science may be simply cutting across the totality of things at a particular angle; and it may well be that at whatever angle they were cut across, they would equally exhibit a regular construction and a constant sequence. But that sequence may be simply a sequence to certain faculties, and the facts of which it is only one aspect may be determined by entirely independent causes.

In fact, in these scientific objections to the moral action of the Divine will in determining the events of Nature, there seems to be a continual confusion between the order in which phenomena occur and the phenomena themselves. It is connected with the old dispute whether antecedents and consequents are equivalent to causes and effects. It depends upon my will which of two possible occurrences shall ensue ; but whichever ensues, the order of Nature is equally obeyed, and a sequence is equally apparent to the scientific observer. It is probably, therefore, an entirely inaccurate mode of expression to speak of miracles, and still more of ordinary interpositions of Divine Providence, as interferences with the order of Nature. They are an interference with what would otherwise be the course of Nature by the introduction of an unusual cause ; but an order is neither suspended nor interrupted because it is prevented by the appearance of a new agency from producing its ordinary results. Moreover, all objections of this class seem to assume that the physical order of Nature is finite, and that its manifestations are confined, so to speak, within the limits of a definite beginning and end. If, on the contrary, as Science herself would seem to bear witness, the order be infinite, any partial disturbance may find its counterbalancing adjustment. Nature may be like the ocean, which, after any storm, always finds its own level.

In the Book of Wisdom there is a beautiful simile in illustration of miracles, derived from music. "For," says the author, "the elements were changed in themselves by a kind of harmony—like as in a psaltery notes change the name of a tune, and yet are always

sounds;" as though a miracle might be conceived
as a change of tune, or an alteration of a key. The
ordinary moral action of the Divine will might, perhaps, receive a similar illustration.   Suppose yourselves for the first time listening to a perfect com-
position in music, played by an invisible musician,
and with nothing open to your observation but the
tones you hear, and the movements of the strings
which you perceive.   You would find it possible, after
due observation, to determine that the sounds were
combined according to regular laws ; and though you
might not penetrate to the essential law of the melody,
you would yet perceive that there was such a law, and
that it determined the course of the successive notes.
But who is not sensible that, in addition to the strict
law of musical harmony or melody, there are possible
in music an infinite variety of shades of personal influence, which depend entirely on the will and feeling
of the musician, and which have a more subtle influence than can be referred to any but the most intimate
and delicate feelings of our nature ?   The harmony of
Nature, regular as it is, is surely capable of being
similarly supplemented in its action by the subtle
touch of a Divine hand, often only perceptible to those
who have spiritual ears to hear, and a pure heart to
feel.   There seems nothing inconceivable in the supposition of the physical order of nature remaining
unchanged, and yet being perpetually varied in its in-
cidence on that moral part, at least, of our constitution,

to which physical tests and physical observations do not reach.

But, to take a still stronger case, consider the human body. If we observe certain portions of it in action, we shall find them presenting a regular sequence of phenomena, depending on the circulation of the blood, just as much as other natural bodies. If you suppose a scientific being confined in his view to a particular organ or function, he might regard it as nothing but a system of sequences. He would not see, and he might deny, if it were suggested to him, that the movements he observed could be modified, and were modified, by the action of the will and intelligence of the man or woman of whom they were a part. The human body is claimed, and necessarily claimed, as subject to the same physical laws as those which govern other bodies; but this does not hinder, as a matter of fact, but that the human will and reason are present, by their influence, in every part, and modify the action of each. If the analogy be extended to the universe, you have some resemblance to the conception which, apprehended from a moral point of view, is revealed in the Psalms. Nature, if the expression may be for a moment allowed, is like a part of the Divine organism, and the laws and sequences we observe are but the appearances to our senses of that which is really the personal act and will of the Creator.

The scientific objection, in fact, proves too much. It

claims to apply to every part of nature and of human nature the principle of Conservation—an extension of the primary law that action and re-action are equal and opposite. Every physical action by a human being must have had, as the extreme form of this supposition declares, a physical antecedent, and must have a physical consequent; and these are necessary parts of one vast system. I am not concerned to dispute the assertion. But it is nowise inconsistent with the conception of the Divine agency in question. One of two alternatives must be accepted: either the human will is a force external to the order of nature, and interposes in it without disturbing the harmony of natural action; or it is in itself, in its physical aspect, a part of that order. In the former case, there is no reason why a Divine will should not similarly interfere without any disturbance of harmony; in the latter case, it is quite certain that the human will remains, for the practical purposes of Conscience, as much a moral agency as ever. Explain it as you like, analyze it physically as you please, the Conscience of man retains its moral character, and must retain it by its very nature. No good man of science would wish it to be otherwise. But if the physical order of nature is thus compatible with human moral agency, why not with Divine?

In short, whatever may be the value or interest of these illustrations, on a matter where all illustrations can be only approximative, I do not know that they

are necessary for the argument. In claiming the existence and action of a Personal God, I am only claiming
a personality for Him and His agency similar to that
of which I am conscious myself. If my personal will
and deliberate reason are not incompatible with the
order of Nature, why should His be ? In this, as in all
other points of this argument, we need only throw
ourselves back upon our personal experience. Whatever Science may demonstrate respecting the fixity of
natural laws, human nature will love and hate, will
praise and blame—will exert, in a word, personal acts ;
and consequently, the further Science pushes its con-
quests over the phenomena of human life, the more
evident must it become that that life has an entirely
distinct aspect from that which is purely scientific.
This conclusion must be extended to Nature at large ;
and the moral aspect of the world which the Scriptures
disclose must be admitted as distinct from, and cor-
relative with, the scientific.

LECTURE V.

THE MORAL WITNESS TO JESUS CHRIST.

I JOHN i. 3.

" That which we have seen and heard declare we unto you,
that ye also may have fellowship with us : and truly our fellowship is with the Father, and with His Son Jesus Christ."

THE preceding Lectures have, I hope, illustrated
the manner in which our belief in a personal God
of infinite power, wisdom, and goodness, is founded
upon the simplest and most imperious dictates of the
Conscience ; and so far as this has been successfully
done, we are now in a position to pass to another
division of the subject, and to consider the grounds of
our specific faith, as Christians, in the divinity of the
Lord Jesus, and in the revelations made by Him and by
His prophets and apostles.   Everything, it is obvious,
turns upon the validity of those primary considerations.
Unless men have some real knowledge of God, antecedent both to the Christian and to the Jewish Revelation, they cannot have adequate ground for accepting
either of those Revelations, because they can have no

touchstone by which to try them. The experience
which is interpreted for us in the hundred and thirty-
ninth Psalm is accordingly treated by St. Paul as
essentially that of all mankind ; and he says it is " because they did not like to retain in their knowledge "
a God who thus searched and tried their hearts with a
judgment according to truth that they were given over
to a reprobate mind. Whether addressing Athenians
or Romans, St. Paul bases his appeal upon the knowledge of God which is already attainable by his hearers,
if not already possessed by them, and he claims cre-
dence for his revelation as consistent with that knowledge, and as its necessary complement. In this, as
in all other subjects, we can only advance from the
known to the unknown. As it is only from simple
acts of reason that we can advance to the more complex, so it is from the simple acts of faith, which are
prompted by the elementary instincts of conscience,
that we must advance to those lofty heights of faith
which reach their culmination in the Christian creed.

It is in this spirit that we must proceed to consider
the question, whether the belief of Christians that
Jesus Christ is God rested originally, and may rest
still, on any such broad, experimental grounds as those
we have adduced for faith in God Himself. Here
again, unless we can discern such grounds, Christianity
must be a speculation and a philosophy, rather than
a living force. The original Apostles themselves, and
the poor to whom in so large an extent they appealed,

were not learned people, capable of logical analysis and of scientific demonstration.   Similarly the great mass of men at the present day cannot be effectually reached, unless we can address to them some appeal which has a legitimate claim upon their simplest and most common instincts.   A vital religion, like a vital morality, must appeal to men and women rather than to philosophers, and must strike its roots in ordinary experience.   Now, it must be admitted that, especially to those who view it from the outside, the Christian creed does seem to make an immense demand—a demand to which nothing but a supreme conviction can justify us in surrendering ourselves, as we are called upon to do, with all our hearts and all our souls.   To recognize a person appearing in human form as God, to render to Him the homage, the obedience. and the trust, which are due to God alone, are acts of faith which must needs appear momentous in proportion to the purity and the force with which the idea of God is realized in our mind and conscience.

In order fairly to appreciate the actual and historic reality of this belief, we must place ourselves, in imagination, in the position of a Jew like St. Paul, at the time when the divinity of Christ was first proclaimed.   To the Greek, perhaps, there was only too little theoretic difficulty in the proclamation.   The Cross of Christ, indeed, was to him a stumbling-block. But the mere idea of God appearing in the likeness of men was in harmony with all his traditions.   His

R

difficulty was, as I have said, too small; because he
had so utterly inadequate an idea of God.   His gods,
no doubt, might be fitly described as "magnified
men;" and it was a comparatively small descent that
they should appear in the likeness of men.   The
heresies which the Church had to encounter during
the first three centuries may, indeed, be instructively
regarded less as declensions from the truth than as
approximations to it, and as successive stages in the
elevation of the Pagan mind towards an adequate
conception of God.   Arianism was the last step in the
process; and its defeat was the final emancipation of
Christian thought from Greek and Pagan conceptions
of the Godhead.   We cannot well realize in the
present day this fatal facility of apotheosis in Greek
and Roman thought; but we may understand, in some
measure, the opposite difficulty, as it would have at
first presented itself to St. Paul, and as it still presents
itself to Jews, and probably to Mahometans.   The
whole drift and burden of the Jewish religion had
been, as we have observed, to render more lofty, more
spiritual, more transcendent, their conception of God.
In proportion to the greatness of a Jew, did he enter
into the words, "For my thoughts are not your
thoughts; neither are your ways my ways, saith the
Lord.   For as the heavens are higher than the earth,
so are my ways higher than your ways, and my
thoughts than your thoughts."   Suddenly—it may
be at a distance from Judæa, and without any due

description of the attendant circumstances—he hears
that one of his own race is advancing a claim to be
one in nature and will with that awful and mysterious
Being whose very name he shrank from pronouncing.
That this man was reported to spring from a despised
district, or even that he had at last been crucified as a
malefactor, would scarcely heighten to his mind the
inconceivable and awful presumption, that any one,
being man, should make himself God.   It is not sur-
prising—it is most natural, and in perfect harmony
with the deep religious sincerity of St. Paul's subsequent character—that his first impulse should have
been one of intense indignation and fury against what
would appear to him an intolerable blasphemy.   Had
he not, indeed, like the majority of the Jews of his
day, been " slow of heart to believe all that the pro
phets had spoken," this difficulty would have been
obviated.   But, as a matter of fact, his eyes were
closed to the profounder spiritual meaning of the
prophetic intimations.   He felt or acted "ignorantly,
in unbelief ;" and it must be regarded as a gracious
condescension to such ignorance that nothing less
than the miraculous appearance of the Saviour Himself should have been vouchsafed, in order to overcome
this intense prejudice in the intensest of Jews.

But St. Paul does but offer a peculiarly forcible
illustration of the difficulty which had, as a rule, to be
overcome by the Jews in accepting the claims of our
Lord.   To us also, as to them, so long as we remain

outside the circle of influences to which I am about to refer, a similar difficulty has its pardonable, and even laudable, side. It is well, at all events, that we should realize the immeasurable import of the confession that Jesus Christ is God ; and should ask ourselves most seriously upon what convictions so momentous a belief either was originally based, or can be based now. Simple and familiar as are the opening words of the Epistle from which the text is taken, there is something inexpressibly astonishing in their statement. " That which was from the beginning, which we have heard, which we have seen with our eyes, which we have looked upon, and our hands have handled of the word of life ; (for the life was manifested, and we have seen it, and bear witness, and show unto you that eternal life, which was with the Father, and was manifested unto us ;) that which we have seen and heard declare we unto you, that ye also may have fellowship with us : and truly our fellowship is with the Father, and with His Son Jesus Christ." How could St. John, a Jew of the Jews no less than St. Paul, venture on the statement of his calm and mature belief that his eyes had seen, and his hands had handled, that eternal life which was with the Father ? It is only by realizing the magnitude of the realm of thought thus traversed that we can appreciate the intensity of the conviction which could alone sustain the soul in such a flight.

With this view, let us pursue the course we have

hitherto adopted, and consider what, as matter of fact,
was the process of Christian conviction.   Now it will, I
think, appear that, however dependent on miracles, however indissolubly bound up with the great historic fact
of the Resurrection, the life and soul of that conviction are everywhere essentially moral—using the word
moral in that large acceptation which I have claimed
for it in these Lectures.   In proportion as the belief is
genuine, it is the dictate, not merely of the intellect, but
of the heart, and it addresses its main appeal to the
Conscience. Consider, for instance, the wonderful assertion in the text : " That which we have seen and heard
declare we unto you."   What had St. John seen and
heard, which he thus identified with the eternal word of
life ? He proceeds to explain, repeating his expression :
" This, then, is the message which we have heard of
Him, and declare unto you, that God is light, and in
Him is no darkness at all.   If we say that we have
fellowship with Him, and walk in darkness, we lie, and
do not the truth ; but if we walk in the light, as He is
in the light, we have fellowship one with another, and
the blood of Jesus Christ His Son cleanseth us from
all sin."   The Apostle is evidently giving the very
essence of that revelation which had compelled him
to render to his Master the homage and love due to
God ; and this essence is a moral one : it is that God
is light, and that in Him is no darkness at all.

Those words, in their natural simplicity, suggest
with intense vividness the vision which overpowered

the soul of the Apostle. He felt himself, in that
sacred Presence, in an atmosphere of pure and undimmed light. No veil of secrecy, no shadow of evil,
no momentary gloom, affected for an instant the ra-
diation of that moral and spiritual sun, which gleamed
upon him without variableness or shadow of turning.
He had ascended a mount of transfiguration, above all
the clouds and mists which here darken the intercourse
of soul with soul, of conscience with conscience ; and
in spirit he ever discerned his Lord with the fashion
of His countenance altered and His raiment white and
glistering. He was like some inhabitant of a narrow
valley, suddenly placed on a mountain peak, so lofty
that it was perpetually illumined by the undimmed
rays of the sun. He was brought under a moral and
spiritual illumination which penetrated to the recesses
of his being, and refused to endure in him the least
shadow of darkness. Compare this language with
that of the Gospel, and its intense moral significance
will in both places be the more apparent. " In Him
was life, and the life was the light of men. He was
the true Light, which lighteth every man that cometh
into the world. He dwelt among us, and we beheld
His glory, the glory as of the only begotten of the
Father, full of grace and truth." That, be it observed,
is the idea, in the mind of St. John, of the Only Begotten of the Father—One who is "full of grace and
truth." Grace and truth, moral and spiritual life and
light—these in their essence were the qualities which
commanded his adoration.

This, it will be seen, was not a matter of speculative argument, nor of arbitrary revelation. It was a matter of plain experience, which could fitly be described as having been "seen, and heard, and handled." This glory of grace and truth had been as vividly perceived by St. John as the sun at unclouded noon. It had dawned on him in daily intercourse, when leaning on his Master's breast, watching His eyes, listening to His words, attending His footsteps. It had shone upon him in every act and word of ordinary life, as well as not unfrequently in gleams of splendour which revealed a miraculous power in full harmony with this grace and truth, and able to subdue to itself whatever, either in nature or in man, was inconsistent with them. It is, alas! scarcely possible for us adequately to realize the immeasurable and over-powering glory of this revelation; but we may form some estimate of it by the effect which has been produced by means of those four reflections of it which have been preserved to us in the Gospels. Those outlines—for they cannot, however admirable, be more—of the Lord's life, and character have sufficed to command the homage not merely of the Church, but of the world; and their reflected rays have, in every age and in every country, acted like the sunlight of the moral sphere, awakening in the soul of man a new life and beauty. Conceive all that influence infinitely multiplied, and brought to bear upon pure and true souls, and you may then form some distant conception of the supreme influence

which led them, through love, to the profoundest
adoration which can be offered by the human heart.
Imperfect, moreover, as may have been in some respects their apprehension of their prophets, their moral
sensibility was, doubtless, intensely enhanced by the
long spiritual training of their race ; and they would
discern, even if half unconsciously, how the profoundest and noblest visions of their Scriptures were being
realized before their eyes. Miraculous grace and
truth, combined with miraculous power—this it was
which sufficed to convince a Jew that the very Lord
of life was incarnate before him.

But to illustrate the matter further, let us apply to
it the considerations we have been reviewing in the
preceding Lectures. We have there seen that the
natural interpretation of the voice of Conscience
within us is to regard it as the voice of God. Searching and knowing us, understanding our thoughts afar
off and the words of our tongues before they are
spoken ; pursuing us in darkness and in light, in
heaven or in hell ; and ever in the same imperative
tones commanding the right and rebuking the wrong
—what can it be but the utterance of a righteous personal Being, by whom we, and the world of which we
are an essential part, have been fearfully and wonderfully made ? Whatever the force of this conviction, it
may now be pressed a step further. Conceive this
voice not merely within you, but without you ; conceive it speaking to you in human tones, penetrating

you with human eyes, awing you by human acts,
present with you, not merely in the recesses of your
souls, but as a living human companion—in one word,
conceive yourselves in the presence of a Conscience
Incarnate, and then try to realize the awful homage
which would be extorted from your souls! Such, in
instance after instance recorded in the Gospels, was
the effect of our Saviour's words, and looks, and deeds,
upon the men and women around Him. With Na-
thanael, or the Samaritan woman, or Nicodemus, or
the Apostles, He touches the secret springs of their
thoughts, and they are instantly overcome, like Jacob
when wrestling with the angel. Whatever, in short,
the Divine claim of a Conscience within us, such is
the natural claim of a Conscience personally incarnate
before us ; and those who felt themselves to be in the
presence of a Man who, in every word and act, revealed Himself as their Judge yielded allegiance to
Him just in proportion as they yielded allegiance to
their secret Conscience. This was the first step : but
when they further found that this Being, in whom
their very Conscience seemed made flesh, also possessed that power which, as we have seen, is inseparable
from the God of Conscience ; when they saw Him
commanding at His will all the elements of nature,
but always commanding them (if I may use the word)
conscientiously—never, that is, without a moral purpose, nor beyond the moral necessities of the occasion
—it was at this perfect display of power, wisdom, and

goodness combined, that they recognized the Ruler alike of their own spirits and of the world, and acclaimed Him, with the Apostle, their Lord and their God.

Let me now observe that it is this great practical conviction, and not, as has been recklessly alleged,[1] any "poor stuff" of metaphysics, which is involved in the language of the first chapter of St. John's Gospel. Among the misfortunes inseparable from translation, none, perhaps, is more to be lamented than the loss we have unavoidably incurred by having to render *Logos*, in that chapter, by the term Word. It was, perhaps, the best translation that could be made— especially after the Western Church had for centuries used the translation *Verbum ;* but the effect is certainly to obscure very grievously, to the general mind, the natural and human signification which the language of the Apostle involves. He is, indeed, revealing mysteries of the Divine Nature ; but he is doing so only so far as they come home to human nature, and are inseparably bound up with the experience of our own souls. The word *Logos* implied, to a Greek ear, not merely the speech of man, but the reason which animated it. It is explained by one of the early Greek fathers, in connection with this language of the Apostle, as embodying at once the highest rational and moral principles—the practical as well as the scientific reason of man. In short, if we translate it "The Word," we

---

[1] By Mr. Mill, in his Essay on Theism, p. 254.

have to bear in mind that it means the Word of
Conscience and Reason ; and consequently, when I
spoke just now of Conscience Incarnate I was but
translating one aspect of St. John's expression, "The
Word was made flesh." When he says that "In the
beginning was the Word, and the Word was with
God, and the Word was God," whatever further
meaning his language may carry, he is at all events
expressing, in its simplest form, the truth we have
been contemplating in the course of this argument—
that a moral purpose runs through all creation, and
that the Conscience of man, his sense of truth, and
of right and wrong, are an essential part and a final
cause of the whole design. "All things were made
through this Word of Conscience and Reason ; and
without it was not anything made that was made."
"The Lord," that is, "is righteous in all His ways, and
holy in all His works ;" and without this righteousness
and truth, and except in subordination to it, no part of
the universe was made.

We must consider, therefore, the Conscience of man
as being the reflection of the Divine reason and
righteousness. "In Him was life, and the life was
the light of men ;" or, as the same truth is expressed
in other terms by St. Paul, "In Him were all things
created, that are in heaven, and that are in earth
whether they be thrones, or dominions, or principalities, or powers : all things were created by Him,
and for Him ; and He is before all things, and by

Him all things consist." This is the mystery of
which St. Paul said that, from the beginning of the
world, it had been hid in God, who created all things
by Jesus Christ.   Thus St. John and St. Paul are not
describing a mere theogony of metaphysical mysteries
beyond our ken.   They are explaining, justifying,
deepening, and finally establishing, that profound conviction of the human soul that, as was once said from
the point of view of a mere man of the world, " Morality
is in the nature of things."   Accordingly the Apostle
justifies his own belief in the Godhead of Christ, and
claims a similar belief from others, on the ground that
the Light which had illumined his existence, in his
Master's Person, was the Light which lighteth every
man that cometh into the world.   This revelation of
the Evangelist is the only adequate fulfilment of that
vision, which we have hitherto traced in the hundred
and thirty-ninth Psalm, of a God of Conscience, who
is also the Creator of the whole frame of man and of
nature.   Thus only could the Apostle speak, with the
intense conviction expressed in the text, of having seen,
and heard, and handled the Word of life.   To speak
of having seen, and heard, and handled Eternal Life
in its mysterious creative or absolute nature might,
indeed, have been the wild speculation of a Gnostic.
But St. John, even in these supreme and lofty flights
of his eagle's wing, keeps close to the Moral Sense of
man, and appeals to the witness of his reason and his
conscience.   It is remarkable that a similar mode of

appeal, and similarly broad human sympathies, are
apparent in the great Christian fathers, so long as
Greek influence remained dominant, and wherever
this word *Logos* touched that chain of human consciousness on which I have been dwelling. I need
only quote some memorable expressions of Justin
Martyr, written about the middle of the second
century: "Whosoever have lived conformably to
reason and; the ,Word are Christians, though deemed
atheists and worshippers of no divinity, as among
the Greeks were Socrates, Heraclitus, and the like.
..Whatever, things were rightly said among all
men are the property of us Christians; .. for all such
writers were able to see realities darkly, through the
seed of the implanted word which was in them."[1] We
have not, alas! to wait for modern times before
this evangelical, human, and reasonable principle
became obscured; but no one who bears this truth in
mind will be much disturbed by objections which
treat the first chapter of St. John's Gospel as a piece
of Alexandrian metaphysics.

Such, in its essence, then, appears to be the nature
of that conviction which established in the minds even
of Jews, like St. Paul and St. John, the belief that
Christ was nothing less than the incarnate Wisdom,
Truth, and Righteousness of God. It will be understood that I am not attempting to limit the particular
methods by which, in varying individual cases, the

[1] Justin Martyr, "Apologies," i. 46; ii. 13.

conviction might be reached, or to assign the exact
relations of miraculous and moral considerations in
Christian evidences.   On that subject it is enough, for
the present, to observe that the two must of necessity
be taken together; that power without goodness is
not Divine ; and that supreme goodness without power
is imperfect.   It was a combination of the two in one
and the same Person which created, and which alone
can explain, such a conviction as that which possessed
the soul of St. John.   Perhaps one of the strongest
incidental evidences of the truth of the miracles recorded in the Gospel is that, notwithstanding the immense difficulties which I described at the outset, St.
John and St. Paul should have reached the conviction
which, beyond all historical doubt, they did possess
respecting the person of Christ.   But that which con-
vinced them is expressed in one brief phrase of St.
Paul—that Christ was " declared to be the Son of God
with power, according to the spirit of holiness, by the
resurrection from the dead."   His sufficient witness is
the spirit of holiness combined with power.

But that which, perhaps, is chiefly necessary, if we
would fully appreciate such considerations, is to realize
more clearly than we are wont the supreme grandeur
and the overwhelming force which moral influences
and revelations exert over souls familiar with their
contemplation.   " Two things," said the German philosopher, " fill the mind with ever new and increasing
admiration and awe : the starry heavens above, and

the moral law within."[1] The observation is a profound
one ; but it had been anticipated many thousands of
years before by the author of the nineteenth Psalm,
who, by one of those rapid transitions which constitute
so great an element in the force of the Scriptures, describes the law of God in the heart as not less marvellous than the law of God in the firmament. "The
heavens declare the glory of God, and the firmament
showeth his handiwork.". ..."The law of the Lord
is perfect, converting the soul." If you are impressed,
in the present day, with the grandeur and magnificence
of the visible universe, conceive those pure souls
among whom our Lord lived not less awed, over-
powered, and overwhelmed, by the vision of the moral
universe, the firmament of the soul, which He revealed
to them. "The pure in heart," He said, "shall see
God ; " and it is to this faculty of spiritual vision that
the Gospel and our Saviour Himself address their
main appeal. From hence it arises that, both in the
Gospels and in the Epistles, the sum and substance of
Christian faith and Christian life is expressed as consisting in belief in the Person of Jesus Christ Himself,
as Man and as God. It was felt that no man could
say that Jesus was the Lord but by the Holy Ghost.
The full meaning of that acknowledgment was then
more vividly appreciated than in days like the present,
when it is apt to be the result rather of a tradition
than of a direct conviction ; and it was recognized as

[1] Kant, "Critique of the Practical Reason:" Conclusion.

a moral act of the highest significance, pregnant with vital consequences to the whole moral being. When St. Paul, for instance, sums up the whole of his message in the words, "Believe on the Lord Jesus Christ and thou shalt be saved," he is not merely inviting the acceptance of a dogmatic revelation; he is also calling from his hearer for the surrender of his conscience and heart to a Person whose influence had a moral claim over them, and would perpetually regenerate them.

The essence of the Gospel in this respect cannot be altered; and as these Lectures, though apologetic, are delivered in a Christian church, it may not be out of place to observe that the depth of our own Christian faith mainly depends on the degree in which our acknowledgment of the Lord Jesus Christ as God is rooted in the moral convictions of our hearts and souls. Our faith is vital so far as, in the first place, we realize the absolute identity of God with righteousness and truth; and, in the second place, so far as we discern in the Person of Jesus Christ the perfect embodiment of that moral and spiritual goodness. To enter into the character of Christ is to enter into the character of God ; and to identify the two is to know what God is, and to have communion with Him. This is the spirit in which the Apostle declares that "Whosoever shall confess that Jesus is the Son of God, God dwelleth in him and he in God." From hence follow, by necessary sequence, all the other influences of the Gospel, and that mysterious communion and fellow-

ship by which, in our whole nature, we are united to
Christ. "If a man love me," says our Saviour, "he
will keep my words; and my Father will love him,
and we will come unto him, and make our abode with
him." Just in proportion as we love Him shall we
keep His commandments, and the depth of our love
must needs be proportioned to the depth of our appreciation of His "grace and truth." "This," accordingly,
says Christ Himself, "is life eternal"—in this consists the moral and spiritual vitality of the soul—
"that they might know Thee, the only true God, and
Jesus Christ whom Thou hast sent."

LECTURE VI.

GENERAL EVIDENCE OF REVELATION.

HEBREWS i. 1, 2.

"God, who at sundry times and in divers manners spake in time past unto the fathers by the prophets, hath in these last days spoken unto us by His Son."

I ENDEAVOURED last Sunday to explain and to justify that momentous act of faith by which our Lord Jesus Christ was recognized by His Apostles and disciples as the Only Begotten of the Father, the eternal Word of Life and Truth, made flesh and dwelling among them. If that explanation be valid, it is sufficient to sustain, in principle, the whole Christian edifice. The authority, of course, of the teaching of Christ, when this character is once assigned to Him, stretches both forwards and backwards; and it becomes our main task to apprehend and unfold His words. For the general purpose of Christian life and instruction, we may treat this consideration as independent and self-sufficing. The

collateral and historical arguments which co-operate in
establishing the divinity of our Lord are, indeed,
essential to a comprehension of the Divine Revelation
as a whole.   But Christ would not be the Son of Man,
He would not appeal to men in all countries and in all
times, unless His claims were adequately asserted by
His own personality and His own words, previous to
their corroboration by other facts of revelation and
history.   St. John, in his first Epistle, and in the
opening of his Gospel, appeals, as we saw, to broad
facts of human experience, human reason, and human
conscience—not to that which could be established by
a chain of argument, however valid, but to that which
he had heard, which he had seen with his eyes, which
he had looked upon, and his hands had handled, of
the Word of life.   In this, as in the other great points
we have been discussing, the Gospel rests not on any
recondite considerations, but on the moral constitution
and the broad moral instincts of man.   We are concerned, however, at present not merely to deduce from
this general truth the verity of religion in other particulars, but to consider those particulars independently, and to show that they have a like conformity
with reason, and a similar claim on our belief.

The Apostle in the text specifies the general claim
of what has recently been called "supernatural religion."   It is not merely that God has spoken to us by
His Son ; but that the same God, at sundry times and
in divers manners, spoke in times past to the fathers

by the prophets. The Church puts forward a continuous series of revelations as having been made by
God to men from the earliest times—from the days of
Noah and Abraham to the times of Christ and His
Apostles ; and a question is very fairly asked respecting these, similar to that which we considered last
Sunday with respect to Christ Himself.   On what
principle could the persons who are said to have
received these revelations rely on their being revelations from God ?   It does not seem sufficient, however
true in certain senses it may be, to say that the
Divine interposition which conveyed the revelation
created, at the same time, a miraculous conviction of
its origin.   To rest satisfied with such a plea is
to escape the necessity of rendering any reason for
our faith whatever, and indeed to admit that any such
reason is unattainable.   This is not, at all events, the
method of the Scriptures.   They treat the acceptance
of such revelations by those to whom they were vouchsafed as moral acts, as righteous exertions of faith, as
winning the approval due only to reasonable and
conscientious conduct.   " Abraham," we are told,
" believed God, and it was counted unto him for
righteousness "—it was a display of the righteousness
of faith—" and he was called the friend of God."
Similarly, in the great chapter which follows the text,
all the patriarchs and prophets are described, not as
persons removed by a miraculous interposition from
the possibility of doubting the successive revelations

on which they relied, but as men of like passions with
ourselves, who clung to those revelations by faith, in
spite of the strongest temptations to the contrary—
choosing, like Moses, rather to suffer affliction than to
enjoy the pleasures of sin, or, like Noah, condemning
a world which refused a similar obedience, and thus
becoming heirs of the righteousness which is by faith.
It follows that these revelations, in each case, appealed
to a moral principle and had a moral basis. Let us
endeavour to apprehend the nature of this appeal.

But with a view to thus vindicating these successive
revelations on independent grounds, it should, in the
first place, be borne in mind that the principles involved in our acceptance of Christ, and of which that
acceptance is the highest application, relate to the
whole field of Revelation, and are sufficient to render
it both possible and probable. These principles consist in the declarations of St. John that the Word of
reason and of righteousness, of moral and intellectual
truth, was in the beginning with God, and that without
it was not anything made that was made. These statements, so majestic in their simplicity, are, as we have
seen, the final echo of that voice of the human Conscience which, in the elementary religious consciousness of the hundred and thirty-ninth Psalm, testifies
to the whole frame of man being constructed with a
moral purpose, and which imperatively dictates a faith
that the whole world, of which he forms a part, is
similarly moulded with reference to moral and spiritual

aims.   The moral universe is superior, after all, to the
physical : marvellous as are the heavens, the work of
the Divine fingers, the moon and the stars which the
Creator has ordained, still more marvellous, to those
who can appreciate other measures than that of size,
is the soul which reflects them, which penetrates into
their laws, and which discerns their unity with the
physical, and consequently with the moral, constitution of man.   The words of St. John are a republication of the primary revelation of the Scriptures : " God
said, Let us make man in our image, after our likeness,
and let them have dominion over all the earth."

These, certainly, are not the days in which that
sublime vision should be disparaged.   If you seek a
comprehensive description of the task which Science
in this day claims to fulfil, you have it, as you have it
in no other philosophy and no other religion, in these
simple words : " Be fruitful and multiply, and re-
plenish the earth and subdue it, and have dominion ; "
and the founder of modern philosophy discerned the
Divine wisdom of this description when he gave, as
the second title of his " Novum Organum "—" Concerning the Interpretation of Nature and the Dominion
of Man."   But if this describes the work of Science,
the words of St. John are no less the noblest expression of its essential principle : " In the beginning was
Reason, and without Reason was not anything made
that was made."   The belief, in other words, which
sustains every philosopher in his labours is that there

is nothing in Nature which does not correspond to the
faculty of reason with which we are endowed. St.
John in this declaration lays down the very charter of
scientific thought ; and it is a fact which should arouse
attention, that such thought has not permanently
flourished except where the unity of God with reason
and conscience has been thus proclaimed. In Maho-
medanism, for instance, it is the will, and not the
wisdom, of God which is the dominant thought ; and
consequently men feel themselves the subjects of an
inscrutable fate, and not sufficiently in harmony with
Nature to pursue her secrets through all her labyrinths.
St. John, however, further requires us to include in the
reason we thus attribute to the Divine constitution of
Nature moral as well as intellectual principles ; and
to open our eyes, not merely to the rational order of
the physical world, but to its moral and spiritual order.
In Religion, accordingly, no less than in Science, we
start with the principle that man is made in the image
of God ; that his mind, in other words, is adapted to
the reflection of the spiritual and eternal, no less than
of the material and temporary, constitution of things.

From this point of view we have a great advantage
in approaching the subject of this Lecture, since Revelation is at once relieved of that almost unnatural
character which seems often associated with the idea
of what is supernatural. It appears as only the
clearer manifestation to men of the spiritual order of
which they form a part, and to which their whole

constitution is adapted, Revelation becomes probable, not because the truths it makes known to us are so distant, but because they are so near ; not because we are compelled to base our belief on bare authority, but because it is in such complete congruity with our conscience and our reason. The realities we seek after and feel for are not far from any one of us ; and the moment a corner of the mysterious veil which shrouds them is lifted, we feel ourselves, not in a strange and unknown land, but in one of which we have dreamed long before. This is the essential characteristic of religious truth. The heart and mind of man and the will and wisdom of God are always in intimate, though obscure, communion ; and nothing, consequently, is so natural as that a revelation, when made by God, should be at once recognized by man. The protest of Bishop Butler against the false use of the word *nature* is still too frequently neglected ; and it has sometimes been even represented as a testimony to the Divine origin of Christianity that it gained its victories in opposition to human nature. Whereas, on the contrary, it is its comformity with human nature, in the highest sense of the word, which gives it its most irresistible claim, and constitutes the irrefragable proof of its divinity. That the martyrs, for instance, in the primitive Church should suffer every torment, rather than be false to the Lord and Master whom they loved, was far more natural, infinitely more in conformity with the deepest impulses of the

heart, than that they should return to the vice and the
selfishness from which they had been freed. In the
same way, the visions vouchsafed to us of Divine
realities have a native attraction for the soul in proportion to the clearness of its spiritual sight, and they
assert over it the claims which St. John describes
as irresistible in our Lord's own Person—those of
reason, of grace, and of truth.

But while these considerations justify the idea of
Revelation considered as the unveiling of spiritual
truths, there is a further aspect of the question, which
requires more specific elucidation. The revelations
recorded in the Bible are not merely, like the Ten
Commandments, moral truths, or, like the doctrine of
the Trinity, spiritual truths; they are often statements
of fact, which may, indeed, in the course of experience,
prove to be essentially in harmony with the order of
life, but to which, in the first instance, no direct moral
test can well be applied. The most conspicuous case
is that of those promises to Abraham, on trust in
which his whole life is described as having been based.
St. Paul treats him, on the ground of his faith in
those promises, as the father of all them that believe ;
" Who," he says, " against hope, believed in hope, that
he might become the father of many nations, according to that which was spoken, So shall thy seed be.
. . . He staggered not at the promise of God through
unbelief; but was strong in faith, giving glory to God ;
and being fully persuaded that, what He had promised

He was able also to perform. And therefore it was imputed to him for righteousness." Now, adds the Apostle, "It was not written for his sake alone that it was imputed to him, but for us also, to whom it shall be imputed, if we believe on Him who raised up Jesus our Lord from the dead." It would be impossible to express more clearly the conviction, in the mind of St. Paul, of the identity in principle of Christian faith with the faith of Abraham in the promise vouchsafed to him. But how, it has been asked, could this faith in a prediction respecting the future bear that moral character of righteousness which attaches to faith in the Person of Christ? Assume that, whether by vision or by voice, whether "in a dream, a vision of the night, when deep sleep falleth upon men," or in some calmer but more mysterious communications by day, these assurances of facts beyond all expectation were impressed upon the patriarch's mind—how was he to identify their origin with the word of a Being to whom his faith and trust were due?

Even admitting, that is, in accordance with the considerations adduced in the last Lecture, that a life which, in human form like our Lord's, was seen and heard and handled might be identified with the eternal life and light of the conscience, still what could warrant, either in the case of Abraham, or of Moses, or of the Prophets who succeeded him, their claiming for the words with which they were inspired, and for the visions by which they foresaw the future, the authority

of God Himself? They did so, it is clear, without
hesitation, and without systematic reasoning, by a sort
of instinctive conviction. St. Paul himself affords the
latest and the most unquestionable historical instance.
We have it on his express and reiterated assurance
that, after his conversion by the miraculous appearance
of our Saviour, visions and spiritual intimations were
vouchsafed to him, guiding him in the course he should
take in several exigencies of his life, and revealing to
him, not merely moral truths, but mysterious facts of
the Divine Dispensation respecting the Person and
office of our Lord. By what means, it is asked, could
such witness be in any case authenticated ?

The answer to this question appears suggested by
the very comparison we are seeking to explain, drawn
by St. Paul between the faith of Abraham and that of
Christians in their Lord ; and its validity depends on
the force of that appeal to the Conscience, as the
primary revelation of God, on which I have so urgently
insisted. David, we have seen, believed in God, because his Conscience bore continual witness to him
that he was in contact with a righteous Will. St·
John believed that Christ was God, because he discerned in Him righteousness, truth, and power incarnate. Now consider whether a precisely similar
association of thought be not a justification of the
patriarchal and prophetic visions. If these visions and
inspirations had been experienced as mere physical,
or even intellectual, influences, they might, indeed,

have been credited; they might have been regarded, especially if justified by evidence, as the result of a mysterious faculty of foresight or intuition in certain men; but it would seem that no such sense of obligation would arise as that which, in the minds of the prophets, is attached to faith. Even if accompanied by miracles, they would rather, it would seem, be subjects for the critical than for the moral faculty. Power, of whatever kind or degree, if it be only power, may convince the reason, but does not appeal directly to the heart. But suppose that all these visions, and any miraculous manifestations with which they were accompanied, were invariably and indissolubly associated with moral influences. Suppose that they were but incidents, though inseparable incidents, in a life-long course of moral education. Consider them, that is, as inseparably blended, in each instance, and on the whole, with intimations which spoke to the Conscience, which aroused and deepened the perceptions of right and wrong; let them, in a word, be invariably united in a man's experience with the voice of Conscience, and we may then understand that the obligation of obedience to Conscience itself is reflected upon them According to the old fable of dreams being true or false as they came through the gate of horn or that of ivory, so let us suppose that, in the experience of the patriarchs and prophets, their visions all came through the gate of Conscience, and not merely through that of imagination. Visions of the latter class might

be the subjects only of criticism or curiosity ; to
visions of the latter class their moral allegiance, or
their faith, was due.

Now it will be observed that this is invariably the
case, and is the distinct mark of the revelations recorded in the Bible, from the first to the last. The
revelation assigned to Noah commences with the
words, "Come thou and all thy house into the ark,
for thee have I seen righteous before me in this generation ;" and it has reference to a great moral judgment. Noah is accordingly viewed by the Apostolic
writer, not simply as a man endued with a special
vision of the future, but as a preacher of righteousness,
as thus condemning the world, and as becoming the
heir of the righteousness which is by faith. It is the
inheritor of this tradition of righteousness whom the
Lord called out of his country, and from his kindred,
and from his father's house ; and the revelation is
again addressed to the same moral sense : "The Lord
appeared to Abram, and said unto him, I am the
Almighty God ; walk before me, and be thou perfect ;
and I will make my covenant between me and thee."
The question, in fact, why a revelation should be
vouchsafed to the patriarch, is expressly asked and
answered : "Shall I hide from Abraham that thing
which I do ? Seeing that Abraham shall surely become a great and mighty nation, and all the nations
of the earth shall be blessed in him ; for I know him,
that he will command his children and his household

after him, and they shall keep the way of the Lord, to
do justice and judgment." Similarly, when the covenant is renewed to Isaac, it is "because that Abraham
obeyed my voice, and kept my charge, my commandments, my statutes, and my laws." St. Paul describes
the vision which converted him as marked by a similar
appeal : "I said, Who art Thou, Lord ? And He said,
I am Jesus whom thou persecutest . . . for I have appeared unto thee for this purpose, to make thee a
minister and a witness of these things which thou hast
seen . . . delivering thee from the people, and from the
Gentiles, unto whom now I send thee, to open their
eyes, and to turn them from darkness to light, and from
the power of Satan unto God, that they may receive
forgiveness of sins, and inheritance among them which
are sanctified by faith that is in me." The vision
which stops the Apostle in his full career as a zealot
for the righteousness which is by the law is a vision
which reveals to him the source of a deeper and a
better righteousness. It is not, in one word, a mere
revelation, but a righteous revelation, which, both in
his case and in that of all the great seers who had
preceded him, commanded his trust and his obedience.
In some instances the revelation thus granted is
authenticated by means of a miracle ; but in others
the demand for such authentication is rebuked, and
the appeal is that of our Lord : "If I say the truth,
why do ye not believe me ?" It will be observed,
accordingly, that these appeals are uniformly made

not merely to deep feelings, but to deep obligations—
not to that which is peculiar to one man, but to that
which, by its very nature, is common to every man.
The prophet or seer to whom the appeal was addressed or the vision vouchsafed felt that he could not
reject either without being false to the permanent
dictates of his conscience, and in proportion as the
people were prepared to yield to his moral appeal did
they accept the authority of his prophetic vision.

This moral aspect of the revelations of the Scriptures is, moreover, enhanced when they are viewed in
their historical succession. The appeal is based, time
after time, upon larger and more eternal moral principles. The range of the morality successively ex-
pands till it embraces the relations of the whole
human race. It begins with an individual man :
"Walk thou before me, and be thou perfect." It then
extends to the family ; and God becomes regarded as
the God of Abraham, Isaac, and Jacob. Under Moses
it extends to the nation ; and his revelation concentrates its appeal to the conscience in the Ten Commandments, which are the statutes, not merely of
individuals, but of a people. From that time, the
revelations of the prophets, and all their predictions,
are bound up, not only with the morality of the individual and of the family, but with the moral education
of the nation as a whole, and with its discharge of
the spiritual and moral functions entrusted to it. But
whether personal, or social, or national, every revelation

comes through the same gate of Conscience and of
moral obligation ; and the authority which speaks
within every man's soul demands submission and trust.
In proportion as we can appreciate the vividness with
which moral influences were apprehended by the
Jewish prophets, in proportion as we can realize the
intensity with which they apprehended the fact of
righteousness being the final object of their whole
history, shall we see the force with which the Divine
origin was authenticated of revelations which led them
on from point to point in the development of this
righteous purpose.   At length, with St. Stephen and
St. Paul, their conviction that the life and work of
Christ explained and fulfilled the whole course of their
history became to them, as Jews, the final evidence
of the truth of His claims ; and when St. Stephen is
called upon to defend his faith, he at once appeals to
what I may venture to call this cumulative historic
argument. He recounts the successive revelations
made to his nation ; he shows that they had a moral
aim, and pointed before to the coming of " the Just
One ; " and he describes the uniform cause of their
partial rejection in the words, " Ye do always resist
the Holy Ghost : as your fathers did, so do ye."   This
first Christian apology had, indeed, peculiar force as
addressed to the Jews.   But the force and weight of
the evidence for Revelation has similarly accumulated
age by age ; until now its appeal is to the fact that it
answers the moral demands, not merely of one man,

or of one nation, but of mankind as a whole. There is not a single doctrine of the Gospel which has not a direct bearing on the Conscience of man as man, no matter what his nation or his circumstances. Christianity goes, indeed, beyond what the Conscience could itself apprehend ; because, like all previous revelations, it deals not merely with truths, but with facts. The successive revelations of which we have been speaking have each gone just a step beyond that which could be actually verified, leading men, as it were, point by point, under the guidance which their Conscience afforded them. The revelation, in other words, spoke so truly to their Conscience, up to the point where vision failed and faith began, that they were compelled to yield it a conscientious allegiance, and to be led by it beyond the limits of their experience.

It is for this reason that the demand for faith is a moral appeal, and applies to every man to whom it comes a moral test. Abraham believed God, and He counted it to him for righteousness, because, had he not believed God, he would have been untrue to the deepest convictions of his conscience. The Gospel makes a similar appeal in the present day. Far be it from me, indeed, to say that every man who rejects it is false to his conscience! The appeal may have reached him in a perverted form, and with its best evidence obscured by traditional misconceptions. But speaking generally, and on principle, Christianity, and

T

all the previous revelations of the Bible, have claimed
faith because, so far as they can be tested, they are
authenticated by Conscience, and because, in the
points on which they go beyond our experience, they
have a moral purpose, and, so to speak, a moral limitation. We ask for faith, but not for a blind faith.
We claim submission to authority, but to an authority
which is, in the first instance, the voice of God within
us; and to other authority, so far as it can successfully
appeal for its primary authentication to that supreme
guide.

LECTURE VII.

THE DOCTRINE OF THE TRINITY A MORAL REVELATION.

2 CORINTHIANS xiii. 14.

"The grace of the Lord Jesus Christ, and the love of God, and the communion of the Holy Ghost, be with you all. Amen."

WE have now considered the moral basis on which we rest our faith in the elementary truths of Revelation in general, and of the Christian Revelation in particular. We have seen that the belief in a personal God is founded upon the experience and the imperative dictates of our Conscience ; that our Lord Jesus Christ makes a similar appeal, and claims our allegiance as Conscience Incarnate, "full of grace and truth ; " and that all previous revelations have a moral claim on our belief by virtue of their appeal to the same faculty. Prophets and Apostles, like our Lord Himself, ask us, indeed, to believe that which we can neither see nor verify ; but it is because, up to the point where sight fails, they are in harmony, not merely with our deepest feelings, but

with our feelings of obligation ; because they appeal
to a manifestation of righteousness and power indissolubly combined ; and because the further revelations
on the faith of which they ask us to live are marked
by a righteous purpose, and may be said to have a
moral limitation.   The Christian creed, as has been
seen, is no mere collection of mysteries inaccessible to
human experience, but is an interpretation of that
experience, appealing, in its main principles, to the
only faculty which asserts over us an imperious
authority.

There remains, however, one cardinal doctrine to
which this consideration has not yet been shown to
apply, and which, perhaps, at the present day is apt
to be regarded as peculiarly remote from such practical experience.   I mean the doctrine of the Trinity.
That doctrine is generally represented, by those whose
objections we are now considering, as a purely metaphysical speculation on a subject utterly beyond our
ken ; and even among Christians themselves considerable difficulty is sometimes felt in acknowledging
the paramount importance which the Church attributes to the recognition of this verity. It is not exactly
the mystery of the doctrine from which this difficulty
seems to arise ; it is not simply that men are unwilling
to believe what they cannot understand ; it is that
they feel there ought to be some practical ground for
their belief, and a broad moral reality in it.   They
fail to see how the acknowledgment of three Persons

in one God affects their daily duties and their moral life ; and it is to be feared that too often the doctrine receives rather the assent, than the conscientious adhesion, even of believers.

Now it is at least evident that this state of feeling is out of harmony with the spirit and genius of the early Christians. Without assuming the authenticity of particular texts—against most of which, however, none but theoretical objections can be urged—it is unquestionable, as a matter of history, that from the earliest period an acknowledgment of three Persons in one God was the essential condition of admission into the Christian Church. From the date of the first records to the present moment, Christians have been baptized in the Name of the Father, of the Son, and of the Holy Ghost. The declaration of faith implied in the acknowledgment of that Name has been regarded as the sum and the substance of the truth to which their allegiance was rendered ; and every other doctrine has been, as a matter of fact, centred round it. It would seem equally unquestionable that nothing but an elaborate process of explanation can obscure the fact that the same truth lies at the root of apostolic thought. The manner in which the Apostles continually assume it is even more significant than the definite statements which might be adduced from them. It springs to their lips, as in the text, in their most earnest utterances, in the benedictions and salutations of their letters ; and it seems to determine

almost unconsciously the mould of their thoughts.
They do not state with formal precision that the Lord
Jesus Christ is God, and the Holy Spirit is God, and
yet that They are not three Gods but one God ; but
it is their habitual and natural language to speak of
the Lord Jesus Christ and of the Holy Spirit in the
same terms, and in the same associations, as those in
which they speak of God, while at the same time
exhibiting their perfect adherence to the cardinal truth
of their Jewish faith—that the Lord their God is one
Lord. You do not meet distinct and prominent
statements of the doctrine of the Trinity, for the same
reason that you do not see the roots of a tree or
the foundations of a house ; but it may none the less
be discerned that the whole mind and heart of the
Apostles are baptized into the name and the life of
the Father, the Son, and the Holy Spirit. "There are
diversities of gifts, but the same Spirit ; and there are
differences of administrations, but the same Lord.
And there are diversities of operations, but it is the
same God which worketh all in all." Similarly, the
confessions of the martyrs and the writings of the
early fathers reveal the constant presence of the truth
to their minds with at least as much clearness as the
most express teaching. In subsequent history, special
applications of the truth, in such doctrines as those of
the Atonement and of Justification, have been most
prominent in Christian thought ; while the doctrine of
the Trinity has fallen back, as it were, rather into the

place of a scientific assumption on which practical truths are based. But in the first age of the Church it was the revelation of the Trinity itself, of the mutual relations of Father, Son, and Holy Spirit, and of their gracious relations to man, which inspired Christian thought. In those days, at all events, the doctrine was the greatest of all practical truths; and here again, if we would fully enter into the spirit of our religion, we must endeavour to apprehend the spirit of its first teachers and believers.

Now to realize this practical and moral aspect of the doctrine, it becomes necessary to lay further stress on a consideration which the nature of this argument had, until the last Lecture, thrown somewhat into the back ground: I mean, the historical character of Christian faith. It has been pointed out in that Lecture how each successive Revelation recorded in the Scriptures was, as it were, imbedded in the life of the Prophet to whom it was vouchsafed, and in the circumstances of the age in which it was delivered, and that its authority was in no slight degree dependent upon the manner in which its historic coherence appealed to the Conscience. But the moment we pass to the specific truths of Christianity, this consideration obviously becomes of paramount importance, for they are united with the greatest of all lives and with the most momentous of historic events. They are, above all things, indissolubly bound up, not merely with the teaching, but with the Person and the life of Christ.

The first and cardinal act of Christian faith is that
which has been already vindicated—the recognition of
Jesus as God Incarnate, and as the Lord to whom, in
soul and body, we must for ever surrender ourselves.
But that step having been taken, the life of Christ
becomes the most essential element in our own lives.
That which He was, that which He did, that which
He is, become the very law and mould of our existence. When our Saviour says, "Abide in me, and
I in you; as the branch cannot bear fruit of itself,
except it abide in the vine, so no more can ye,
except ye abide in me," His words must, of necessity, be applied to the whole of His relations
towards us, and especially to those of which we have
direct historical cognizance. He is, indeed, in permanent relation with us by means of His Spirit;
but our only means of knowing this are those acts
and words which, during His life on earth, were seen
and heard and handled. Our Conscience tells us that
we are in relation with a personal God; but that this
God is related to us also as man, is a matter not
of direct experience—however the soul may dimly feel
after the truth—but of historical fact. As our Lord
said, "He that hath seen me hath seen the Father,"
so it is only in the actual life of Christ that He is
Himself to be seen.

The Christian, therefore, is not merely a person who
believes in Jesus Christ as his unseen Lord and future
judge; but he is one who lives in the light of that

illumination which radiates from the life of Christ on
earth.   He cannot any longer, even if he would, rest
on the independent dictates of his conscience, or even
on the precepts of his Lord.   The life of Christ is a
revelation in itself, which must needs determine, control, and animate his own life and all his thoughts.
To a certain extent, indeed, this is the case with all
men, whether Christians or not.   It is not only un-
christian, it is unreasonable and scientifically impracticable, to deal with the problems of the nature of man
and of God without reference to the life of Christ.
That life has become a fact in human experience.
Whether or not you accept the Christian interpretation of it, interpreted it must be.   You cannot put it
aside, and live and act as if it had no bearings on
you.   The Gospels alone, independently of the agency
of the Christian Church, bring that life, in an ever-
increasing degree, to bear upon the thoughts and the
conscience of mankind ; and the world cannot evade
the questions which it arouses, or the claims which it
asserts.   It may reject them, but it cannot avoid
dealing with them.   To the Christian, however, such
considerations have a supreme and overwhelming
force.   It is his characteristic quality to abide in his
Master—to live, to think, to act in conformity with
the life, the thoughts, the acts of that Master.

Bearing this in mind, we may express in very brief
words the moral basis of the doctrine of the Trinity.
It is the interpretation of the life of Christ.   It is a

revealed doctrine, not merely in the sense of its being a communication to us of a truth which we could not ourselves have discovered, but in the sense of its being a doctrine which arises entirely out of certain facts of human history and experience. For such reasons as we have already explained, we believe that the Lord Jesus Christ was Himself God. But He also spoke of God being His Father, and He lived in an intense personal relationship with God. These two facts we find ourselves equally compelled to accept; and they reveal to us at once a plurality of Persons in one God. Let it be particularly observed, in the light of our previous considerations, on what this conclusion is based. The objections urged and felt against the doctrine of the Trinity are connected with an impression that it is an intellectual speculation, resting on metaphysical arguments. Whereas, on the contrary, it rests on a simple recognition of two facts ; both of which arise out of historic experience interpreted by the human Conscience, and still appeal to that experience and that Conscience for their support. It is precisely because we prefer facts to metaphysics, that we are impelled to accept the doctrine of the Trinity. Did we trust simply to logical deductions, we might withhold assent from the doctrine in spite of those lofty philosophic speculations which, from the days of Plato, have been thought by the few minds which could follow them to point to it. But it is because we think our Conscience a safer guide than our intellect, it is because we distrust our power of reasoning in a matter so infinitely above us, and because we deem it safer to accept, even where we cannot understand, convictions which our moral sense forces upon us—it is for these practical, simple, and moral reasons that we believe in a plurality of Divine Persons, yet in One God.

. Regarding the question, indeed, from a merely argumentative point of view, there is something almost extravagantly unreasonable in the assumption often made, especially by the most prominent—and I must add, the most flippant—of recent assailants of this belief, that it is a pure intellectual figment. Argue against it and reject it, if you please. It is a doctrine of the most momentous character, not to be accepted upon any but the most weighty grounds; and every conscientious objection to it deserves the most serious answer. But let it equally be recognized that our faith in it is founded on the deepest convictions of the Conscience. We can only believe that Christ is God by the absolute submission of our conscience to His claims; and it is therefore essentially our conscience, rather than our understanding, which dictates our acceptance of the baptismal confession of the Father and the Son. Overthrow the primary Christian conviction that the Christ of the Gospels is the God of the Psalms, and the doctrine of the Trinity passes, at all events, into the regions of metaphysical speculation. But what the objector has, in the first instance, to deal

with is that conviction of the Conscience, and not any
speculations which have been founded upon it. Accordingly, the doctrine of the Trinity is found to start into
life, not out of any school of philosophy, but out of the
Christian Church. This observation is independent of
the question how far philosophical speculations may
have provided its verbal expression. It is historically
certain that, so long as it remained in philosophical
hands, it was a speculation and no more. But long
before Christianity was recognized as a philosophy,
before it had attracted into its service the genius of
Alexandrian thought, before Athanasius, before Ori-
gen, before Clement of Alexandria, in the first Christian apologists and the earliest Christian martyrs, the
truth of the Trinity is found to be a living and
operative belief. It is thus historically traceable to
the facts of Christian consciousness—not, as I have
before explained, to the consciousness of each Christian considered individually, but to the conscience of
Christians applying itself to the life of Christ.

What else, in fact, could explain such language as
that of the text and of the other apostolic teaching to
which I have referred? To appreciate those expressions it must be remembered, as has been observed in
a previous Lecture, that those who use it were Hebrews
of the Hebrews, men to whose instincts—the traditional instincts of a long history—the very name of
God was exceptionally awful, scarcely to be uttered,
incapable of association with that of any human or

created being. It is these men—not philosophers but earnest Jews—who are found blending together in their customary salutations the name of God, the Father of all, with that of Jesus Christ His Son, and of the Holy Ghost; imploring simultaneously and equally the gifts and the blessings of the Three, and declaring that "to us there is but one God the Father, of whom are all things, and we in Him, and one Lord Jesus Christ, by whom are all things, and we by Him." There is nothing but the facts of the life of Christ to explain this astonishing revolution of thought. But look at those facts in the light that has been suggested, and the development becomes natural and intelligible. The profound conviction of those vivid consciences, that Christ was God, revealed a new aspect of the Divine nature. It was contrary to every principle or their minds to admit that a mere man, however holy, could be in essential union with God; and when they were forced to acknowledge the Divinity of Christ, they were forced, at the same time, to acknowledge that the Godhead contained within it mysteries of personal relationship which could not by mere thought or meditation have been conceived.

It is further to be observed that this relationship thus revealed as an historical fact, between the Father and the Son is not only based on a moral conviction but has the most intimate moral bearing on Christian life. It possesses that bearing by virtue of its moral value in the life of Christ Himself. The characteristic

of His life, whichever Evangelist we follow, is an absolute devotion to the will of the Father.   The Lord's
own prayer—" Our Father which art in heaven,
hallowed be thy Name, thy kingdom come, thy will
be done"—embodies the spirit of that life from its
commencement to its close.   The opening temptation,
in its three forms, is conquered by submission to the
will and word of God ; and the victory is won in the
last agony of temptation in the words, "Not my will,
but thine be done."   The Gospel of St. John does but
interpret for us more fully the spirit which is thus
dominant in the other three.   " I thank thee, Father,
Lord of heaven and earth," He exclaims in St.
Matthew, "that thou hast hid these things from the
wise and prudent, and hast revealed them unto babes :
even so, Father, for so it seemed good in thy sight.
All things are delivered unto me of my Father ; and
no man knoweth the Son but the Father, neither
knoweth any man the Father, save the Son, and he to
whomsoever the Son will reveal him."   "Verily
verily, I say unto you," He exclaims in St. John, "the
Son can do nothing of himself, but what he seeth the
Father do ; for what things soever he doeth, these
also doeth the Son likewise :" or again, " He that hath
seen me hath seen the Father ; and how sayest thou
then, Show us the Father ?   Believest thou not that I
am in the Father, and the Father in me ?   The words
that I speak unto you I speak not of myself, but the
Father that dwelleth in me, He doeth the works."

It would be impracticable, within the limits imposed
on the present argument, to make the least pretence
of developing the significance of these utterances.
But this may at least be said, and it is sufficient
for our immediate purpose. They reveal a relation
between the Father and the Son of the deepest moral
import, and pregnant with the profoundest moral influences on the human heart. Let us reflect for a
moment, by the light of other human experiences, on
what they imply. Such words are not to be interpreted
by their mere logical force ; and the weight of the
testimony in the Gospels to the doctrine of the Trinity
has been, it is to be feared, grievously weakened by
the stress which has been sometimes laid on verbal
deductions. It is the thought and the sentiment which
reveal the reality behind them. There was, as we
see in the narrative, something which to the Jews
of our Lord's day was inexpressibly presumptuous in
the familiar and intimate relationship implied in such
expressions. That a man should be speaking—to take
only St. Matthew's account—"of all things being revealed unto him by the Father," appeared to them
intolerable ; and there is still something in it infinitely
above the reach of unassisted human belief, when once
an adequate conception is attained of the inscrutable
infinity of God. If men degrade the idea of God, as
the Greeks did, and as the heathen still do, they may
find no difficulty in believing in communion between
God and man ; though the conception of that communion

itself becomes at the same time degraded.　But let
the idea of God be raised and sublimed as it is by the
Mahomedan ; and then the idea of complete union,
and of intimate familiar communion, between the will
of God and the will of man becomes almost inconceivable.　A supernatural revelation may be conceived ; but
language which, like that of our Lord, implies essential
and continual harmony between the will of God and
the will of a Son of Man touches an infinitely higher
strain.　Such words cannot be treated as figures of
speech.　There is a seriousness, a simplicity, and an
authority about them which compel us to take them
in their fullest and most direct meaning.

To appreciate that meaning further, consider, in the
first instance, what has been their effect on the consciousness of Christians.　Has there not been developed in Christian saints, instead of a mere submission
to the will of God, as to that of a higher Power, a
deep, calm, and ennobling conviction that that will is
at one with the most human, the most obligatory,
impulses of their souls, and that they could not merely
submit to it, but could love it, and unite their own
wills with it in the intimacy of the deepest human
communion ?　How profoundly that conviction has
influenced the whole life of Christian nations, what
fearlessness, what patience, what gradual destruction
of superstition, what faith in nature, what science, as
well as what morality it has stimulated, history will
perhaps some day recognize more fully than it has

yet done. But, at all events, it is a noble moral conception: and on what does it rest? On what but
this evangelical and apostolical conviction that we can
claim fellowship with One who, as the Son of God,
could enter into the will of God, could reflect it, love
it, and unite Himself with it, not as a mere creature,
but with the filial devotion, the reasonable and moral
submission of a Son? This is the conviction in which
an Apostle exclaims that "Ye have not received the
spirit of bondage again to fear; but ye have received
the spirit of adoption, whereby we cry, Abba, Father.
The Spirit itself beareth witness with our spirit that
we are the children of God; and if children, then heirs;
heirs of God, and joint-heirs with Christ." It is only
so far as we are united to Christ by His Spirit that we
can share, in our degree, in this spirit of adopted
sonship. But the essential moral unity between the
will of Christ and the will of God implies an essential
equality of nature; and it is thus that the doctrine of
the unity of the substance of the Father and of the
Son has a moral foundation far stronger and more
profound than its philosophical justification.

If the reality of the doctrine of the Trinity on moral
grounds be thus discerned with respect to the Son of
God, it will be felt that no difficulty in principle can
remain with respect to the Third Person in this
Trinity—the Holy Spirit. It will be sufficient to
indicate briefly how on this point also the doctrine,
while resting primarily on the authority of Christ,

at the same time appeals directly to the evidence of history and of conscience. As before, we have again to consider the Christian Conscience in its application to the historical facts of Christianity; but in this case, while starting from the life of Christ, we advance a step beyond it. That life revealed to us, on the one hand, a Divine Father with whom our Lord lived in filial, and at the same time equal, communion. But our Lord spoke also of a Spirit, proceeding from the Father, whom, after His departure, He would send to His disciples, who would guide them into all truth, who would teach them all things, and bring all things to their remembrance, whatsoever He had said unto them, and who would take His place in His personal relations towards them. It is a matter of historical fact—for testimony to which we again appeal, not to speculation, but to the conscience —that this promise was fulfilled. We are so familiar with the Epistles, that the miracle of inspiration and illumination which is contained in them loses some of its wonder and its greatness to us. But we have before us, in the Gospels, the evidence of favourable witnesses as to what the Apostles were before our Lord's ascension, and up to the very moment of it; and the Epistles tell us what they were after it. We know also what the life, the philosophy, and the moral elevation of the loftiest spirits was in the world at large in their day; and if we compare the spiritual and moral elevation of the Epistles with that which

was previously discernible either in Gentiles or in Jews,
we are able to judge whether the promise was fulfilled
that a new Divine influence should descend upon the
Church and inspire a new moral and spiritual life. In
a discussion of the Method of Sanctification in the previous course of Lectures, the characteristics of this new
moral creation have been exhibited with more detail ;
while it has also been shown how profoundly the truth
of the personality of the Holy Spirit answers to the experience of the Apostles and to the necessities of the
Christian life. It is enough here to point out that it
is to the witness thus borne by the Epistles and by
the experience of the Christian Church to the personal operation of the Spirit of God, that we appeal
for confirmation of our Lord's assurances respecting
the mission of the Holy Spirit, the Third Person in
the Trinity. The influence is an historical fact, rely-
ing for its recognition upon the testimony of the conscience, and it is interpreted to us by the previous
declarations of our Lord, and by the statements of
the Apostles.

Thus interpreted, the doctrine appeals for confirmation to other convictions of the human conscience,
which have been powerful enough to be the source of
the most elaborate theosophic systems—systems which
did, in fact, contend with Christianity at its outset
for empire over the soul. It touches that conviction,
everywhere revealed in those struggles after God
which are embodied in other religions, of the immense

distance and separation between man as a creature
and God as a Creator; and of the enormous difficulty
of supposing that man, merely as man, can attain
that communion with God, that unity with His will,
that harmony with His wisdom, that love of Him in
His whole nature, for which, nevertheless, our souls
crave. The revelation of the Holy Spirit declares
that, as God has revealed His grace and truth in the
Person of His Son, in an embodiment which unites
Him with us, so He does not leave us as independent creatures to approach Him; but He Himself, in
the person of the Holy Spirit, lays His hand upon
our hearts, draws us to Himself, and moulds us into
conformity with His will and His wisdom. "Likewise," says the Apostle, "the Spirit also helpeth our infirmities; for we know not what we should pray for
as we ought; but the Spirit itself maketh intercession
for us, with groanings which cannot be uttered." In
a word, whether the mysterious truth be morally or
philosophically considered, God alone can be worthy
of the society and communion of God; and consequently, if our communion with the Father is to be
anything but a mere figure of speech, God Himself
within us must present us to God without us; and we
must, in language which the Apostle permits us to
use, be rendered by God the Spirit fellow-heirs with
God the Son, and thus be associated with the very
communion of the Godhead itself.

One cannot speak upon this subject without im-

ploring forgiveness from that awful, yet gracious
Trinity, alike for what is said and for what is unsaid;
but the purpose of these considerations has been
answered if they have shown, however unworthily,
that whatever the difficulty connected with the doctrine of the Trinity, the ground on which it claims our
faith is a moral rather than an intellectual one. Accordingly, it is to be observed that all the terms in
which the doctrine is revealed in the Scriptures are
moral, and not philosophical. The sacred writers do
not speak of the Unity in Trinity, or of three Persons
in one Substance; but they speak of the Father, of
the Son, and of the Holy Spirit—of the Son being
one with the Father, and of the Spirit proceeding from
the Father, and being sent by the Son. Some great
divines have regretted the necessity, if such it was, for
investing these moral terms with the garb of abstract
expressions. But the fact that the doctrine has a
philosophical aspect cannot alter its essential significance; and it is by its moral and spiritual character
that it must be estimated. It is not as theosophic
speculation—it is as the interpretation of a Divine and
human life, of the most momentous facts of human
history, and of the deepest convictions of the human
Conscience, that we confess that "THE FATHER IS
GOD, THE SON IS GOD, AND THE HOLY GHOST IS
GOD; AND YET THEY ARE NOT THREE GODS, BUT
ONE GOD."

ſ

LECTURE VIII.

THE TRAVAIL OF THE CREATION.

ROMANS viii. 19.

" For the earnest expectation of the creature waiteth for the manifestation of the sons of God."

OUR reflections in the course of these Lectures have, I hope, conducted us to a conclusion in harmony with the principle from which we started. That principle was the sense of Right and Wrong—a sense of which we observed the supremacy to be admitted by all with whom, in the present day, it is necessary to discuss the claims of the Christian Religion. We have been asking, throughout these Discourses, what is the meaning of that sense, or conscience ; and we have been considering whether the truths of the Gospel do not afford its only adequate interpretation. The main result of such inquiries has been, so far as the argument may be relied on, to enhance our appreciation of that supremacy, and to show that it necessarily involves the introduction of moral and personal relations into the whole range

of our experience, both here and hereafter, in the
physical no less than the spiritual universe. We have
seen with what singular force the most characteristic
speculations of modern science tend to this result.
Whether their particular hypotheses be right or wrong,
they bear witness to the manner in which all nature
co-operates in the development of Man, and, consequently, in the development of Morality. Within the
sphere of our observation, the Conscience is the
highest and finest achievement of that fearful and
wonderful mechanism of which we are a part. Human
civilization is a vast and complicated phenomenon ;
but just as three laws of motion and a few axioms of
geometry suffice to explain the movements of the
whole celestial universe, so do a few laws of morality
control the order and development of the human race.
Human civilization, moreover, tends more and more
to become the predominant part of Nature. The
" minister and interpreter of Nature," man is for that
reason her lord : he develops her riches ; he modifies
her products ; he transforms her very aspect ; and
thus, on the observance by a race, or a nation, of a
short code of moral commandments may depend immeasurable consequences both to the animal and to
the vegetable world. Man, in a word, is the lord of
Nature, and Conscience is the lord of Man ; and consequently the chief power which is at work in that
vast manifestation of wealth and dominion, to which
the most distant kings of the earth now pay their

homage in this city, is that moral force which alone
maintains men in their due relations to each other
and to the great realities amidst which they have their
being. Even in physical nature, the most potent
forces, as we are daily learning, are those which are
apparently the most insignificant, and which are the
least open to a superficial observation. The gigantic
forces of the ocean or of the winds are themselves dependent upon the most minute molecular agencies, or
the most subtle electrical attractions ; and similarly,
it is not the physical power of modern machinery, but
that still, small voice of the Conscience, by the aid of
which the constructors of this machinery are organized,
which is the real master of all the mechanical and
muscular, and even rational, force it embodies.

But the force of these considerations became
infinitely enhanced when we proceeded to consider
Conscience as the faculty which brings us into direct
and conscious communion with a righteous and reasonable Being, who is the Maker and Preserver of all
things, both visible and invisible. The extent as well
as the depth of this revelation must be regarded, if its
force is to be appreciated. It is not merely that
Conscience reveals to us a righteous God, with whom
we ourselves have to do ; it reveals to us a God whose
righteousness and reasonableness, or, in the language
of St. John, whose *Logos* is the law of creation. A
righteous God must be Almighty by virtue of His
righteousness ; for a Right which could not assert its

Might would be a mockery. It is consequently one of those utterances of Revelation which are scarcely discernible from the utterances of an enlightened conscience, that "in the beginning was the *Logos*, and the *Logos* was with God, and the *Logos* was God;" that "all things were made through him, and without him was not any thing made that was made."

It follows, however, that so far as a man, by means of his Conscience, is in union and harmony with a righteous and reasonable, and therefore personal God, who is the Maker of Heaven and Earth, so far is he also in union and harmony with nature and with the whole constitution of the universe. The true interpretation of the voice of Conscience, the habitual recognition of a personal God, the acceptance of His righteousness, and, above all, faith in that Being who, as Conscience and Reason Incarnate, claims to be regarded as the Son of God—these moral acts become, not mere incidents in religious consciousness, not mere conditions of spiritual life here or hereafter, but circumstances which determine how far we are in a true relation to the world, whether physical, moral, or spiritual, in which we are placed. Accordingly, the revelation of Christ is to St. Paul not merely a revelation of the Saviour of mankind, but, as including this, it is a revelation of the moral centre of the whole creation. Import, as we are required to do, moral considerations into the whole of the Apostle's language, interpret him as we have been interpreting St. John, and we discern the momentous moral force of his re-iterated declarations of that mystery of the Divine will, "that in the dispensation of the fulness of times, He might gather together in one all things in Christ, both which are in heaven and which are on earth, even in Him : in whom we also have obtained an inheritance." Such, for instance, is the mighty grasp with which the Apostle welds together the whole spiritual, moral, and physical universe, when he thanks the Father, " Who hath delivered us from the power of darkness, and hath translated us into the kingdom of his dear Son ; in whom we have redemption through his blood, even the forgiveness of sins ; who is the image of the in-visible GOD, the firstborn of every creature ; for by Him were all things created, that are in heaven and that are in earth, visible and invisible, whether they be thrones, or dominions, or principalities, or powers ; all things were created by Him and for Him : and He is before all things, and by Him all things consist." These expressions, as I have said on other occasions, are no dreams of a speculative philosophy ; they are the utterances of a deep moral conviction that Righteousness is the law of the universe, and that Christ, as the Lord of Righteousness, is also the Lord of all.   The import of these grand and comprehensive statements is, however, necessarily reflected in the most elementary action of the Conscience, in its primary consciousness of Right and Wrong, and of its relation to a personal God.   That which is involved in

this sense of obligation is nothing less than the whole
relation of man to God on the one side, and to Nature
on the other—and consequently, since man is an
essential part of Nature, the very order and harmony
of Nature itself. Men who are not true to the dictates
of their Conscience are like planets which break away
from their sun, and they involve a similar anarchy in
the whole constitution of the system of which they
form a part.

Now I would ask you to-day, as I hope a not
unfitting close to these discussions, to turn the light of
this moral revelation upon that dark problem of imperfection, of pain, and of death which Nature forces
on us, and which, in age after age, has equally dis-
tressed the simple and baffled the wise.   The problem
has recently been stated with singular force in the
posthumous essays of Mr. Mill ; but it is as old as the
book of Job : it has been the starting-point of philosophies and the foundation of religions.   There is,
indeed, a strange and instructive contrast between the
complacency with which the order of Nature is sometimes dwelt upon by her modern worshippers, and the
strains of distress and indignation which are wrung by
her disorder from a philosopher like Mr. Mill, or which
a poet like Pope struggles to appease.   "All," we are
told, "which people are accustomed to deprecate as
'disorder,' and its consequences, is precisely the counterpart of Nature's ways.   Anarchy and the reign of
terror are overmatched in injustice, ruin, and death, by

a hurricane and a pestilence."[1] Pope expresses a
similar sentiment in the lines,

> " If plagues or earthquakes break not Heaven's design,
>   Why then a Borgia or a Catiline ?"

We need not go to the Scriptures to learn that, to
the apprehension of men, in proportion to the keenness
of their appreciation of reasonable moral order, something like a curse appears to weigh upon creation ; and
that not merely man, but all sentient nature, seems
groaning and travailing under an unequally distributed
burden of pain and death. A Revelation which failed
to face this mystery, and to throw some light on its
relation to the righteousness of God, would fall very
far short of the claims of Christianity, and would leave
untouched one of the greatest perplexities of the
human spirit. The Scriptures accordingly deal with
the problem alike in their earliest and in their final
revelations ; and, though they deliberately leave us still
in the presence of a mystery, they transfer the mystery
from the world at large to our own spirits, and to the
very constitution of morality itself.

Let us recur to what has just been said respecting
the supremacy of the Conscience, not merely over
individuals, in their individual capacities, but as the
ultimate law of the universe. Bear in mind that man
is an essential part of nature, and that conscience is
the most essential part of man, and then consider
what must needs be, and what ought to be, the result

---

[1] Mr. Mill's " Essay on Nature," p. 31.

of the disobedience of man to the dictates of his Conscience.   Such disobedience becomes the destruction
of the keystone of the arch.   By the very supposition,
it involves nothing less than a break between God
and Nature ; it interrupts the communion of the
Creator with the creation, by dividing Him from that
reasonable and moral creature, through whom He
Himself designed to display His moral dominion over
all other creatures.   From this point of view we may
say, in all soberness, that when the first act of disobedience was committed, when faith in God first
failed, the heavens fell.   Such is the truth which, too
often presented in a hard and arbitrary form, is enshrined in the Scriptural doctrine or allegory of the
Curse following the Fall.   However that doctrine may
have been travestied, and whatever excuse there may
consequently be for the repulsion which it sometimes
arouses, it must appear, from our present point of
view, the deepest homage ever paid to the supremacy
of Conscience and of Morality.   It proclaims the moral
order of the world to be supreme over the physical to
such an extent, that its violation entails the inevitable
anarchy of the whole.

It will be observed that the weight of this consideration is uniformly ignored in such attacks on the
injustice of Nature as that of Mr. Mill, or in such
imperfect defences of it as that of Pope. The injustice
of which they speak is, indeed, often only that which
appears to them to be injustice in each particular

case; and even these particular cases are judged with sole reference to the present life. Nature is treated as something external to man, and its essential connection with his moral constitution is disregarded. But the cardinal error of such arguments is that they treat the apparent order of nature as the real one; and that, leaving out of account the possibility of its disorganization by moral causes, or by the human will, they attack it or defend it as displaying, in its present state, the will of its Creator. In order to meet such objections, and to understand the teaching of the Scriptures, it is necessary to shift the whole aspect of things to a point of view which modern thought and discovery have rendered unfamiliar to us. We must even go further than regarding morality as a part of nature—we must look upon it, as we have been describing it, as the crown or keystone of nature. The view taken of life in the Bible, and the view taken of it by science and philosophy, are, indeed, we must recognize, entirely distinct. The scientific conception, more or less clearly developed, is that we live in a physical universe, of which the moral world forms a part; the Hebrew and Christian conception is that we live in a moral universe, of which the physical world forms a part.

I have quoted, on a former occasion, the famous saying of Kant, that two things filled him with amazement: the starry heavens above him, and the law of conscience within him. But to the Jew, and to a

Christian Apostle like St. Paul, the conscience within him held the very place of the starry heavens above. There was a firmament ever present to his moral and spiritual eye, which far transcended in vastness and in influence the visible vault of heaven. His vision pierced that physical vault to discern, encompassing it, the Lord of heaven and earth—a Lord who was righteous in all His ways and holy in all His works, and whose Righteousness and Holiness utterly overwhelmed, in the potency of their influence, even the mightiest and most vivid of the forces of nature. "The earth," they exclaimed, "shall tremble at the look of Him"—not at His mere look of power, but at His look of righteousness: "if He do but touch the hills"—touch them with His righteous sceptre—"they shall smoke." Prophets and Apostles dwelt consciously in a world which had no need of the sun, neither of the moon, to shine in it; for the glory of God did lighten it, and His righteousness was the light thereof.   Once thus transpose the whole mental attitude to that of the moral sphere, and the manner in which the Scriptures subordinate physical to moral evil appears equally natural and moral.   The mystery is, as I have said, transferred from the world without to the soul within; and a double problem is reduced to a single one.   To the mere philosopher—unless, indeed, he be a materialist—there are two distinct problems : that of physical imperfection without, and of moral evil within.   To St. Paul, on the other hand,

regarding the whole universe as centred in Christ and
in Righteousness, the sole problem is that of moral
evil—the depravation of the human Conscience and
Will.   That, indeed, remains an unsolved and insoluble
mystery ; and it is no reasonable objection to a doctrine that it fails to explain the origin of moral evil.
But we can at least discern that the absence of
physical evil, in the presence of moral evil, would be
inconsistent with a constitution of things which makes
morality paramount.   As long as the wills of moral
beings, who are the most essential part of nature, are
imperfect, so long must nature be imperfect ; and
there is no remedy for its imperfection, but in the
creation, or re-creation, of harmony between the will
of Man and the will of God.   Accordingly, St. Paul
declares that "the earnest expectation of the creature
waiteth for the manifestation of the sons of God."
Possibly, these words may be applied to remove a
difficulty which might be raised as to the existence of
pain and death before the appearance of man on the
earth.   The Scriptures reveal to us other moral
and spiritual beings, with whose moral corruption
on the principles we have been considering, physical
imperfection may be not less connected than with
our own.   But, however this may be, the expression
in the text would almost seem to imply that the creation could not but be imperfect, could not display a
perfect order, until the sons of God should be manifested—until, that is, in the mysterious working of the

Divine wisdom, a church of Saints, conformed to the image of the Son of God, should be gathered together and revealed, who, through faithful hearts and righteous wills, should establish harmony between heaven and earth.

Such, then, are the principles upon which the Gospel deals with this great problem ; and it will be seen that, so far from their being out of harmony with a moral view of things, their difficulty lies, not in their throwing too little stress on morality, but on their laying so much stress upon it. Let us pass on, however, to consider the manner in which the principles of the Gospel, in this respect, are illustrated and confirmed by its facts. Now it will at once be observed that the miracles recorded in the Gospels are in strict harmony with this view of the relation between the physical and moral spheres. The only instance in which complete power over physical evil is displayed is in the life of One whose will was so entirely righteous, that He could say, " I and my Father are one." The moment a perfectly holy Person appeared, then, but not till then, was complete control over the curses of humanity exhibited.

The miracles have sometimes been used too exclusively as testimonies to a supernatural mission ; but their value, even in this respect, is immensely enhanced when they are further regarded as the unique testimony of experience to the moral fact, that the highest Might has never been seen on the earth apart from Right, and that unlimited mastery over the whole forces of evil has only been exercised by perfect holiness. Miracles are, indeed, revelations of power ; but the power is that of a Righteous Will. The force of this consideration, moreover, is strengthened, when it is borne in mind how constantly the exhibition of the power was rendered dependent, not merely on the righteous volition of the Saviour, but on the righteous condition of those for whose benefit it was exercised. The faith which was exacted of those who appealed for help was, as we have seen in a previous Lecture, essentially a moral act, carrying with it a recognition by the Conscience of the claims of Christ as the Lord of the soul, and therefore as the Lord of nature. It was when men and women were thus placed by their faith in a true relation to Christ, and consequently in a true relation to God, that His righteous will could operate without obstruction upon them and for them, and that the true order, which moral corruption and spiritual faithlessness had interrupted, could be restored. A kindred co-operation, it may well be believed, has united, and will ever unite, the prevalence of Christianity with the power of perpetual advance in the sciences which aim at the relief of man's estate ; and it is only by the agency of those sound moral, as well as intellectual, habits which the Gospel fosters that the secrets of nature can be successfully penetrated. By a profound moral connection, the very Science which repudiates the miracles

of Christ has its root in them, and, could it possibly
be separated from their influence, would wither and
decay.

But there is one fact of the Gospel which has done
more to furnish a practical solution of this problem
for the conscience of man than any other, and which
brings its message of comfort to millions who could
never follow the profound reasoning of the Apostle.
That fact is the suffering of Christ. It is a fact which
has thrown a new and intense illumination over the
long agony of the human race. It has established for
ever the music of that awful minor harmony, in which
the bitterest pain is blended with the deepest peace
and joy. In all nations indeed, and at all times, the
way in which men have met death, and women have
met suffering, has been a testimony to the conviction
that pain, when endured for a moral purpose, may be
transformed from a curse into a blessing, and may
elevate the nature on which it seems to inflict a
wound. But this conviction has been established as
one of the supreme laws of human nature by the cross
of Christ. Here, again, as I showed in the last Lecture with respect to our Lord's relation to His Father,
His relation to suffering must for ever be borne in
mind as an historical fact in human experience. That
which, in reference to this subject, the story of the
cross reveals is that the most perfect of human souls,
the soul most in love with righteousness, the most
perfectly in harmony with the Divine will, embraced

the deepest agony as essential to its own perfection, and as the only means of fully displaying the glory of the Son in whom the Father was well pleased. From thenceforth men might not know the mystery of pain and suffering; but this they did know, as an unquestionable historical fact to which their deepest moral convictions bore testimony—that the highest moral and spiritual excellence the world had seen was indissolubly connected with the deepest suffering. Let it not be supposed that the fact of those sufferings being borne for us interfered with their actual and natural effect on the Saviour's own soul. On the contrary, it was the very reality of His experience which rendered Him our representative. "By the grace of God," says the Apostle, "He should taste death for every man." "For it became Him, for whom are all things, and by whom are all things, in bringing many sons unto glory, to make the Captain of their salvation perfect through sufferings. For both He that sanctifieth and they who are sanctified are all of one; for which cause He is not ashamed to call them brethren." Those sufferings were, indeed, more conspicuously than all others, the result of sin—the last injustice of human nature and nature combined. But, the sin existing as the curse of that nature in which Christ took part, the sufferings are none the less the means of revealing His perfection, and in that sense of refining, with the last fire of purification, the exquisite beauty of His soul. From thenceforth, when aspiring, with

the Apostle, to be heirs of God and joint-heirs with
Christ, men and women have been constrained to add,
" If so be that we suffer with Him, that we may also
be glorified together."　Well might the Apostle speak
of all things being gathered together in Christ! for
they could only be gathered together in One, in whom
not only the joy, but the travail of the world, had
been concentrated in an intense agony and a joyful
resurrection.　It is in view of that supreme revelation
of the capacities of the soul that the Apostle exclaims,
and that Christians have exclaimed after him, " I
reckon that the sufferings of this present time are not
worthy to be compared with the glory which shall be
revealed in us."　" We know that the whole creation
groaneth and travaileth in pain together until now :
and not only they, but ourselves also, which have the
firstfruits of the Spirit, even we ourselves groan within
ourselves, waiting for the adoption, to wit, the redemption of our body."　The travail of our souls and bodies
is but a part of the travail of the whole creation, and
it is one with the travail of the soul of Christ ; and if
He, with His perfect insight into holiness and justice,
His perfect innocence, and His bitter agony, yet, " for
the joy that was set before Him endured the cross," shall
we deem it too much to conclude, with St. Paul, not
merely that we hope, but that " we *know* that all things
work together for good to them that love God ? "

Such is the answer offered by the Gospel to this
" enigma of life."　It is not, indeed, a clear, dogmatic

solution ; and in that respect it is in conformity with
the whole spirit of Christianity. It is an appeal to
faith, based on moral convictions ; and what it asks of
us is not to submit, on mere miraculous authority, to
an incomprehensible revelation, but to trust and follow a living Person, who has Himself experienced the
mysteries and sounded the depths amidst which He
asks us to have faith in Him. Mystery on this subject,
as on all subjects connected with the moral constitution of man and of the world, you cannot escape. The
question is whether, to sustain you amidst such mysteries, you will await the tardy support of the speculations of Science, or accept at once that of the convictions of Morality. It is not difficult to construct
such indictments against the order of nature as those
to which I have to-day referred, and the scientific or
philosophical answer to them has not yet been
returned. But while your intellect is thus baffled and
perplexed, and equally baffled and perplexed from
whichever side you approach the problem, a Person
appears who appeals to your heart and conscience with
all the force of truth and righteousness and all the
light of love, and who implores you, in the tones of a
fellow-man and in the accents of a fellow-sufferer, to
have faith in Him, and to believe, as He did, that, in
spite of all appearances, God is for us, no matter what
may be against us. Such assurances come from One
who has tasted, not only death, but every moral and
physical agony ; who has been victorious over them

all, and who appeals alike to His voluntary suffering
and to His victory as the ground for our trust.   Upon
this, accordingly, the Apostle falls back as he concludes, in the Epistle I have chiefly followed, his review
of the great outlines of Christian faith.   " Who shall
separate us from the love of Christ ? "   He is not
merely addressing the feelings, but appealing to sober
facts.   That love is still to us, as it was to him, the
most potent moral force in human history.   It is an
eternal spiritual reality; and the ultimate question involved in such doubts as I have been discussing is
whether you prefer to trust that love, or to follow the
comparatively feeble experience of others and the tentative speculations of the intellect.   May God grant
that in these Lectures, now concluded, in spite of the
imperfections for which I here entreat His pardon,
something may have been done to enable us the
better to join, with a similarly sober conviction, in
the declaration of the struggling but believing Apostle :
—" I AM PERSUADED, that neither death, nor life, nor
angels, nor principalities, nor powers, nor things
present, nor things to come, nor height, nor depth, nor
any other creature, shall be able to separate us from
the love of God, which is in Christ Jesus our Lord."

www.ingramcontent.com/pod-product-compliance
Lightning Source LLC
Chambersburg PA
CBHW030922050726
47498CB00003BA/868